"Dear Michael, I just want to say how much I enjoyed working with you in *Harlow*."

Love, Carol Lynley - Actress

"If you look up 'tall, dark and handsome' you'll find a picture of Michael Dante. Michael has always had the amazing good looks and world-class talent that real movie stars are supposed to have. I loved working with him in *Born Reckless*. In addition to being easy on the eyes, Michael is interesting and fun to be around. If his book is half as cool as he is, it will be a huge hit."

Mamie Van Doren – Actress

"I remember Ralph Vitti (not named Michael Dante yet) when we used to sit around the clubhouse in Orlando, Florida, during spring training with the Washington Senators. We'd talk about baseball, mostly hitting. Ralph had a good swing and it was too bad he came up with a sore shoulder. I still believe that if it wasn't for his injured throwing arm he would have made the ball club. After that he went on to greater heights in the movies, television and radio. He became a big star. Ralph Vitti, it's great to call you my dear friend."

Roy Sievers – Outfielder, Washington Senators, Major League Baseball Player

"Michael, Good luck with your book. You have had a great and impressive life; professional baseball, television and motion picture actor, celebrity radio talk show host and a writer. I have always enjoyed our friendship and all the good times we have shared together. God Bless."

Ken Venturi – 35 years CBS Golf Analyst /2013 World Golf Hall of Fame

"Michael Dante has been a friend of mine for many years. We were both raised in the suburbs of Stamford, CT. Michael has been a professional athlete and motion picture and television actor and has appeared in numerous movies and TV shows since the 1950s. He was under contract with three major studios; MGM, Warner Bros. and 20th Century-Fox. The title role that Michael played as the star of the movie *Winterhawk* was a particular favorite of mine. My wife Joan and I wish Michael much happiness and success in future years."

Marty – Martin Ransohoff Productions, Inc.

Michael Dante
From HOLLYWOOD to
MICHAEL DANTE WAY

Written by Michael Dante

Edited by Marshall Terrill

Kathy & Bob,

Enjoy!

Michael Dante

BearManor Media

2013

1/13/19

Michael Dante: From Hollywood To Michael Dante Way

© 2013 Michael Dante

Library of Congress Registration: TXu 1-856-615
Effective July 31, 2012 / Certification: Michael Dante

For information, address:

BearManor Media
P. O. Box 71426
Albany, GA 31708

bearmanormedia.com

Typesetting and layout by John Teehan
Cover Design by Mary Jane Dante and John Teehan

Published in the USA by BearManor Media

ISBN— 1-59393-756-3
978-1-59393-756-0

Dedication

Mom, Dad and the Good Lord gave me the gift of life and my wife Mary Jane enriched it with her love and support.

Table of Contents

Foreword

My first meeting with Michael Dante happened in March of 2008. It was my sixteenth year as moderator of the celebrity question and answer panels at the Festival of the West in Scottsdale, Arizona. Since 1992 I've had the pleasure of interviewing many of the stars I grew up watching on television and at the movie theater. Little did I know at the time that all those hours I spent watching them would prepare me for what I'm doing now.

My father had our family television installed on a large Lazy-Susan between our family room and dining room. When it was time for dinner he could swivel the TV around on the turntable and we would spend dinnertime watching our favorite shows. When dinner was over the TV was turned back to the family room where the evening's schedule would continue. Because of this, I could tell you who most of the past and present actors were before I reached my teens.

Back then films at the movie theaters would change every Wednesday, not Friday as they do now, and very rarely were they held over for a second week. A weekly trip to the Mesa Theater in Mesa, Arizona, or a local drive-in, where I would see a double feature, was always on the agenda. John Wayne, Elvis Presley, and Audie Murphy were among my favorites. But even at an early age I was intrigued by Michael. I just couldn't pin him down like I could other actors.

Michael's role as Crazy Horse on ABC's *Custer* (1967) was just one of many that intrigued me. The show lasted only one season, but Michael left a lasting impression. His Crazy Horse was noble and honest, unlike many presentations of Native Americans at the time. It was refreshing and Michael was the chief (no pun intended) reason to watch the show. I'm sure it came from the way Michael carefully studies each character he plays to find the real essence of what's conveyed on screen.

As I stated before I had already enjoyed Michael's work alongside Elvis in *Kid Galahad* (1962), and Audie Murphy in *Apache Rifles* (1964) and *Arizona Raiders* (1965) so I was very aware of him, yet there was a mysterious quality about him, possibly due to the variety of characters he chose to play. He was always mesmerizing on screen.

While preparing for my panels with Michael I found some very interesting facts. What I share with you here might seem a bit vague but that's only because I want to simply whet your appetite for what you'll read from Michael himself.

Before becoming a successful actor Michael was an up and coming professional baseball player under his birth name Ralph Vitti. An unfortunate injury caused Michael to eventually look elsewhere for a career. Due to his good looks, Ralph soon found himself signed to a contract by MGM, arranged by a very famous bandleader; no names because Michael will fill you in later. Ralph

Vitti became Michael Dante when he later signed contracts with Warner Bros. and eventually 20th Century-Fox. Not bad being signed by three major film studios.

Looking at his career it's easy to see that it was calculated on Michael's part never to be typecast. As a small example of his variety of roles take the years 1962 through 1967: A boxer in the musical drama *Kid Galahad* with Elvis. Action film heroics World War II-style in *Operation Bikini* with teen idols Tab Hunter, Frankie Avalon, Gary Crosby, Jody McCrea, and stalwarts Jim Backus and Scott Brady. A vile millionaire with a terrible secret life in *The Naked Kiss* helmed by revered director Samuel Fuller, a Native American in *Apache Rifles* alongside Audie Murphy, an arrogant but comedic James Bond type spy on *Get Smart*, a proud Hispanic who claims his father owns the rights to the Ponderosa land on *Bonanza*, and the alien Maab on *Star Trek*. And this is just a sampling of roles he took during this period.

The *Bonanza* role would bring an offer to star on another popular NBC Western series being created at that time. Michael wanted to avoid typecasting and turned the offer down, something he had also done a few years earlier. What TV shows were they? Again, Michael will tell you. The one exception to playing a starring TV role came with Crazy Horse on *Custer*. Why did Michael change his mind with this offer? Read on and find out.

Throughout his career Michael made sure that he played a variety of characters in every genre imaginable; however, he is proudly remembered for his starring title role in *Winterhawk*. Once again Michael did honor to the Native American in a role he was meant to play.

But back to March of 2008. I was looking forward to meeting Michael but what would the real Michael Dante be like? Frankly, I've interviewed a few people that I would just as soon never interview again for one reason or another. In Michael's case he's genuine, honest, kind, warm, and extremely friendly, putting you at ease immediately. Over the years I've crossed paths with Michael and his lovely wife, Mary Jane, and I always receive a warm welcome. Michael tells their story within these pages as well.

He'll also share the many deserved awards he has received, which are numerous and they haven't stopped yet. All of them given in gratitude for the many quality hours of enjoyment he has given us.

I'll also tell you that he is simply one of the best panel guests you could ask for, and I am proud to call him a friend.

As I stated before, I have been evasive on some points while having the privilege of writing this Foreword. It's because I want you to enjoy every page like I did as Michael tells his own story. This is a great read and I am proud to be a part of it.

Thank you, Michael, my friend. Little did I know when I saw you singing with Elvis on the big screen that I would one day have such an honor. To all of you readers all I can say is enjoy the ride *From Hollywood to Michael Dante Way* will give you!

– Charlie LeSueur, actor, author and
Western film historian

Introduction

Dear Reader,

You are about to embark on a literary journey filled with romance and adventure, traveling along with the writer of this remarkable journal as he pursues the American dream. But before you leave there are facts about the author you may not discover in your travels – only because this journalist's modesty forbids him to sing his own praises. So, I feel obligated to tell you that not only is he an impeccable actor and a gifted athlete (innumerable awards and trophies decorate his mantel), he is a devoted husband, a church-goer with strong religious convictions, a patriot and the most charitable human being I know. Knowing the above, you're sure to find the journey with Michael as inspiring as I have found his friendship for over half a century.

Bon Voyage,

James B. Harris – Motion Picture Producer, Director, Writer

Acknowledgements

What a gift it is to be given life and to be born healthy, both mentally and physically. To be blessed with the parents I was blessed with and to be born in America. The clarity in which I appreciate the above has allowed me to embrace life and my responsibility to grow as a human being every day. I always knew whatever gifts the good Lord gave to me, I would develop through hard work and dedication in order to leave something of value behind after my days on earth are gone.

The house where I was born, located at 96 West Avenue in Stamford, Connecticut.

I have to thank my wife Mary Jane, first, for encouraging me to write my memoirs. Without her understanding, patience and assistance, I could not have completed what I set out to do. It has been yet another part of her devotion to our teamwork and our marriage.

When author/biographer Marshall Terrill offered to edit my book, I knew I was sent a gift from heaven. I was inspired to write my biography because I knew I was working with the best. I will be forever grateful for Marshall's many contributions, but most of all for his friendship.

My thanks go out to copy editor Patricia King Hanson for her contribution.

My special thanks go out to Gregg and Austin for their time and talent.

I've always said, "Timing is not important, it's everything." Therefore, I have to thank my teammate with the Washington Senators, Mickey McDermott for introducing me to Tommy Dorsey. I met Tommy through Mickey, which eventually led to my first screen test and signing a seven-year contract with MGM Studios.

At that point my whole life changed. I transitioned from a professional baseball player to an acting career. I'm grateful to producer Jack Cummings, who, thanks to Tommy Dorsey, arranged the screen test at MGM. I can never thank them enough.

After leaving MGM, I signed a contract with Warner Bros. Studios and was given the opportunity to star in my first motion picture, Westbound, directed by Budd Boetticher.

I shall always be indebted to Budd because that opportunity advanced my career in an upward direction.

Early in my career I was represented, very well I might add, by agent Sy Marsh at the William Morris Agency. Unfortunately for me, he left the agency business to become a partner and produce projects with Sammy Davis Jr. It was my misfortune because I never had an agent or a manager that I respected as much as Sy Marsh. He was the best.

I would also like to thank the many fans who have supported me throughout the years, and those who encouraged me to write my autobiography. They would say wherever I went, "Mr. Dante, you should write a book." So for my fans, this one's for you!

I've been a member of the Screen Actors Guild since 1955 and a recipient of its many benefits to the present day, which I am grateful for.

This book is also about all the "larger than life" people I had the opportunity to work with and get to know along the way. My journey in pursuit of the American Dream has been interesting, educating, exciting and still going strong.

My only regret is what you're about to read went much too fast.

At three years old, riding a pony in Stamford, Connecticut. I always wanted to be a cowboy.

Introduction: Drowning

At the age of nine I almost drowned. On a very hot and humid summer day in Stamford, Connecticut, my sister Rose and next door neighbor, Anna Campana, and several of my friends went to Spelke's Beach on the east side of town to swim. When we got there my friends and I decided to walk out on the breakwater. These were huge round boulders piled one on top of the other that penetrated out from the sand to break the waves and separate the channel from the swimming area. The four of us decided to venture out on the rocks and not one of us knew how to swim.

Spelke's Beach.

At that time we thought it was low tide but it was higher than we anticipated. We decided to play a game, so we bet a quarter to make it interesting, daring one another to dive into the water. I dove from the rocks into the water and went right to the bottom; at that point I was drowning. I can only tell you that there is no pain in drowning—it's like watching a television show, one picture after another of your life unfolding before you. One subliminal image after another of whatever of my life I had already experienced at that age. I saw all these beautiful pictures, these images were coming across so vividly beneath the surface.

Suddenly someone miraculously grabbed my hand as I was going down for the third time and saved my life. That person was Anna Campana, who drove us to the beach that day. She and my sister Rose were watching us from the shore while sitting on a beach blanket. She saw what was happening and ran into the water. She grabbed me by my hand and pulled me up from underneath. I came to the surface after engulfing an awful lot of water and was choking and gasping for air.

There was an older person swimming not too far from us and he saved my buddy's life, so we were both saved and were brought to shore and given artificial respiration. I went home in a daze as it was a traumatic experience coming so close to death. However, I was determined to learn how to swim. The following day, I went back to Spelke's Beach alone, walking five miles to get there. I immediately went to the shoreline and stood in about three feet of water and began to kick up one leg at a time until I was able to stay above the water. Before the day was over, I learned to swim. No one showed me a thing. I just kept kicking and kicking until I could stay afloat; I did that all day long.

The next day I returned and swam across the channel. The smell of the salt in the air and the taste of the salty ocean water remained in my taste buds and nostrils for many years and always reminded me of that near fatal day. This was the first of many times the dear Lord saved my life.

1

The Circus

Every summer the circus came to town and it was a big deal. Under the big top we saw all the animals, the jugglers and the tightrope artists. We rode the merry-go-round, tried to hit the dolls down with a ball for a prize and ate lots of popcorn and ice cream. The circus people would solicit youngsters to work; it was quite alluring. When I was eleven, I applied and discovered that I had to compete with two other boys who were my same age.

The circus boss was rather strange and a tad mercenary. He pitted the three hopefuls against each other and wanted us to duke it out for the job. The winner would be given the job of taking care of Ken Maynard's horse, 'Tarzan.' I didn't like the idea of having to fight someone I didn't know and who hadn't done anything to me. The boss found that to be humorous. He set the stage by telling one person the other said something terrible about him. He instructed each of us to beat each other up, and we went at it. Despite my reluctance, I won both fights and got the job.

I was given a dollar a day and one ticket to the big top. My job was to clean the manure in the stalls, stack up fresh hay, curry Tarzan and assist Mr. Maynard with his props. When he came to work we immediately saddled up Tarzan in preparation for the show in the center ring. He was, after all, the star of the circus. Most of the time the star came in intoxicated and needed me to help him get up on the horse.

The moment he sat in the saddle he miraculously sobered up, it was something to behold. He did every show to perfection. When he finished, he brought the horse to the stall, and practically fell over every time. In the meantime I was able to get all my friends in the neighborhood a ticket to the big top. That was good because no one could afford the admission. I found out where they kept them in the trailer and developed a system to pilfer the tickets. It was really quite simple: while I went into the trailer and grabbed the stash of tickets, my buddies would watch to see if anyone was coming in our direction. During the first two weeks I was employed, every one of my buddies was able to see the show. It was a thrill of a lifetime to meet Ken Maynard in person. Every Saturday we went to the Strand or Palace theatres to see Western movies and serials. Ken Maynard was one of our favorite cowboys, and to this day we all could not believe our luck.

I gave the job to one of my buddies when a sideshow barker walked by and saw that I had quite a few friends. He had something in mind and got the bright idea to assist him barking. His sideshow went something like this: "Alright, alright, step right up. The one and only Little Jo Jo, the dogface man; he has two sets of teeth in his upper jaw. When he bites, he bites twice. Give 'em a little bark, Jo Jo." And with that, someone pulled the string and allowed this fearful sound that came out like a ferocious bark. He asked me to work for him, and rewarded me with $2.00 a day

3

At the circus, Ken Maynard on his horse Tarzan.

and a pair of tickets to the big top. I immediately accepted. I was asked to come to work that night and told to wear a sport coat and a bow tie. It didn't take long, I learned fast and the crowds were gathering more and more around the sideshow. I became instantly popular with my buddies and neighbors throughout the stay of the circus. The barker was the happiest camper in town and none the wiser regarding the missing tickets.

We were doing terrific business and I was having a lot of fun. And that was my indoctrination to show business. I forgot to add that I wore a derby, which made me look like a mini version of the barker. My mom, dad and relatives got the biggest kick watching me perform. When the circus left town I immediately went back to my regular life, which included lots of baseball.

Freefall

With the circus on my resume, it didn't mean that I was quite ready to perform death defying stunts. That same year I fell from a 20-foot pole and there was no net to catch me. Allow me to explain.

My next-door neighbor, Mrs. Campana (the mother of Anna Campana, the girl who saved me from drowning) asked me to attach her clothesline from one pole to another in her backyard. It was the summer, which meant it was hot and muggy. The grass was neatly cut and there were grapevines growing in the yard. The vines were attached by wire to wooden railings that were in several rows near the clothesline. Mr. and Mrs. Campana had twelve children, six girls and six boys. None of the boys were home at the time. Mrs. Campana saw me playing in the street in front of her house and asked me to hang up the clothesline in her backyard. I said, "Sure" and she replied prophetically, "Ralph, I know you'll do the job right and you won't fall." Hello!

I climbed to the top of the pole just fine; attached the line, but on my way down I caught the hammer loop on the side of my overalls. It threw me off balance and I plummeted to the ground. Twenty feet doesn't sound like much on paper, but it was a miracle I didn't kill myself. I got up thinking I broke my hip or my leg. I never told anyone what happened. I didn't want my mom and dad to worry or take me to a doctor. At home I moved around the house so gingerly when my parents and my siblings were not looking. I was sensitive and concerned because we didn't have insurance. That would have been more painful. I knew we could not afford a huge doctor bill. It took a few painful weeks but I got through it. The most pain I felt was not from the fall itself, but not being able to run without discomfort for quite some time. Mrs. Campana was busy inside the house taking the clothes out of the washing machine to hang on the newly erected clothesline and never knew I fell from that 20 foot pole.

The good Lord saved me again.

3

Go, Yankees!

I was just a kid when I saw Yankee Stadium for the first time. The New York Yankees were playing the Cleveland Indians, and it was a big deal to any kid growing up in that era. I went with the Boy Scouts, Troop 18, on a bus despite the fact I was not a member. A couple of buddies of mine told me about the journey and that I should tag along by sneaking me on the bus. It would be easy because there would be about a hundred youths going and all I had to do was follow their instructions. They gave me a troop hat and shirt for starters, and told me to answer when the scoutmaster called out Al Peluso's name, "Here!" The guys were right—it was easy. The scoutmaster never lifted his head when he called out the names from a clipboard. After roll call I could finally relax and enjoy the experience. We were each given $1.00 for hotdogs, ice cream and sodas. In those days a dollar went a long way.

For the next few hours I was mesmerized. Hall of Famer Bob Feller was pitching that afternoon against the Bronx Bombers. The team included the greatest all-around player of all time, the legendary Joe DiMaggio. To this day, he was the most graceful ballplayer I ever saw. He just loped after the ball and made everything look so easy.

We sat in the third tier of the old Yankee Stadium, in the highest seats, close to baseball heaven. I felt like I could touch the sky. We could see every inch of the ballpark as we looked down on our heroes, playing that All American sport. For me, it didn't get any better. Joe had his usual stellar day against Feller: three hits, a homerun, double, a single, scored two runs, made two great catches and picked off a runner trying to take an extra base. Halfway through the game, I knew I wanted to be a big league ballplayer. I couldn't wait to get home to tell my parents where I went and informed them of my new ambition.

Upon our return to the Sacred Heart Church parking lot, I said my goodbyes, and ran two miles home as fast as I could and didn't stop until I got there. I knew I was late getting home. Once inside the house, I told my father, "Dad if you buy me a glove, I'll work hard for eight years and I'll be a big league ballplayer." My father looked at me like I was crazy. He couldn't even get his employees to work eight hours with such dedication. After I calmed down and told him in detail what I had experienced and where I had been, I was forgiven. The next day my father bought me a baseball glove—and not just any glove—an infielder's glove, a Marty Marion model. I was the happiest kid alive. From that moment on I never stopped dreaming and practicing what I set out to do. In addition, I prayed every night for the Lord to help me along the way and even took my glove and bat to bed with me for good measure.

With a large silhouette panel of Joe DiMaggio at the new Yankee Stadium in 2012.

Many years later I interviewed Bob Feller on my radio show and talking with this Hall of Famer for one hour was one of the highlights of my career. We met at Harmon Killebrew's celebrity golf tournament in Scottsdale, Arizona. For ten years we met annually to support Harmon's Foundation. It was a great tournament with all the money going to various charities. We always enjoyed ourselves and of course most of the players were Hall of Famer's from the NBA, NFL and Major League Baseball. Bob was there every year for the entire decade and we had some nice conversations. Many years later I was invited to play in Joe DiMaggio's Bocce Tournament in Las Vegas. Joe was a big fan of TV and western movies, and I had appeared in several. The tournament organizers contacted me and I immediately accepted to play. As a matter of fact, my partner and I finished third and won $2,500. My partner was Ralph Branca, the ex-pitcher for the Los Angeles Dodgers. I set a trend by donating half of it back to the charity, and the others followed suit.

The extra benefit was my friendship with Joe DiMaggio. We met at the Warner Lambert Celebrity Golf Tournament in Florida and alternate years in Palm Springs. We grew close and he liked my wife Mary Jane as well. Whenever we saw each other Joe would insist Mary Jane and I sit with him. He followed my career just as I idolized and followed his until Joe's last game. Joe was sensitive, private and particular about the people he shared his time with. He loved drinking coffee, smoking cigarettes and was an impeccable dresser. He wanted someone around he could trust to buffer the fans and strangers. He enjoyed his privacy and practically demanded it.

Which reminds me of the time when I was sitting with Joe in Las Vegas at a cocktail lounge along with a good friend of Joe's by the name of Sugar Brown, a retired middle-aged "Runyonesque" type character. We were in the middle of a conversation when a young attractive lady and her husband approached the table. She obviously had too much to drink. In a very inebriated way she began to spew out loud how well she knew Marilyn Monroe and that she went to school with her when her real name was "Norma Jean." She kept repeating how well she knew Norma Jean, which made Joe extremely agitated. I was sitting on one side of him and Sugar Brown on the other side, and her motor mouth was just getting revved up. It was embarrassing, so I spoke up and told them we were in the middle of a very important meeting. Her husband finally pulled her away, but Joe was still uncomfortable. About five minutes later he excused himself from the table and said he was going up to his room and would be right back. About twenty minutes later, he did not return. Sugar and I went to the house phone to call his room. The operator said he just checked out. We weren't surprised that he was on the next plane to San Francisco. Throughout the years we spent time together and that subject matter was never brought up.

I really had to pinch myself from time to time because no matter where I saw Joe, he would immediately wave me over to join him. It was an extraordinary boyhood dream come true to spend quality time with my idol, an unbelievable gift.

But what are the odds that 70 years later in June 2012, my wife and I were given two tickets as an anniversary gift to the new Yankee Stadium and watched the Yanks take on the Cleveland Indians again? And the icing on the cake was that my team won that day, too!

Mrs. Calhoun

I was in the fourth grade when my teacher Mrs. Calhoun, a slender, dark-haired, attractive woman, made me aware that I read differently than the other students in class. Each one of us was more self-conscious than the other, particularly me. Everyone was asked to read a paragraph except me. Mrs. Calhoun was theatre-oriented and saw something different in me and allowed me to read a few pages. It was painful though because I was so shy. I was not aware that I read differently. I didn't know then that I was really performing, not just reading. The book was by Jack London and entitled *Barry*. I remember one scene went something like this: "It was a pitch dark, windy and cold night. You could hear wolves howling off in the distance. Barry was perched by the fire and beginning to react nervously to the cries of the wolves getting closer and closer. The wind was howling through the trees and the wolves again inching closer and closer. Barry was getting very tense because the wolves were getting too close for comfort."

I was sweating bullets when I finished reading because I was so self-conscious and embarrassed. I didn't even realize the class was watching me perform. Mrs. Calhoun said gently and with an assuring manner, "That was very good."

I didn't see words when I was reading. I saw pictures. My mind quickly transferred the words to images. Something magical was taking place as the words seemed to flow freely without any hesitation. Miraculously, I didn't feel shy when I was performing. The next day Mrs. Calhoun asked me to read for a play that Ms. Brown, the sixth grade teacher, was directing and producing. Ms. Brown looked and was built exactly like Eleanor Roosevelt and ruled with an iron fist. We were all frightened to death of her and called her "Mamma Brown." Mrs. Calhoun said she would give me an improved grade in English and Reading if I would just audition for the part. I thought it would be an easier way to get better marks, so I had nothing to lose. It was a win-win situation, because I felt I wouldn't get the part.

It was my hope to get turned down immediately so I could go and play baseball with my buddies, who accompanied me to Ms. Brown's room and waited outside. I went inside thinking that I would read and make a fool of myself, she'd ask me to leave and I'd be on my way.

I purposely walked in and was rude. I wore a pork pie hat and disrupted everyone. Ms. Brown told me to, "take off that hat and pick up the sides on the table!" I didn't even know what sides were or what she was talking about. She scolded me and told me to sit down and prepare myself to read the part of Joey. I picked up the sides and sat down with just two pages of dialogue. Before I knew it, I was on my feet reading the part of Joey. The dialogue went something like this: "Ah Ma, what 'ya boder me for? Every time you ax me to do somethin' I'm going out to play ball. Can I throw

Stevens Elementary School.

the garbage away when I get back?" I purposely read the lines like one of the Dead End Kids, and everyone started laughing, even Ms. Brown was smiling.

"Young man you have the part of Joey," she said. "That accent was perfect!" So there I was stuck doing the play, which was put on stage for the rest of the school to see and enjoy. Not in my wildest dreams did I ever think that I would get the part. But I thought all I had to do was open my mouth and try to speak like a streetwise thug, thinking I would get thrown out on my ear. Instead, it was perfect for the character of Joey. My buddies never let me forget my introduction to the stage. Everyone and their brother and sister got to see me perform. And lemme tell you, it was a lot more difficult than taking care of Ken Maynard's horse or working as a barker in the circus. Interestingly enough, it didn't stick in my youth. It would be many years before I made my return to the stage.

5

Cloonan Junior High

I attended Cloonan Junior High School for seventh, eighth and ninth grades. It was located about three miles from our house at 637 Fairfield Avenue, two blocks from the Old Greenwich city line. Every day I walked past rows and rows of New England style single-family houses with lots of trees and traffic in both directions. I made the 45-minute trek to school in the heat, rain and snow. Sometimes I walked with my schoolmates that I met along the way.

I remember having growing pains around this time. I was growing so damn fast I could feel myself actually sprouting. At one point I became really concerned after I added another three inches to my frame. I went to my father and asked him, "Dad, am I going to be a giant?" I used to measure myself every day. I went through shirts and sweaters at a rapid pace. My dad assured me that I wasn't going to be a giant. I went out and bought a set of barbells and began lifting weights to put on a little

Cloonan Junior High School.

11

muscle. I became very active with the athletic programs they had at the school; baseball, basketball, boxing, wrestling and gymnastics. By the time I entered the eighth grade I was the captain of the baseball and basketball teams, a member of the boxing, wrestling and gymnastics teams as well as the Captain of the Leaders Corps. In order to train for the boxing, wrestling and gymnastics teams, I had to be in the gymnasium no later than 7:30 every morning. Baseball and basketball practice took place after school, so my entire youth was wrapped up in athletics, which I loved. I didn't realize later how important that discipline and training became in my life. Needless to say, I ate like a wolf when I got home and got to bed early because I was so darn tired.

One thing I didn't overcome was getting over my shyness. Only when I was on the basketball court, baseball field, or in the gymnasium, did I feel confident about myself. In fact, upon graduation I was voted as the most athletic boy in school and the shyest as well.

We had a one-hour study period which took place in our homeroom. I used the time wisely and studied so I didn't have much to do when I got home. I was a pretty good student. I was proud of the fact that I had never failed a subject in all of my school years. I took great pride in getting the best grades possible and learn as much as I could to make my parents proud. That was very important to me because I loved my parents dearly and would never let them down if I could help it.

It wasn't all athletics. I thoroughly enjoyed my history and science classes throughout the three years I attended Cloonan. I was always curious and anxious to learn about something scientific in the past or in the future. My science teacher did a good job communicating with us because we all looked forward to attending his classes. He spoke slowly to make sure that we understood everything. He also made us feel comfortable if something was not clear.

My history teacher, Mr. Littleworth, was my favorite be-

Receiving a plaque and trophy for the Most Athletic Boy at Cloonan Junior High School.

Quarterback and captain of the Westside Hawks Football Team.

cause of his verbal intelligence, beginning with the Grecian civilization, the Roman Empire, the epic wars and their great leaders throughout history. I used to hang on every word he said. He was so descriptive and delivered his stories with a soft voice that was pleasing to the ears. Everything seemed to sink in so effortlessly.

Mr. Littleworth was tall and very thin, and for good reason—he told us how he was gassed in World War I and was never able to put on any weight for the rest of his life. It certainly didn't affect his mind. He always stood up, in front of a large world map with a pointer in his hand to indicate exactly what country he was historically talking about at that time. We were always able to understand better, because we could see precisely the movement of the armies against one another in various territories throughout history. Each student had the same enthusiasm when it was time to enter his classroom. He was a master teacher because his method of teaching made you see and understand more than with words. We all loved and respected him. He was such a good teacher and a wonderful human being. Just the kind of person I wanted to be when I grew up.

6

Home of the Braves

During my sophomore and junior years at Stamford High School, I didn't audition for any of the school plays. I didn't have the confidence or the inclination and I was still shy. I put all my energy and time into practicing to make the high school baseball, basketball team and a semi pro football team called the Stamford Aces. I never deviated from my boyhood dream of becoming a major league baseball player.

By the time I became a senior, I played on four championship baseball teams. Our high school team won the Connecticut state championship in 1949. I played for the Sacred Heart team in the Twilight League and the American Legion team in Stamford and we won the championship for both teams. I also played for the Stamford Advocate in the New England Newspaper League and we won the New England Championship. I was singled out as the most valuable player and signed a $6,000 bonus with the Boston Braves along with my teammate outfielder Joe Morelli. We played our playoff games in 'Beantown' and it was the first time I left home since I ventured to Yankee Stadium. We played the series at the old Boston Braves ballpark and it was an incredible experience. It had a traditional ballpark feel with all the players, managers and umpires on a neatly manicured field,

Returning with team from Boston, Massachusetts, after winning the New England Newspaper League Championship.

Shortstop on the Westside Eagles baseball team.

and of course, the crack of the bat, the colorful sales pitches of the vendors and the smell of the popcorn. The Waltham Company made their clocks in Boston and was one of the sponsors of the Braves. Their huge clock remained in place in centerfield even after the Braves moved to Milwaukee in the 1950s.

I had never been away from home for a length of any period. Our team stayed at the famous Somerset Hotel where all the major league clubs lodged and commuted to the park from there. The hotel had a nostalgic and fun atmosphere, and the food was the best. After each game we spent time at the swimming pool, enjoying each victory. We had to win three games to take the championship, and we did just that. Two Boston Braves scouts stayed in the same suite with me for fear that I might sign with another team. To assure themselves that I wouldn't sign with anyone else, they accompanied me home to Stamford to sign a contract in the presence of my parents since I was underage at that time. The Boston Braves head scout Jeff Jones signed me to my bonus contract.

My high school graduation picture.

Now in those days a $6,000 bonus was the maximum that they could give to anyone, because they would have to keep a player two years on the major league roster before they could option you out if you received a penny more. They gave me the maximum, which was fine. That was a lot of money back then. Not much longer after I inked the deal, major league baseball eliminated the $6,000 maximum bonus so they were able to give more money to prospects entering professional baseball instead of going to college. I missed it by one year. Otherwise, I would've received a bonus in the neighborhood of $100,000.

With the bonus money I bought the family our first car. It was a brand new four-door Buick with whitewall tires, radio, heater…it was a real beauty and cost somewhere around $2,500. I told my mom and dad I would like to reserve some of the money to go to college to study drama at the University of Miami in case I got injured. Little did I know a year-and-a half later how wise that decision was. What I didn't know at the time was that fate was dealing me a slow hand providing a path toward my lifelong vocation—acting.

My Rookie Year

At the end of March 1950, I left for spring training to Myrtle Beach, South Carolina. It was an old army base that was converted into a baseball spring training facility for the Boston Braves' minor league players to get in shape for the coming season. There were approximately eight hundred players in camp, representing every minor league club in the Braves organization. We were put up in World War II army barracks and it was not the cleanest or most comfortable place in the world. As a matter of fact, about half of us got the crabs during our stay! It was a long and drawn out process with too many players vying for spots. I barely got any batting practice.

I was on the roster and at that time Atlanta was the Boston Braves Double-A club in the Southern Association League. Our manager was Tommy Holmes who played eleven seasons in the major leagues, ten with the Braves and his final year with the Brooklyn Dodgers. He was a strong leader who went on to manage the Boston Braves in 1952. I knew I was not going to make that club and was looking forward to getting assigned to a team that I was going to play for the coming season. When we broke camp I was sent to play in Olean, New York, in the Pony League. The Braves had a working agreement with Olean. I was doing well, but for some reason the organization had a falling out with the Olean front office and four of us who were property of the Braves were sent to other affiliated clubs. I was sent to Owensboro, Kentucky who were owned by the Braves. For an 18-year-old I was beginning to travel quite a bit, seeing places I never had seen before. I wasn't a happy camper with the Braves organization, but I enjoyed playing in Owensboro much more than I did in Olean and certainly a lot better than spring training in Myrtle Beach, South Carolina.

Travis Jackson was the Owensboro manager and was a talented major league player in his day. He played the infield for 15 seasons with New York Giants 1922 to 1936, left with a lifetime batting average of .291, and was inducted into the Hall of Fame in 1982. I learned a lot from him. Just wish I could have played for him the entire year. I got off to a slow start and finished with a batting average .231 as opposed to hitting over .300 in Olean earlier in the season. While playing in Owensboro, I bought a 1936 four-door Dodge. I paid $120 for it and had more fun with that old jalopy than I could imagine.

I was able to drive to and from the park and around town. As matter of fact, when the season was over, I drove home with two other players that were living in Pennsylvania and Maryland. Talk about an adventure! I had more guts than brains but we did get home safely. We had fun along the way and stayed overnight at one of my teammates, Ed Melisevich's farm in Pennsylvania. The farmhouse didn't have many modern amenities and it still had a hand-cranked well for water.

17

It was an early gothic-style home with a rambling one-story floor plan. There was a big fireplace and a large kitchen. Ed's family had emigrated from Poland to the United States, and they were very friendly and welcoming to us. They owned several cows, chickens, goats and pigs. Our breakfast was fresh and delicious, and as they say "right off the farm." The next morning I went on my way and drove my other teammate to his home in Marysville, Maryland. We had more laughs about that car. When we left Owensboro all of our teammates thought we were crazy to take a chance to travel all those miles in that loveable heap.

When I finally arrived home I received some heartbreaking news. The girl that I dated in high school for three years and the woman I thought I would marry was seeing someone else while I was away. I immediately

Rookie year at spring training with the Atlanta Braves of the Southern Association League in 1950.

called her when I arrived and arranged to take her to the movies. The next evening I picked her up in my Kentucky heap and the moment she sat down in the car and got comfortable, she told me without a trace of emotion that she no longer wanted to go steady. That was pretty shocking because I thought she was in love with me. I must say I recovered rather quickly. I drove around the block and took her home. I wished her the best, headed home and remembered another favorite line of mine, "You never lose anything you never had!"

Neither of us knew at the time that she did me a big favor. I was now free to pursue my life without the encumbrance of someone I could not trust. I was going in one direction and she was going in another.

Despite my single status, I had a prosperous winter. I stayed in good shape, went to the gym three times a week and played basketball three nights a week. I even refereed some basketball games for the Stamford High School Recreation Board. The following March I went to spring training again to Myrtle Beach, South Carolina. At least this time I knew what to expect. There wasn't much improvement, but there weren't as many ballplayers as they were the year before.

Hanging out with Atlanta Braves teammates Tito Francona and Marty Keough.

I guided my own work ethics and schedule. I was aware and knew what to do and not to do as that first year taught me an awful lot about myself and what spring training was all about. Several coaches and players said I was the most improved player in camp. It was unfortunate; a few weeks later I hurt my arm. The Braves sent me to their local doctor, who really didn't know anything about sports medicine.

He administered diathermy treatments, which in hindsight was the worst thing he could have done. It was like putting fire to fire and instead of helping the arm, it only got worse. I couldn't throw across the room without pain. It got to the point where tears would roll down my face after I threw over the top. There isn't anything worse than playing injured. It was unfortunate for me that sports medicine was behind the times in the early fifties. Today that kind of injury could have been easily treated and I might've been out of action a week or two at most. Not knowing how to treat the injury made everything psychologically more painful.

The best advice that one of the doctors gave me was to go someplace where the weather was warm. Since I couldn't throw, I really couldn't play. I went to Boston to ask for my release. I wasn't happy with them and they felt the same way with me. So they gave me my walking papers. I took my doctor's advice and decided to go where the weather was a heck of a lot warmer, and, saw sunshine twelve months of the year.

California, Here I Come

Looking back, the timing of my departure from the East Coast was near perfect. My aunt, uncle and niece were leaving Stamford, Connecticut, to live in Van Nuys, California, a suburb of Los Angeles in the San Fernando Valley. I went along for the ride in a comfortable four door Cadillac and enjoyed all the beautiful sites along the way.

The California climate was pleasant and I immediately started running, hitting, throwing, and fielding ground balls at a local park. To my surprise there were several professional ballplayers working out during the week participating in the Southern California Semi-Pro League on weekends with a lot of ex-pros and young players like myself. I was in good company and my arm was beginning to come around. It wasn't 100 percent, but I was able to throw and make the plays without much pain for the first time in over a year. It was getting better and at nineteen years of age, something had to heal. I didn't realize at the time I needed to stretch the ligaments in my shoulder from the point where it was inflamed to healthy tissue. It had to be done by a good professional trainer. I didn't learn this simple way of treating it until much later.

Bill Hoyt, my manager for the Stamford Advocate team, wrote to Hollywood Stars catcher Mike Sandlock that I was coming to California and explained my situation. When I felt I was ready as instructed by Bill, I went to Gilmore Field, the home field of the Hollywood Stars of the Pacific Coast League, to meet Sandlock a few hours before game time. The Stars were playing a night game against the Los Angeles Angels and Mike was there early to get treated by the trainer for a nagging injury. He was expecting me along the way and asked me how I felt and if I wanted to suit up. I brought my gear and was ready to work. I cautiously took my time warming up and went to the shortstop position and fielded a few ground balls. I worked up a good sweat and I felt better about my arm than I did a couple of weeks before.

The coach called me in to take some batting practice and standing nearby were two Pittsburgh Pirates scouts, Howie Haak and Rosie Gillhausen. When I finished hitting they invited me to workout with the club for the duration of the Stars home stand. That first weekend I played in a game at Southgate. I met Herman Reich who was the former first baseman for the Chicago Cubs and played in the Pacific Coast League for a number of years. He was scouting and looking for professional players for Hermosillo, one of the Mexican Coast Winter League teams. I had a good game and afterwards he asked me if I was interested in playing south of the border. I told him I was and we exchanged phone numbers. He kept in touch to give me all the info to get to Hermosillo when the time came to leave. This was the last week of the season for the Hollywood Stars and I continued to work out with the club. I met with manager Fred Haney and told him I was going to play in the Mexican Coast Winter League with Hermosillo. He told me to be sure to see him in his office at the ballpark on my way back home.

He gave me his blessing and in short order I was in Mexico.

9

Baseball South of the Border

I flew from LAX to Hermosillo, Mexico, and arrived on time. Much to my dismay, there was no one at the airport to pick me up. Not helping matters was the fact I didn't speak the language. I managed to get to my destination, the San Alberto Hotel, by speaking Italian. When I made contact with the club's business manager, apologies were in order. It was all new and strange for this wide-eyed 20-year-old kid. I had dinner that night with Herman Reich and our manager, Virgilo Arteaga, and the next day we were at the ballpark getting ready for the upcoming season.

It was extremely hot and humid; my arm was loosening up and getting better every day because of the heat. The ballpark was in good shape and our home field was one of the best in the league. Most of the infields in the league were skinned with pebbles making it very tough on the infielders, with bad hops all over the place. When we finished the first road trip, the second baseman, Howie Philips and I had black and blue marks all over our chests! Howie was the property of the St. Louis Cardinals organization and played several years with Rochester in the International League. He was a good all-around veteran player.

I got off to a good start. I became an instant fan favorite, because they played Lamacarena, the bullfighter entrance song at the ballpark and I was the next batter on deck when the music started. I was inspired by the music and thought I would ham it up a little and did a "Veronica Pass" the crowd absolutely went wild. Guess it was those acting instincts coming out. The fans immediately began yelling, "Oye muy guapo." I thought they were calling me a "Wop." Well, the joke was on me because they were complimenting me. "Guapo" in Spanish means handsome, good looking or attractive. We all had a big laugh and the nickname stuck. The fans treated me well and the town was one of the nicest in the league. In those days we played four games a week; one game on Friday, Saturday and a doubleheader on Sunday. The other three days we were free to workout, play golf, go fishing or just rest up before the weekend. That was the main reason they were able to attract quite a few "name" American ballplayers for their winter league. Sad to say, those days are long gone. Nowadays it's just like any other professional major league schedule, play six days a week and only one day off.

To keep it in perspective, they only allowed six Americans on each team; it still was the Mexican Coast Winter League. So you can imagine how thrilled and how fortunate I felt playing with so many more experienced players. Besides, the extreme hot and humid weather was healing my arm and I was getting more confident every day. For the first time in more than a year I was enjoying playing the game I loved. I was learning fast and playing on a much higher level. I even found a bat I could control for the first time in my career. It was an old S2 Luke Appling model, 35 inches in length and weighed 32 ounces. I used that model until the last game I ever played, and what a difference it made. It took all my high school years and two years playing professionally to know what bat I could handle, I was never that comfortable at the plate until I found that ol' Luke Appling S2.

The second weekend of the season, Mr. La Brada, the owner of the Hermosillo ball club, asked me if I would like to go with a couple of the other players to his beach house in Guaymas.

He said he had a terrific chef and plenty of help. We were welcome to spend our off days there to fish and cook. He soon came to discover that players liked to drink a lot and eat a little. I accepted the invitation and was looking forward to this new experience as well as enjoy the seafood they would be preparing for us. He said there would be a couple of players from the Guaymas ball club there as well. It was a large spacious beach house, maybe fifty yards from shore with five bedrooms and a huge kitchen loaded with all the cooking utensils you would need, hanging from wrought iron racks.

I recall Bob Moncrief was there, the ace pitcher for the Guaymas team and had several good years in the big leagues, particularly with the St. Louis Browns. In his prime he had one of the best curveballs in baseball, a nice guy and a great storyteller. Guaymas was noted for its shrimp. The chef did a fabulous job frying all the seafood in beer. It cooks fast and the beer flavor melds into the food. Again it was something new, different and delicious.

That was the first time in my life I had eaten food cooked in beer. By the way, Mr. La Brada was the only distributor of the Miller Highlife beer in all of Mexico, and was an extremely wealthy man. He was also a good customer as his chef cooked everything in beer.

A few hours after our scrumptious meal, I decided to go for a swim in the ocean. It was low tide that day so I walked out and swam out quite a distance. Before I knew it I was far from the beach house. I turned around to see how far I was offshore and noticed one of the employees waving a white towel and yelling as loud as he could. I was beginning to get tired and I was no longer perpendicular to the beach house. I had drifted along with the current and at that point, I started to work back to shore as fast as I could towards the house. He was still waving the white towel and yelling continuously, "Tobonero, Tobonero!" By this time everyone in the house came out on the beach, and they were all yelling and waving me to shore. It took me a while, but I eventually made it. Completely exhausted, I walked to the shore and everybody surrounded me. They informed me I was swimming in shark-infested waters and insinuated how lucky I wasn't attacked. That's when I learned that Tobonero means "shark" in Spanish.

Our first road trip was to Mazatlan. They had a good team and the two clubs were rivals ever since the league started. We stayed at a very old hotel in Mazatlan, which was ornate; everything was made of wood and the front doors were all hand-carved. A guard stood by the door with a pistol at his side. The doors stood about 15 feet tall and made an impressive entrance. Three of us—Howie Philips, Fletcher and me—were put into a huge room on the Mezzanine floor with three antique hand-carved bed frames that had tall bedposts and carved headboards. They were beautiful antique works of art.

En route to the ballpark for a day game the next day, we were bombarded by loyal Mazatlan fans throwing oranges and lemons at us. We traveled in an open bus, leaving us a vulnerable and easy target. The fans were very emotional, yelling at us and calling us all kinds of names. The American players learned later this was a tradition.

Their ballpark was not a pretty one. The infield and outfield lacked grass and the surface was rough and filled with rocks and pebbles. To make matters worse, that day we were facing the best left-hander in the league, Lino Donoso, who was one of the starting pitchers for the Pittsburg

Playing for the Mexican Coast Winter League Team Hermosillo.

Pirates that year and he threw BBs. Although he beat us, I had a good day against him with two hits and some nice plays in the field.

On the way back to the hotel, we got bombarded again. That night after our day game Howie Philips, Fetcher and I went to an amphitheater not far from the hotel where they served good food and beer. It was hot and humid that night but we did enjoy the atmosphere, the food, the beer and the stories were all interesting. I guess we stayed there until about 11 P.M. and walked back to the hotel, which was only about ten minutes away. There was the guard with his pistol at the hotel entrance, he opened the huge door as we approached and we went up to our massive room on the mezzanine floor.

Again, the doors were huge and took a big key to open. We entered the room like three tired ballplayers needing rest. I locked the door from the inside with the large old-fashioned key, turned out the lights, took off our clothes and hit the sack. Before going to sleep we all hung our pants over the bedposts at the edge of the bed. We got paid just before we left for Mazatlan, all American cash. I took my wallet out of my pants and put it inside my pillow, way back into the far end. My street smarts went to work when I first laid eyes on that armed guard at the front door.

The room was so huge and the beds were located in each corner, I had no idea where Howie or Fletch put their wallets. The next morning, about seven o'clock, I heard a commotion coming from the lobby down below. I was closest to the door and was awakened by loud yelling and bickering going back and forth. All three of us woke up and looked for our pants. We put them on the bedpost, and they weren't there. Sensing something was wrong, we bolted out the door to the mezzanine balcony and looked down to the floor of the lobby and there lay the three pair of pants.

The police, the hotel management and the officer who was supposedly on guard that night were going back and forth, like a question and answer time about what happened or what could've happened. Obviously the guard must have been in on the deal. There was a rope at the other end of the mezzanine balcony to our right about twenty yards from our door attached to the bars. The

The Three Amigos: with teammates Olney Patterson and Royce Lint in the Mexican Coast Winter League.

rope led to the street level. Whoever came into our room had to have a weapon. We were three big athletes and to have the nerve to open that locked door had to be a professional and an inside job. Turned out I was the lucky one for having put my wallet in my pillow. Fletcher and Philips left their wallets in their trousers. Fletch was calling them every name in the book.

In no time our manager, Virgilio Arteaga, came to the lobby where he discovered everything on the floor and people yelling at each other. Somebody had to know we had just gotten paid and got paid in American money. Fletcher told him they had broken into our room and stole all of our money even though the door was locked from the inside.

He told our manager in no uncertain terms what he thought of Mexico and if he didn't have his money by the time we got to the ballpark he'd be on the next plane to the States. Now you have to imagine this is all said very emotionally with a harelip. It was really funny but we didn't dare laugh. Even Philips had to pinch himself to keep from breaking up. After all the questioning with the police and having had our say with our manager Virgilo Arteaga, we went to breakfast and took a cab to the ballpark.

I wasn't so lucky this time. I had to pick up the tab because they didn't have any money. To listen to Fletch bitch and moan all way to the ballpark with his harelip was classic. To this day I don't know if Fletch ever got his money from the club but the next day he left for home. I had the feeling he got paid and went home anyway.

Playing in the Mexican Coast Winter League was really a special experience for me. I was the youngest American player in the league, competing against some of the most outstanding big league athletes in all of Mexico. Getting to know and understand the people, culture and what it meant to be a minority for the first time. Everything was new and a first for me.

It was a short season, although I was playing well and beginning to put it all together. However, they dropped the American athletes and I was one of them. We were not winning, our pitching was not very good and we didn't have much power in our lineup. I was not disappointed. I was there long enough to get my arm to where I could throw without pain. I was playing at the highest level possible and absorbed all that Mexico had to offer. I was looking forward to stopping to see Fred Haney, the manager of the Hollywood Stars, as he instructed me to do so.

I flew to San Diego from Hermosillo, where my ex-teammate Olney Patterson picked me up at the airport. We spent a couple of days visiting with he and his parents before I left for Los Angeles. Olney was our centerfielder for Hermosillo until he was released a couple of weeks before me. I enjoyed the visit, and seeing several military ships that were docked in the San Diego Harbor, an awesome sight of huge, magnificent aircraft carriers. Another first in my life, thanks to baseball.

10

Layover in L.A.

Upon arriving in Los Angeles, I immediately went to see Mr. Haney at Gilmore Field, home of the Hollywood Stars. The ballpark was located near Fairfax Avenue near the famous Canter's Deli in the heart of Hollywood. I sat down in his office and he told me I was invited to spring training with the Hollywood Stars in March. He said he didn't think he'd be managing the Hollywood Stars because he was in negotiations to helm the Pittsburgh Pirates. He said, however, I would be in good hands if Bobby Bragan managed the club if all went well with his negotiations with the Pirates.

Mr. Haney said I would be hearing from the front office with all the instructions about transportation and when spring training would commence. He then took me to the Stars' business office and arranged for my plane transportation home. It was an incredibly thoughtful gift. At that moment I was the happiest ballplayer in the whole world, looking forward to spring training with the Hollywood Stars. He was not only a terrific manager but one hell of a sincere man. It was a pleasure to know him and my only regret is that I wish I could've played for him. I left the office and headed for the airport and home, one happy young man.

11

Going Home

I arrived home and before long I shared all of my experiences with my family and buddies. I was feeling great with all the expectations before me. I thought the needed rest for the next couple of months before spring training would be perfect, especially for my arm and shoulder.

I started running and throwing two weeks before I left for spring training sometime in March or April with the Hollywood Stars. Little did I know at the time, resting my shoulder did not help. I eventually learned the ligaments in my shoulder contracted. I soon found out by throwing and preparing those two weeks before I left for spring training that I was back to square one because no one at the time knew anything about sports medicine to be of any help.

All the pain and frustration I endured along the way, just to think that all I needed was a simple stretch of my arm which would have taken care of all the problems. If I only knew to continue to throw indoors to keep those ligaments stretched until I went to spring training.

It was the first time I doubted what I was doing and thought that maybe the good Lord might have had something else in mind for me. Leaving for spring training and knowing I couldn't throw, my only hope was that their doctor or trainer could help me. Wishful thinking…

I revisited my childhood home at 637 Fairfield Avenue almost seven decades later in 2012.

Hollywood Stars of the PCL

The time had come to say my goodbyes to my family and friends. I hopped on a plane bound for Fullerton, California, the spring training camp of the Hollywood Stars baseball team of the Pacific Coast League. The PCL was an unclassified league before the major league teams came west. Fullerton was not far from Los Angeles with its plentiful citrus orchards and the future home of Disneyland, about an hour's drive from the Los Angeles Airport.

California orange and lemon groves in the 1950s.

All the ballplayers stayed in a charming, early California Spanish-style hotel where many of us gathered in the main lobby to watch television and commiserate. The hotel was a short distance from the ball park and the team supplied round trip transportation to and from the park. The journey was a pretty sight. There were orange and lemon trees row upon row all the way to our home field. You could smell the aroma of the fruit blossoms for miles. Since my father was in the wholesale produce business, it was even more interesting and educational because California oranges and lemons were a big part of his sales to his customers. When I spoke on the phone with my dad, I shared with him my new fascination with produce and it tightened our bond.

Our sports facility was huge and well-groomed. No one had the power to hit one out of the park during the entire training session. It was about 450 feet in dead center and 400 feet down the left field and right field lines. The moment I started to throw I knew I was in trouble again.

Picture of the original entrance to Disneyland in Anaheim, California, in the 1950s.

Our trainer, Jake, was a grumpy old tobacco-chewing, ex-fighter who only catered to the veteran ballplayers. I asked for help but his reply was typical, "A big young strong guy like you? Just keep throwing and you'll be alright." Well, I wasn't alright. He didn't know my history and cared even less. Again, all I needed was to stretch those ligaments beyond the point where there was no inflammation, but unfortunately, I didn't learn that until much later. The good weather conditions were perfect along with a bunch of talented guys trying to make the club. It was sad. I was so ready to show them what I could do.

Unfortunately, it was not to be. What it boiled down to was if you can't throw you can't play. I became a good hitter by using the right length and weight of my S2 Luke Appling bat, relaxed my hands and learned what kind of stuff the opposing pitcher had to offer, all of which I learned on my own playing in Mexico. The team sent me to a local doctor and he gave me a shot of cortisone, which was something new in those days. The shot did not help and before I knew it a month went by, spring training was over and I was on my way home.

I was told to stay in touch and to let them know how my arm was coming along. They didn't completely give up on me and thought I was still an outstanding prospect at only twenty years of age. Inside, I was heartbroken again. My instincts told me not to give up, just hang in there no matter what and not lose hope. I believed the good Lord was going to show me the way one way or another.

Twilight League

I went home and stayed in shape by playing in the Twilight League, a good local semi-pro league in Stamford, Connecticut. I had to play first base and throw underhanded because of my shoulder. I did all the things to stay in good condition; took as much batting practice and fielded as many ground balls as I could, hoping and praying my arm would come around.

The summer seemed to zip by but my arm was not getting any better. Toward the end of the summer season I spoke with the Pirates organization, which was the parent club of the Hollywood Stars at that time. Joe L. Brown was the general manager of the New Orleans Double A Ball Club in the Southern Association. He invited me to spring training in March with their club in Huntsville, Texas, managed by Danny Murtaugh, former second baseman for the Pittsburgh Pirates. I learned later that Joe L. was the son of Joe E. Brown, the famous actor/comedian.

I hoped my arm would be okay before I left for spring training with the New Orleans club in Huntsville, Texas. Again I was hoping and praying they had a trainer who knew more about shoulder injuries than anyone previously. They were giving me every opportunity to make the team. Time and chances were running thin!

14

The Heart of Texas

Huntsville, Texas had a nice training facility. I got off to another good start and impressed manager Danny Murtaugh and Joe L. Brown with my good hands, range and my much improved hitting ability. However, my arm continued to be a liability.

I still was not able to throw over the top without pain. I took it upon myself to move to second base, where I could throw side arm and still have enough steam on the ball to throw the runner out. I was now more mature, knew how to go about my business on and off the playing field. I was popular and well respected by the other ballplayers because of the way I performed for my age and how I played the game.

In the middle of our spring training the Pirates organization asked Danny Murtaugh to manage the parent club and also hire Joe L. Brown as the general manager. Danny replaced Fred Haney, who two years before was the manager of the Hollywood Stars club. It created an awful lot of curious dialogue, controversy and distraction during spring training.

Just before we broke camp, the announcement was made about the change in staff. I knew that would help me because Danny and Joe L. liked the way I played the game. But at this point, I couldn't throw overhand, which meant on the relay plays from the outfield suffered.

Before we broke camp I spoke to Joe L. Brown. He said they thought highly of me and that I should see a good orthopedic doctor to have the arm operated on because I had a good future with the organization. He also said he would be glad to have me back next spring if my shoulder was fixed and rehabilitated; as always is the case, easier said than done.

15

Shoulder a Heavy Burden

The time had come to address the inevitable. I went home to Stamford, Connecticut, and upon the advice of the New Orleans trainer contacted Dr. George E. Bennett, head of the orthopedic surgeons at Johns Hopkins Hospital in Baltimore, Maryland. He was the first one to put pins in Ted Williams' shoulder when it separated and was doing groundbreaking work for athletes. I was hoping and praying he could help me.

I went to Baltimore and met with Dr. Bennett, who couldn't have been nicer and more concerned. He knew how much I loved playing baseball. He said he would cut into my shoulder to explore and do everything he could do to restore the use of that throwing arm without pain. He operated on my shoulder but not before he asked my permission to have the trainer for the Montréal and Toronto hockey teams to observe, because it was exploratory surgery.

He didn't know what he was going to find or what he had to do to repair the shoulder. Certainly, I gave him permission and believe it or not, he didn't charge me one penny. He knew I didn't have medical insurance and was sympathetic to my plight. I shall never forget how generous and kind this great doctor was to me. He and the trainers were there to learn something too; he was the best!

He said he scraped a lot of calcium from the area and removed the bursa sac from the front of the shoulder and that I should be okay after the healing process. Upon my departure he said that I should go to a warm climate, someplace like Florida, and allow it to heal. He said I could start throwing gingerly in a couple of months.

I went home to rest and waited for the healing to take place. I applied and was accepted to the University of Miami of Florida for the fall semester. I decided to enroll as a drama major, my second love, and started my formal education on acting. Of course, the good Lord was guiding me in the right direction all along, but I didn't know it at the time.

16
Miami U

In the summer of 1954, I applied and was accepted to the University of Miami in Florida.

About three weeks before the fall semester, I bought an inexpensive four-door Ford. My childhood friend, Donald Zacagnino, who was interested in going to the university, applied and was also accepted. We drove together to Florida and had an interesting time seeing the sights, as we went down the East Coast imbibing everything along the way. We finally arrived in Coral Gables, the home of the University.

College life was another world, an experience I will never forget as long as I live. It was so exciting to be a part of this great university. The campus was located near beautiful Miami Beach and Crandon Park, where all the students gathered when not at classes or studying. There was lots of dancing and drinking at the park and swimming at the beach. It was certainly a different atmosphere than I've ever experienced before.

We moved to an apartment off campus, not far from our classes. The apartment was a historic Spanish building on a street of all things named Calabria. I was already feeling much better about my decision. I took drama classes and enjoyed the coursework.

The university had a well-groomed ballpark. We arrived at the time during football practice. Everybody was excited to learn that we had an outstanding football team, which made the atmosphere around the campus even more exciting.

Perry Moss, a former All American football player at the University of Illinois, was the head football and baseball coach at the time. As soon as I got settled into my apartment, I went to see Perry. He was receptive and could not have been friendlier. My timing was perfect. Perry was looking for someone to assist him with the baseball program because he was so busy running the football team.

He didn't have the time to spend with the baseball players who wanted to begin their training early for the upcoming season. The conversation began with me asking if I could use the baseball facilities. He told me to take advantage of all of the equipment, training room and the ballpark on one condition: that I would work with the ballplayers until after the football season when he would be able to catch up with me. I was just the right guy he was looking for—a professional who could teach the college kids the fundamentals.

It was a deal made in heaven. I asked him for a letter of recommendation and asked my Drama and English professors to allow me to finish by 1 p.m. That was the key, because I needed a flexible schedule to get myself in good condition before the players were finished with their classes. Then on a daily basis I would be able to give all of my attention to them for the rest of the day. My arm was healing and as the doctor ordered me to, I began throwing, slowly. Without a doubt I had the best schedule in the university to do the things I wanted to do and the best professors as well. I posted at the athletic department that we were going to start the baseball program early, and the response was 100 percent.

There were several ballplayers on full or partial scholarship and word got around fast that we were going to be well prepared for the season and have a lot fun doing it. I had recently been introduced to Mickey Grasso at the Hollywood Race Track, where he was working at the betting windows. I told him what I was up to between races. Mickey was a catcher for the Washington Senators for four years, two years with the New York Giants and one year with Cleveland Indians. I asked him to come out in his spare time to help me with the Miami team.

On his off days he came to work out with the catchers, pitchers and the hitters. He was not only a tremendous help to me, but became a dear friend. Mickey wasn't just a hero with me and the other players, but a World War II hero. He was captured and tortured by the Nazis and managed to escape his POW camp with nine comrades. He crossed the Elbe River by boat to reunite with American GIs. He told me when he was captured he weighed about 200 pounds and when he escaped he weighed almost 150 pounds.

In no time word got out that we were working out every day. Several big leaguers and managers who lived in the area came by to observe and began to workout with the kids. I say "kids" but they were not much younger than me. Some of the players included Mickey McDermott, Less Moss, Mickey Grasso and Hall of Famer Jimmie Fox.

Before long we had quite a large audience watching us work out every day. The kids were developing so fast and I had two players that were signed to professional bonus contracts before the college season started. Perry had some mixed emotions about that!

I was also being challenged in my Drama and English classes. It was all so new to me. It was a full class of approximately 35 students for the most part wanting to become actors. I began to gravitate to those who were serious about learning acting technique. I had to find time to read works written by various playwrights, and eventually rehearse scenes with other students. A big bonus was working with all the pretty ladies in class.

My days were filled with schoolwork, baseball and acting. At night we hung out at a beer joint called The Nook. It was a ten-minute drive from the campus and usually packed with students. It was *the* hangout, particularly for those of us that didn't have enough money to spend on good, wholesome dinners. Many nights we filled up on peanuts and beer because the price was always right.

We ate most of the time at the famous White Castle, the best little hamburgers in the world, and an Italian restaurant called the Santa Croce. The owner was a middle-aged Italian man and his girlfriend was one of the waitresses working there. She took a liking to my friends and me, and gave us a lot of food that was not listed on the check. We'd go in for a pizza, and she would give us spaghetti, meatballs and salad, but only charged us for the pizza. She knew we didn't have much money. Many a night that sweet lady kept us from starving. Also, Mickey McDermott, Pete Henderson the jockey, Mickey Grasso and a few of their friends often invited me to dinner.

To this day, I often think of Mickey Grasso, Pete Anderson and Mickey McDermott and appreciate the real meaning of friendship. They cared about me and were rooting for me to make the big leagues or become a movie star. They often said I was the best-looking baseball player they had ever seen. They believed it to the point that if I didn't make it in the big leagues, I could go to Hollywood and have a career there. McDermott and Grasso told me what a good big league prospect

I was and had a bright future ahead of me if my arm would come around. After a few weeks of practice and working out, Mickey called the General Manager of the Washington Senators, Calvin Griffith and told him I was good enough to make the ball club and to invite me to spring training with the Senators in March, which he did.

Mickey never told him about my arm and my operation because we both figured I would be ready by March 1. This was only the first week in October. McDermott came to the park two to three days a week to work with the pitchers, Mickey Grasso and Less Moss with catchers, while I handled the infielders.

We all worked with the hitters and on two occasions Jimmy Foxx came by to help including Less, Mickey and myself. What a thrill for all of us, and no one could believe the program I had set up for the University.

Perry Moss was so impressed that he offered me a scholarship and asked me to be his assistant coach of the baseball team if I chose to stay. I thanked him and told him I was going to spring training with the Washington Senators in March and would work with the team until the day I left. He was disappointed but understood. I had everything going in my favor, all I had to do now was hope the operation was successful.

It was a Sunday morning when I got a call from McDermott, asking me if I would like to join him and Tommy Dorsey, the famous bandleader and his manager Tino Barzie for lunch at a hotel in downtown Miami.

"I'd like you to meet him because he and Tino love baseball. As a matter of fact, the band will be playing at the Orlando Air Force Base and Rollins College in Orlando when we're at spring training with Washington in March," Mickey informed me. "He loves to talk baseball, and every time he has a concert somewhere near a major or minor league ballpark, he loves to go to the park to work out, and he's not a bad ballplayer."

He told me Tommy was a fascinating guy, a no nonsense leader, highly intelligent and knew everybody in show business. Mickey was absolutely right; Tommy and I hit it off. I told him all about my shoulder operation, the situation at the university and my shot at the big leagues. Tommy said he was going to be doing a number of one nighters up the Florida coast, continue up north through Georgia, South Carolina, North Carolina, Maryland, Pennsylvania and back to New York.

He was married to his wife Jane and was living in Greenwich, Connecticut. At that time Tommy was the number one bandleader in the world. He was also the bandleader on "The Jackie Gleason Show," which was the hottest show on television.

We spent a couple of hours with Tommy and Tino and left with plans to see them in February. I left there feeling good about having met the great Tommy Dorsey. Being a jazz lover, I've admired his musicianship since an early age. The next day I couldn't wait to share my meeting with Tommy with the team, thanks to Mickey McDermott.

The activities and excitement was continuous. Now that the football season was in full swing, the whole campus looked forward to all the home games played at the beautiful and spacious Orange Bowl. I knew a lot of the football players because they fraternized with the baseball team. They had heard about all the professionals I had coming out to work with us and were impressed. As a matter of fact, one of the quarterbacks attended a few of the practices, and he could have made the team as a shortstop. He had terrific hands with excellent running speed and a good arm, but his plate was too full with football and academics.

He had a full football scholarship and was studying to be a doctor. I really thought he had the most talent of all the infielders and was definitely a big league prospect. The days, weeks and

MiCKEY McDERMOTT

Former Yankee Mickey McDermott helped me coach the Miami U baseball team in the mid-1950s and served as a great mentor.

months were going by so fast. I was enjoying my life with my drama classes now that I was learning more about preparation, technique and eliminating as much self-consciousness as possible. I was, however, having a difficult time trying to overcome my basic shyness performing before my peers. I think for most, standing up and speaking in front of people is terrifying.

Every once in a while I had the opportunity to spend some time with Mickey Grasso, Pete Anderson and Archie Stone. Pete hosted many a luncheon or dinner at the Jockey Club not far from the track. The jockeys, owners and trainers dined there all the time, the food and the atmosphere was excellent. They were so concerned about me, like a younger brother and wanted to hear a progress report every so often and to make sure I had a big juicy steak once in a while. They were all so generous and I was enriched to have them as a part of my life.

There were many ex-service men and women attending the university on the G.I. Bill and one of them became a good pal of mine, Steve Sintros from Boston, Massachusetts. He was a terrific, colorful ex-athlete who spoke with a thick Boston accent. One day he got a call from a friend of his, who was the trainer of a horse named The Boston Doge and told him to bet on the horse, because he had a good chance of winning his first race. Steve told us to put a few bucks on him and see what happened.

We weren't experienced gamblers and didn't have extra money to bet. Turned out the horse did win. A few weeks later, Steve got another call to tell him he was running again and to bet on the horse once more. Well this time, we gathered as much money as we could and bet The Doge to win. He did, paying a good price. As a result, Steve became the most popular guy on campus, because for the first time in a long while we all had some extra money.

I almost forgot about my Ford automobile that I purchased before coming down to Florida with my buddy Donald Zacagnino. Once we got settled in our apartment off campus, it seemed as if half of the university borrowed my car for one reason or another. It wasn't in the best of shape, but it got us to and from wherever we wanted to go within reason; classes, ballpark, errands, The White Castle, Santa Croce Restaurant and, of course, The Nook.

One day I loaned it to Joe Rein, an acquaintance whom I didn't know very well at the time. Joe said he needed a ride in a hurry. I told him I couldn't leave but he could take the car as long as he had it back in two hours.

We became buddies after that, and later upon graduation Joe became a successful commercial producer in New York and Hollywood. Time was flying by because my schedule was so full every day. Before I knew it the semester came to an end and the holidays were upon us. I didn't go home for the holidays, so I could concentrate on getting my arm ready.

Several of the ballplayers stayed to get a jump start on the season, which made it convenient for me to have enough players to pitch batting practice, shag fly balls and take infield practice. I was so happy to see the dedication and growth in these players.

I registered for the spring semester taking drama classes, despite the fact that I was leaving school the last day in February to be in Orlando for spring training with the Senators on March 1st. I was working on a scene from the play *Golden Boy*. I was playing the part of Joe Bonaparte with a classmate of mine to present before my drama class.

As I was walking out of my apartment with my arms full of props, the phone rang inside. I hesitated for a moment whether to answer it or not, thinking my family might be trying to get a hold of me. So I pushed the door in, threw the props on the couch and picked up the phone. On the other end was the voice of Tommy Dorsey. He said he was trying to get in touch with me all day.

"Your phone number is not in the book and I called McDermott to get your number but he wasn't home," he said. "I finally called administration and got your number. We're off tonight and we'd like you to have dinner with us. Tino will still try to get a hold of McDermott and have him join us." I said I couldn't join him for dinner because I was working on a scene for my drama class, but I could join him afterwards. He asked me where I was doing the scene. I said, "The Ring Theatre on campus, it's an important dress rehearsal and I can't get out of it."

He said, "Okay we'll meet you backstage and we'll all go to dinner later." I was at a loss for words and was so thrilled the great Tommy Dorsey was going to see me perform. I gave him the time and directions before I hung up the phone and rushed off to the theater in delightful anticipation. True to his word, there Tommy and gang were there sitting in the audience to see me act.

I was inspired and my energy permeated to the back of the theater. I really felt good about my performance. There was a special limited audience that responded very positively, and it could not have been better. Tino and Tommy came to see me backstage and told me how much they enjoyed the scene, especially my work. They admitted they were pleasantly surprised and Tommy said that I had a big future in Hollywood if my arm didn't respond to the operation. After I introduced Tommy and Tino to the director and other actors, we took off to have dinner at a nearby restaurant.

We sat down and relaxed a bit before we ordered our food. Tommy gave me a copy of his tour itinerary and said his final stop in California, was at the Pan Pacific Auditorium in Hollywood. The venue was adjacent to the Hollywood Stars baseball park, Gilmore Field.

Tommy then said something I could hardly believe. "I want you to know I only believed in one other guy that much and his name is Frank Sinatra. He did okay." Again I was speechless, I asked Tommy, "Do you really think I have a future as an actor?" He said, "You have all the attributes; tall, handsome, athletic and talent; all you need is experience."

He said he could arrange a screen test for me at MGM Studios in April. "Again, it all depends upon your arm and a decision you and you alone will have to make when the time comes. If your arm is not ready by that time you might take a two-week leave of absence, do the test and see what happens. We'll be in touch to get a progress report on how you're doing from time to time."

"Feel free to call anytime, the hotel phone numbers are on the itinerary. Right now just concentrate, work hard and get your arm in shape." His last words were, "We'll see you in Orlando."

If I didn't answer that phone call, that split-second, that day, I would not be writing this book. Timing isn't important…it's everything.

Before I left Miami, I made sure I prepared the ball club for Perry Moss, the football and baseball coach, before leaving. He couldn't be more appreciative of my dedication and hard work. He asked me again if I would like to be his assistant baseball coach and he would see to it that I got a full scholarship. Again I thanked him, but told him I was leaving for spring training.

I made a deal with my roommate, Donald Zacagnino, to buy the car for $100 but asked him if he would he mind driving me and Mc Dermott to Orlando. The car made it there like a charm. Zack dropped me a line later that Old Reliable made it back, but the transmission was on its way to heaven. I loved that car; it had such personality.

I've always had good taste in automobiles and my first ride was just like this 1946 Ford four-door sedan. Mine was two-tone, tan and brown. A beauty!

Zack graduated with a degree in Education and stayed in Florida, got married, raised a family and taught school in Okeechobee, Florida. I only saw Zack once more when I visited my mom and friends in Fort Lauderdale. We had a terrific time and had lots of laughs about the old Ford car and our school days. I was so happy I was able to see him when I did, because he passed away a few years later. He was a fine human being and a dear friend.

I owe a great deal of gratitude to the University of Miami in Florida for providing a launching pad for me as a major league baseball player and provided the essential tools I needed to make it as an actor. Fate, as it always does, ultimately chose which path I would take.

Senatorial Privilege

Mickey and I checked in that memorable day March 1st at the same hotel, The Orlando Hotel where the Washington Senators had been staying for many years. The hotel was comparatively small and aging, but it was popular because of its history with the team and the fans had easy access to their favorite players to collect autographs. In those days players bunked together, so naturally Mickey and I teamed up.

The following morning, Mickey and I went to breakfast and quite a few of the veterans were already seated at a large table. Mickey introduced me to everyone. It sure was a colorful entrance for me. I was wearing a brown sport coat, tan shirt and a pork pie hat with pegged pants. I looked like I just walked off the sidewalk at Times Square in New York City. That was the style in those days. Frank Shea, the right-handed starter for the club, thought I looked like a gangster out of a James Cagney movie. With a smile, he and the rest of the guys immediately accepted me.

Frank pulled out a chair and said, "Sit here pal." A rookie sitting with the veterans on opening day was one in a million. I sat down with the likes of third baseman Eddie Yost, Jim Busby, Pete Runnels, Mickey Vernon, Jim Lemon, Roy Sievers and Dick Wakefield. Mickey told them all about me, which set me up pretty good, so they'd be giving me a good look when training got under way. My grand entrance was something they never forgot. I became even more popular when Mickey told them about my acting potential. I could not have gotten off to a better start if I wrote the script.

After some fun jokes and interesting conversations took place, we headed out to the ballpark. I didn't want to take anything for granted and get too friendly too soon, so I purposefully grabbed a locker away from the veterans and got fitted for my uniform. I was so surprised, or should I say shocked, that No. 5, my favorite number and my uniform size was available.

We all suited up and ran onto the field for all the photographers waiting for a group picture and individual shots of each and every ballplayer, as well as sportswriters firing away with their pens and writing pads in hand. I can never aptly describe the feeling when I put that major league uniform on for the first time. It was definitely a boyhood dream come true.

With tears coming down my cheeks I turned toward the inside of my locker to thank God for such a wonderful gift. I immediately thought of my father, who went out to buy me a glove the next day after I sneaked on the bus to see my first game at Yankees Stadium. I prayed and worked so hard toward this moment and to think that I was wearing the same number my idol, Joe DiMaggio. It was beyond belief.

Reporting to spring training in Orlando, Florida, on behalf of the Washington Senators.

The team's manager was Charlie Dressen, former Brooklyn Dodger coach and manager. He called for a team meeting in the clubhouse after all the press hype.

Dressen got off to a bad start when he prattled on for close to an hour about the fantastic Dodger clubs he managed in the past. The veterans weren't interested in hearing about the Dodgers and wanted to hear about what he was going to do now as their new manager. I looked across the room and I could see the reactions of Shea, Sievers, Vernon, Yost, Wakefield and McDermott. Finally, Shea pretended to drop a ball from his hand and bounced it in the direction of Dressen, hoping it might in some way change the subject matter.

He picked up the ball and went right on talking without missing a beat. The meeting finally ended, leaving mostly the returning regulars hoping they wouldn't have to hear any more about the Brooklyn Dodgers. The next morning it was time to go to work.

Incidentally, this was the rookie year for two outstanding prospects—third baseman Harmon Killebrew, a future Hall of Famer and Bobby Allison. The workouts were all professionally organized inside this pretty good sized ballpark, and the weather was ideal. When it was my turn in the batting cage, I was swatting line drives all over the place. I got their attention real fast. The conditioning running, fielding and batting practice in Miami paid off, and it gave me a good head start. I was doing everything so well, except throw without pain. I was back to where I started.

I guess I was waiting for a miracle to happen within the next ten days. In the meantime, Tommy Dorsey had called to get a progress report. He also reminded me they were going to be playing at the Air Force Base and Rollins College in two weeks.

About the middle of the first week of spring training some of the veteran ballplayers were getting antsy about having a few beers. There were only a couple of bars in town and manager Dressen didn't want anybody drinking, period. He knew the owners of those bars and the vets knew that and they would be persona non grata in those places and would be fined if they were seen there.

My roommate McDermott earned a well-deserved reputation; he spilled more booze than most people drank. As a matter of fact, Mickey was destined to become a great pitcher, but he couldn't stay away from the hooch. Years later, shortly before he passed away, he wrote a book entitled *A Funny Thing Happened on the Way to Cooperstown*.

Mickey thought the best idea would be to have somebody drive us out to the Air Force base and have a drink there. It was far removed and none of the locals would see us drinking. But Dressen's influence was both far and wide. Mickey had a friend who drove him, second baseman Tony Roig and me, to the base. He knew the drinking hole well. I wasn't a seasonal drinker, but Mickey was my roommate and I went along to keep him out of trouble. I didn't have a problem at all with booze, but unfortunately Mickey did. When we got to the Air Force Base and entered, all the tables were taken by Air Force recruits so we had to sit at the bar. As sure as God made apples, Mickey said something to a recruit who had a few too many. The place was filled with young hotshots looking for a little action. And boy, they were ready to rumble.

It was just about to become a free-for-all. We were sitting at the end of the bar and a few of the locals made a move toward us. I said, "Guys, get up and put your backs against the wall because we're about to get our butts kicked."

Thank God a young recruit from Boston recognized Mickey before the first blow was thrown. He happened to be a big Red Sox fan and Mickey was one of his favorites. He pointed at Mickey and asked, "Aren't you Mickey McDermott who used to pitch for the Red Sox?" Before anyone could get a word out I said loud and clear, "Yeah, that's him." I wasn't going to let Mickey answer before me.

I knew that was our lifeline. From a scary and tense few moments everything changed to one of the warmest, fun and friendliest times I had ever spent in my life with our nation's heroes. We talked baseball with them for the next two hours. Thank God for baseball!

During the next few days I met and talked with Harmon Killebrew, Bobby Allison, Roy Sievers and Larry Ciaffone. They were four of the nicest and most talented guys in camp. Larry was traded during the winter from the St. Louis Cardinals organization to the Senators. He was one of the best right-handed hitters on the ball team along with Roy Sievers, but he didn't have good foot speed, which immediately put him in the doghouse with manager Dressen.

If the designated hitter was in play in those days, Larry would have been their designated hitter and without a doubt would be a .300 hitter. As a matter of fact he would have been the Cardinals designated hitter had they not traded him to Washington.

Larry was born and raised in a tough section of Brooklyn, New York, and had a great sense of humor with an infectious laugh. Mickey, Larry and I hung out together all throughout spring training. We went to dinner practically every night and had a lot of laughs.

Time was flying by and Tommy was due in town any day now to play for the troops at the Air Force Base and the college students at Rollins College.

My arm wasn't getting any better and they were beginning to send players to their AA Club, Chattanooga of the Southern Association League. Later I questioned myself why I didn't move over to second base from the beginning. I could have at least showed off my good hands, range and temporarily gotten away with throwing underhanded from that position. I could have managed more at bats and they would have seen what kind of a hitter I was. I didn't have the background stats for them to sit around and wait for my arm to come around. Time was not on my side and certain decisions—hard decisions—had to be made.

Tommy Dorsey called the night before he arrived in Orlando and invited Mickey and me to join him and Tino for breakfast in the morning. Tommy and Tino arrived much earlier than the band because they traveled by car and the rest of the band traveled by bus including his brother Jimmy, who preferred the bus. Buddy Rich also traveled in his own Cadillac convertible.

I learned about these facts the morning we all had breakfast together and then headed out to the ballpark, but not before a number of the players came over to the table to say hello and or introduced themselves. Tommy and Tino couldn't wait to suit up and throw the ball around. Tommy knew Calvin Griffith, the general manager and Dressen well. They enjoyed the exchange because Tommy invited the whole club to the concert at the Air Force Base that same night.

Tommy and Tino came to the park worked out, chatted with everyone and enjoyed the workout. I really believe to this day both would have traded their professions for a spot on the roster; that's how much they loved baseball. Tommy and the boys were fabulous that night. I think they gave it their best shot with all the servicemen, women and the Washington squad in the audience. In addition to Tommy, the band featured his brother Jimmy Dorsey on the saxophone, the great Buddy Rich on drums and Charlie Shavers on the trumpet.

It was an entertaining and memorable night for all of us. It was fun and a diversion from the grind of spring training in that town in those days where there wasn't much entertainment at all. The following day Tommy, Tino and Buddy Rich came to the ballpark and worked out with us again.

I played catch with Buddy and learned how much *he* loved baseball. He told me all the bandleaders had their own baseball team and would play against each other in Las Vegas and New York when the twains met. Mickey, Larry, and I went out to the concert the next night at Rollins

Posing with third baseman Eddie Yost on left, me and catcher Mickey Grasso of the Washington Senators.

College, surrounded by students and it was another great evening of big band sound appreciation. We all said our farewells and Tommy said he'd call me in a few days. A few days later, Larry Ciaffone and I got the word that we were going to be sent to the Chattanooga Lookouts camp down the road. I was expecting it, but I felt bad for Larry, because he was still one of the best right-handed hitters in the camp along with Roy Sievers. For whatever reasons, he just wasn't manager Charlie Dressen's type of player.

It was tough saying, "see you later" to all the guys but by this time everyone on the team knew what my alternatives were. We left together but not before McDermott called the Chattanooga trainer, Sandy Sandler and told him about my arm. Sandy told him not to worry.

Sporting my Washington Senators uniform at spring training in Orlando, Florida, in 1955.

"I'll check him over and do what I can," Sandy said. Mickey hung up the phone and told me he was the best, and if anyone could do anything for me, it was Sandy. That was good enough for me. I couldn't wait to get there to see if he could help me. I was at my wit's end.

The next morning I was in his training room just as he instructed Mickey to tell me before he hung up the phone. Sandy was very personable, highly professional, and straightforward. Larry made it a point to be there and was rooting for me like a brother. Sandy had me lay face down flat on the table and began to loosen the muscles in my back and shoulders for a good fifteen minutes. Then he began to work on my upper shoulders, loosened them up and began stretching my right arm straight out from the table back and around to a position that I could almost touch the top of my shoulder blade with my right hand for the first time in two years.

He went back and forth, stretching in every direction possible. All of this took about 45 minutes. There was some pain while he stretched as much as he deemed possible. I yelled out a few times but I couldn't have cared less.

I was so anxious and looking forward to getting off that table and start throwing to see if I was ever going to throw a baseball again without pain. This was my last shot Sandy said, "If the operation is successful plus what I'm doing here, you will either throw today without pain or you're done." I got off that table as soon as he finished, picked up my glove and prayed every step of the way until I reached the playing field.

Larry and Sandy were a few paces behind when I picked up a ball and turned around to see Larry with his glove ready to catch with me. I threw a few balls gingerly and got more and more aggressive. With each throw there was no pain at all, I couldn't control the tears that ran down my face. God bestowed another gift. A miracle took place with each teardrop. Larry and Sandy shared in the obvious joy that filled that whole ballpark with every throw. Sandy with all his smiles had to slow me down, because I had to strengthen my arm and not rush it too soon.

I had to treat the arm like I was just starting spring training and gradually strengthen it a little each day. I will never be able to describe that wonderful inner feeling that glowed and flowed through my whole body in those miraculous moments. It was the first time I threw without discomfort or pain in two years and all I needed was to be cranked up by a trainer who knew what to do. I thanked the dear Lord for Sandy Sandler a hundred times for that most precious gift. A half hour later, Larry and I checked in with the manager of the Chattanooga Lookouts, Cal Ermer and we were ready to go. I took a lot of ground balls at second base and everything felt perfect.

The team was already set with their veteran shortstop, Don Grate and I wanted to move to second base and stay there until somebody told me otherwise. Larry shagged a lot of balls in the outfield; we both took batting practice and were hitting line drives all over the place. The three weeks we spent with the club gave us a huge advantage, our timing was way ahead of most, if not all of the Chattanooga ballplayers. I called Tommy that night and told him the good news and the bad news. I told him my timing wasn't very good because I was sent down to the Chattanooga club but the trainer there was able to crank me up and I finally threw without pain. Unfortunately, the Senators were breaking camp and I wasn't able to show them my arm was fine. It was too late. He asked me what I had in mind.

I told him that we had a couple of exhibition games to play in the next two days and I would call him afterwards and let him know what I was going to do. I played well in the two exhibition games had four hits, made some good plays in the field and didn't make any errors. Before I called Tommy, I had a good talk with Larry Ciaffone and he said the right thing to me. "You're young enough to take advantage of Tommy's offer now to arrange a screen test for you, and if it doesn't work out you can always go back to baseball. You may never again get that opportunity; you're still a young guy." That last line really registered with me and was all I needed to make up my mind.

I checked the itinerary that Tommy left with me. They would be just arriving at the Royal Nevada Hotel in Las Vegas that day. I spoke with Tommy that night and told him of my decision and he turned the phone over to his manager Tino Barzie. Tino made the flight arrangements for me to catch the morning plane out of Orlando to Las Vegas. Everything was taken care of. I told manager Cal Ermer of my decision and said my farewells to some of the guys on the club.

I left early the next morning and several hours later Tino picked me up at the Las Vegas Airport and drove to the Royal Nevada Hotel, where Tommy, the band and I would be staying. It was hard to believe that my baseball career might be over. But I was young, had the rest of my life ahead of me and like a good soldier, I was willing to adapt and overcome. Hollywood would prove to be a battleground and I needed a different kind of strength to persevere.

18

Vegas, Baby!

The ride from the airport to the hotel was life changing. I was like a kid in a candy shop, taking in the sights on every block we passed. I was so impressed with the glitz of all the lights throughout the city. It had a kind of certain magic, different from anything I had ever seen or experienced before. This was in 1955 and there still was a great many empty lots on the strip and much more on the periphery. It was nowhere near as densely populated as it is today.

I'll never forget walking through the revolving front doors of the Royal Nevada Casino Hotel for the first time. The sound of the one-armed bandits and the frequent whistling sound of the spinning roulette wheels throughout the casino had a buzz in the air. It was full of people, some laughing, some drinking and all focused on one form of gambling or another. It was magnetic; a sight to behold. That cacophony of sound rings through my memory as if I was standing there today. Tino said for me to call Tommy's room after I got settled.

I thanked him, registered and went to my room. I called Tommy to tell him I arrived in one piece and thanked him for the plane ride. Tommy asked me to come to his room to talk to me about helping Tino. I went to his room and Tino was there. Tommy knew I didn't have much money, so he asked me to work with Tino.

My job was to run errands and pick up any items Tommy needed at the local stores and to make sure his car was clean, serviced and always full of gas. He paid me a salary of $200 a week for the next month, which included the one week in Vegas, a couple of days in Northern California and two weeks in Hollywood during the Home Show.

After Tommy and the band left California, I was on my own if MGM signed me to a contract. So I had to be very frugal and try to save as much as I could out of the salary I was going to earn.

I left the room and immediately went down to the casino; it was like a magnet. It sucked me right in and with the few bucks that I had on me, I decided to play black jack and in about twenty minutes I won $200. It was the worst thing that could have ever happened, because I left the table thinking it was easy money. The next day I lost the entire $200 and had to borrow money from Tino to sustain me until I received my first paycheck.

During the next few days I spent some time with Buddy Rich and we had a lot of laughs. He loved baseball and we lounged around the pool area, played catch and talked a lot about the game. We got along royally. Buddy, without a doubt, was the greatest drummer of all time.

The band played two shows each night and after the last show the second night we were there, Tommy and Tino invited me to go along with them to Hank Henry's late night nightclub on the strip. All the entertainers gathered at Hank Henry's club after they've finished their show at the casinos. Hank was a terrific comedian, a little on the risqué side, but very funny and well liked. Other comedians and singers would get up on stage with him and it was a riot. I never laughed so hard in my life that night. It was a special place and we went there again before we left Las Vegas, enjoying the evening more each night. After every show I was invited to go wherever Tommy and Tino went. After the fourth day, Tommy got a phone call from Bobby Layne, the great quarterback for the Detroit Lions.

He asked Tommy if he would like to go gambling because he felt lucky. Tommy thought it was a good idea and said they would meet back in his dressing room after the second show. Tommy had not done any gambling yet and was ready for a little action.

Bobby and his liquor caddie saw the second show and came back stage afterwards. I kid you not; he had a friend carrying his own bottle of booze with his own label on the bottle that read "Bobby Layne Scotch."

Before we left Tommy's dressing room he made a hand gesture to his caddie, who poured him a stiff one. He downed it all before we left. Both he and Tommy only played craps. I got the feeling they did this before. Incidentally, Tommy quit drinking many years before. We left Tommy's dressing room and headed for the crap tables. The moment Tommy and Bobby arrived, a huge crowd of gamblers and spectators began to gather around their table. There was an excitement that permeated on the whole floor of the casino. Bobby was in a position on the table to shoot the craps. He and Tommy were heavy betters.

They bet the numbers across the table the 4, 5, 6, 8, 9, and 10. Bobby indicated with his hand to his booze caddie, who quickly filled another glass of his private label. He downed a good portion of it and grabbed the dice and covered the numbers across with hundred dollar chips. He rolled out a number and kept rolling numbers for almost twenty minutes to a half hour and he was pretty lit up in the process.

Tommy was betting on his hand the whole time, the same numbers across the board. He rolled an extraordinarily hot hand. He hit every number several times before he stopped rolling the dice. In gambling terms, he finally "7'd" out. People were yelling and rooting and betting on his hand. Bobby was a smart gambler. He picked up all his chips and said to Tommy, "Let's go, I can't top that." Tommy picked up his chips and we all joined them to the cashier's window. Bobby cashed in about $25,000 and Tommy won $15,000. They pocketed their money and Bobby said, "Alright now, let's go over to the Desert Inn. I want to take some of their dough."

We walked through the casino with all eyes on Tommy and Bobby and people all around were talking about his hot hand at the crap table. We jumped in two cabs and went to the Desert Inn for more action. The same reaction occurred when we got to the crap table with gamblers and spectators gathered around the table immediately upon their arrival. Word got out fast that Tommy Dorsey and Bobby Layne were at the crap table. Again his booze caddie handed him another drink. He took a good swig, placed his bets, picked up the dice rattled them in his lucky right hand and rolled them out. Tommy placed his bets, as he did previously at the Royal Nevada.

Again he held the dice over twenty minutes and made a bunch of numbers before he rolled out a seven. At this point in time he put away some serious liquor, I don't know how he was able to function and stay on his feet, but he knew exactly what he was doing the whole time and, more importantly, knew enough to step away from the table a winner. He gathered his chips, Tommy followed suit and proceeded to the cashier's window again.

This time he collected about $20,000 and Tommy won around 10 grand. We all went to the dining room, had a late dinner and headed to Hank Henry' Club to finish the evening off. What a night!

After being around Tommy for several days I observed that he was an impeccable dresser, a true leader on and off stage and did not tolerate anything but a professional performance from anyone in the band. If someone was not performing well, he was gone the next day and someone else was brought in immediately that could do the job right. Jimmy Dorsey was the total opposite of Tommy. He preferred to hang out with the other musicians in the band and ride in the bus when they traveled. He had a tendency to talk to the fans while they were on the bandstand. Tommy didn't care much for his gregarious behavior with so many people.

Jimmy liked to accommodate and please everyone, and played great saxophone. From time to time, he had his own band and traveled, doing one-nighters throughout the country. He too, like everyone else in the band, loved baseball. He and Tommy didn't get along and every once in a while they would have a beef about something and Tommy would remind him that he was writing the checks.

The next day Tommy and Buddy Rich got into a big argument while rehearsing a couple of new numbers they wanted to add to the show. Both of them were cussing at each other and Buddy stormed off the stage and said he was quitting. Both of them were temperamental and bull-headed about what they believed was right or wrong.

In no time, Buddy, was packing his bags to check out of the hotel. Before he left Tino asked me if I would try and talk Buddy out of it. He knew Buddy liked and respected me, and that I could possibly persuade him to stay. I caught up with Buddy before he checked out and spoke with him but to no avail. He made up his mind and off he went. I didn't see Buddy until many years later. He formed his own band, toured with it on and off very successfully. The last time I saw him was at the UCLA Medical Center after he suffered a stroke and was seriously ill. My good friend, singer Jerry Vale and I went to see him there before he passed away. We had a warm reunion and laughed, hugged and cried together. Tino had the unenviable task to come up with another drummer before the first show, which was about to open in just a few hours.

He was so fortunate that a good drummer by the name of Ed Shaughnessy was living in Vegas and available. They were able to secure his services until they got someone permanently. They eventually hired Louie Bellson when they got to Hollywood later on to do the Home Show at the Pan Pacific Auditorium and the rest of the tour.

That same night, Tommy and Jimmy's mother came to visit her two sons for a couple of days from Pennsylvania. Mrs. Dorsey possessed a vivacious and outgoing personality and had a great zest for life. I had the pleasure of escorting her to the dinner show and the late show for the two nights she was there. In the short time I was in her company she was so delightful to be around. Everyone adored her and Tommy and Jimmy worshiped the ground she walked on. There was no doubt she was the boss. She came along with us to Hank Henry's nightclub the first night and Hank introduced her to a standing ovation. She had a terrific time and laughed so hard tears came to her eyes.

The next day Tommy, Tino, some of the members of the band and I went to the local ballfield to hit the baseball around and played catch for the last time until we got to Hollywood. During our stay we had the opportunity to work out a couple of other days as well.

Tommy asked me to ride with him to the next venue in Hanford, California. We left immediately after the last show as the car was packed and ready to go. Tino had to stay to take care of all the closing business and rode with the band on the bus. Tommy drove the entire way. The only time we stopped was for gas or something to eat.

In no time at all, I learned Tommy was one hell of a driver. He took great pride in his driving ability and he moved that car at high speeds like a professional. We were driving through the

Tommy Dorsey with the band.

giant redwood country not far from Hanford and it was foggy and drizzling slightly. Tommy was doing about 90 miles an hour on an old two-lane highway, with a drop off of about two hundred feet on the right side of the road.

It was in the early hours of the morning with almost no traffic and I could see a huge buck deer down the middle of the road. Tommy saw the deer just as I saw it and didn't panic for one second, he held that wheel straight and never hit the brakes. I guess we were both praying at the time for that deer to move. Tommy blew the horn and just about the time we were about to hit the deer head on, he leaped across the highway and disappeared into the wooded area. Had we hit that deer we would've been crushed and possibly thrown over the side of the cliff.

Naturally, we were exhausted after the drive. One consolation was we arrived way ahead of the band and were able to get a good night's sleep. The band played there only two nights at two different venues. Everything went well playing to packed houses and before I knew it, we were on our way down south to Hollywood for two weeks to play the Home Show at the Pan Pacific Auditorium.

We immediately left after the last show but this time, Tino joined Tommy and me in the car. Tommy and Tino talked about the success of the tour and couldn't be happier with the results. It seemed there were always some tweaks that needed to be worked out or improved. Tommy was a perfectionist and had no patience or tolerance for amateurs. The lesson wasn't lost on me because I found out soon enough that Hollywood had no tolerance for amateurs, either.

19

Tinseltown

We arrived the next morning and headed straight to the Hollywood Plaza Hotel, right in the heart of 'Tinseltown.' The first thing I saw across the street when we were unloading our luggage was the famous Bob Cobb's Brown Derby Restaurant on Vine Street near Hollywood Boulevard. It was a square, tan-colored building with the shape and color of a large brown derby hat on the roof. Cobb was the creator of the popular "Cobb Salad."

I must say I was not too impressed with my first vision of Hollywood. I thought there would be much more Tinsel than what I saw. Eventually, I would soon discover there was so much more than meets the eye. We went to our rooms to get some sleep.

Just about the time we got some shut eye, the bus with Jimmy Dorsey and the rest of the band arrived, and it was their turn to get some sleep. After a much needed rest, I got up and had some lunch and took a walk down Vine Street. Just about a block away on the same side of the street was Sy Devore's famous clothing store where many actors and entertainers such as Elvis Presley and James Dean had their clothes made. I went inside and Sy was there. I introduced myself and he couldn't have been more gracious. Sy gave me a cook's tour of the store and he certainly had the best of everything.

The shirts, slacks, sport jackets, suits, ties, tuxedos were all of the best quality. They could tailor anything for anyone for any occasion. We chatted for a while and told him I was with Tommy Dorsey and we just arrived in town to do the Home Show stand. He said, "Tommy always comes in to have some clothing made when he's in town before he leaves and I'm sure he'll be here to see me," he said confidently. I left knowing that I would be back just as soon as I had some money in my pocket. Later that afternoon, Tommy and the band began to rehearse at the Pan Pacific Auditorium, located on Fairfax Avenue in Hollywood next to Gilmore Field, the home of the PCL Hollywood Stars baseball team. It was a nice feeling to be able to return two years later to Gilmore Field even though it was under different circumstances.

It was so convenient for me to work out and stay in shape and Tommy and Tino in their spare time could come and work out with me. On top of everything else, it was only a few minutes away from the hotel. I couldn't have arranged it any better if I tried. After we got settled and took care of business, Tommy brought me to meet producer Jack Cummings at his Beverly Hills home just one block north of the infamous Sunset Boulevard.

His neighbor was the beautiful actress Betty Grable, who was married at the time to the bandleader Harry James. Jack was under contract to MGM Studios and the nephew of Louis B. Mayer. He and Tommy knew each other for many years when Tommy was under contract to MGM Studios.

We met Mrs. Cummings that afternoon and she was the daughter of the great songwriter Jerome Kern. Jack had produced some of the finest motion pictures that MGM ever produced. One of them was a true story about a baseball player starring James Stewart entitled the *Monte Stratton Story*. My favorite musical that he produced was *Seven Brides for Seven Brothers*. Both were excellent films. Jack said he would be making arrangements for the screen test and would be back to Tommy in and a couple of days.

We left feeling positive about everything and I could observe they liked and respected each other a great deal. Tommy said we would be going to MGM studios to arrange the test as soon as he heard from Mr. Cummings. The next day, Tommy, Tino and I went to Gilmore Field to workout. There were three or four other professional ballplayers already there, so we were able to get good batting practice and infield work out.

One of the players was a second baseman, and he and I worked around the bag making double plays and it made for a terrific workout. Little did I know there was a scout in the stands that day. After we finished, he and Tommy talked. Shortly thereafter, Tommy called me over to introduce me to him. His name was Bill Voss and was the head West Coast scout for the Baltimore Orioles Organization. Tommy had already talked to him about my situation and I filled him in on my present status as a free agent, and about to take a screen test at MGM.

He asked me what I was going to do if they didn't sign me to a contract. I told him I that wasn't sure. He surprised me when he said he'd like to sign me to a contract with the Baltimore Orioles organization. He gave me his card and told me he was at the same hotel where we were staying, the Hollywood Plaza. I was in a rare can't lose situation: I was either going to sign a contract with MGM or with the Baltimore Orioles.

Tommy invited Voss to the home show and we saw him the following night when he came backstage. The next day I went out and worked out again and he was there and was more convinced of signing me if MGM didn't.

Tommy got the call from Jack Cummings and we were off and running to MGM Studios, who was the giant of all the studios at that time. I had the thought that possibly a dream might become a reality and this was something I might potentially be a part of. I had never seen or been to a movie studio before. I was humbled, simply by looking at the main gate entrance, all the office buildings sprinkled around the lot and the huge soundstages situated in rows. People were rushing from building to building or riding bicycles from stage to stage. There was a lot of hustle and bustle and the lot was pulsing with excitement. I loved it! If all went well, it would be a giant step in the direction of my transition from my career in baseball to becoming an actor.

We arrived, parked the car and walked through the main gate and the guard there knew Tommy when he was under contract. His name was "Joe Hollywood" and every actress, actor, director and producer knew Joe. He was a fixture at the gate and everybody loved him. Tommy introduced me to him and he had the kind of personality that when you met him, it was as if you had known him for a long time. We scooted off to the commissary and when we walked in it was filled with an electrifying atmosphere. We stood at the podium waiting to be seated and were greeted by the hostess who had been there for many years and also knew Tommy from his contract days at the studio. In the back of the commissary a hand was raised and waving calling our attention to their table. Tommy and I walked to the table and after greeting us and inviting us to sit and have lunch with them was Vic Damone and Lana Turner.

We sat down and had lunch and talked about my being there for a screen test. Imagine me meeting and having lunch with Vic Damone and Lana Turner my very first time in the commissary.

First publicity picture under contract to MGM.

Both of them had some nice and encouraging things to say to me. They made me feel right at home and Tommy brought up the subject of baseball. Vic happened to be a big baseball fan and they were both impressed with the fact that I was a professional athlete and had all the attributes of a movie star.

It was an interesting and exciting experience to be in the presence of two huge stars upon my first visit to any movie studio, no less MGM. They were both filming on the lot and invited me to visit their respective sets any time I wished.

After lunch Tommy and I visited with Jack. We chatted with him for a while and then went to meet with Al Trescony, the head of the talent department. He had been expecting us for the screen test. We arrived at his office and were greeted with open arms since he and Tommy knew each other and the respect was obvious. After we got acquainted, Al decided we should do a photo and personality test first. Rather than do a scene, everyone thought that it would be best for me to work with the drama coach, Lillian Burns, since I didn't have any experience in front of the camera.

It would be to my advantage to rehearse as much as possible and then do a scene in front of the camera only when they thought I was ready. Al then walked us over to the makeup and hair department, where we met Sidney Guilaroff, who would trim my hair the day of the test, which was two days away. I was to report to his department first and then to makeup just before the shoot.

I did exactly what I needed to do and hoped that everything would turn out in my favor. We were just going to do a photo and personality test conducted by Al, who asked me a few questions while he was off camera. I would answer those questions while on camera from different angles to see how I photographed from right, left, center and back.

Two days later I arrived at the hairdresser's department and Sidney trimmed my hair, I then went to makeup and I was ready to go. The questions were rather simple questions about my family history, contacts in show business, likes and dislikes, college, and my professional baseball career. The answers were brief because all the tests ran no longer than ten minutes. It took a couple of days to process the film before we could see the results.

Hollywood in the 1950s was perhaps the most exciting and creative time in the history of show business because television was just coming into its own. That meant opportunities and jobs for writers, directors, producers, actors and the demand for technical people was growing by leaps and bounds. Everything was fresh and new. There was an excitement and electricity just like the studio that permeated throughout the whole town; hotels, apartments, houses and restaurants were all thriving.

The population grew in so many directions with people coming from all parts of the country and around the world to Hollywood. Two days later Tommy and I returned to MGM to see the results of the test. We sat in one of the small screening rooms to see the test with Al and Jack. Everyone seemed to be pleased with the results, which meant the next step would be to pick out a scene to rehearse and prepare for the final screen test with Lillian Burns.

Another new and curious experience was to see myself on the screen. Sidney trimmed my hair a little too much and I wasn't used to wearing my hair short. I usually wore it long because I had a full, thick head of hair. But, I thought I did okay with interview. Jack, Tommy and I left the screening room and went to have lunch in the commissary. Al had to get back to his office but not before he told me to stop by his office before I left the lot. He said he would've made an appointment to see the head of the drama department, Lillian Burns, by the time we finished lunch. The commissary was full and we were soon escorted to the VIP room, Mr. Cummings had already made reservations for us in the executive room. On our way to our table, we stopped to say hello again to Lana Turner, who was having lunch with her makeup man Del Armstrong. She was very warm and friendly. She introduced us to Del and asked how everything was progressing with my screen test. Jack said some positive things about the photo/personality test.

During lunch Jack asked me where I would be staying after Tommy left. He and Tommy talked previously and he was aware I wasn't in a position to rent an apartment, so he asked me if I would like to stay in a guest room above the garage at his home until after the test. All the things that I was worried about were taken care of during our luncheon. He also arranged for me to receive $75 dollars a week for expense money until I was ready to do my test. I couldn't have had anything better happen to me at that time if I tried. I was so moved by his generosity. After lunch, Tommy and I stopped by Al's office and he introduced me to Lillian Burns, who was aware of my upcoming screen test. This all happened on a Friday, and she told me to be back in her office on Monday at eleven o'clock to set up a schedule to work with her. This was the last weekend for Tommy and the band at the Home Show.

Tommy and I said our goodbyes, but not before I thanked him with all my heart for everything he did for me. I told him I would keep him posted. The last thing he said to me was, "Visit Lana Turner on the set. She thinks you're a very handsome guy!"

There was so much I learned by being around Tommy in such a short period of time. He was a class act, a leader and a consummate professional. That Saturday night I said my goodbyes to Jimmy Dorsey and the rest of the band. The next morning Tommy dropped me off at the Cummings residence, but not before I spoke earlier to Bill Voss.

I told him we saw the test and they were pleased with the results. In a few weeks I will be taking the final test, and the results of that test will determine whether they will sign me to a studio contract or not. I said that I would call him as soon as I had a definite answer one way or another. He wished me luck and said the contract was still open.

Jack and his wife Betty were first rate people. They made me feel very comfortable with my quarters above the garage, which was clean and private. They insisted I eat at the house. They had a live-in maid who cooked and cleaned their home and wanted me to share meals with them. I needed a car to get around, so I went and bought a brand new black Volkswagen with whitewall tires for $1,200. It looked just like a Beetle. I had saved about $200 while working with Tommy and gave them $100 in cash and made arrangements to pay $50 a month to pay off the remaining $1,100.

I began working right away with the drama coach, Lillian Burns. I chose to do a scene from a Clark Gable movie script entitled *Homecoming*. I worked with Lillian two to three times a week until she thought I was ready to do the test. Mr. Cummings asked a young director who was under contract to the studio at the time to direct my test. His name was Stanley Donen and he went on to have a great career directing several outstanding films such as *Two for the Road, Singing In The Rain, Seven Brides for Seven Brothers*, and *Damn Yankees* to name a few. It was a memorable and exciting day. I got in my little Volkswagen the morning of the test, drove to the studio and parked in the lot outside the administration building. My heart was racing with anticipation.

I went in and registered at the desk to pick up my pass and walked toward the makeup department, but not before I stopped to say hello to Joe Hollywood at the gate. He knew I was testing that day, and wished me good luck. He said he had seen a lot of actors come and go, and that I would do just fine. He really made me feel confident. I hurried to the makeup department and received many words of encouragement from them, too.

Publicity photo with the legendary Grace Kelly during the filming of High Society (1956) at MGM.

I sat back in my chair and thought about my unbelievable journey to this moment. Before I knew it I was on my way to the set where I met the director Stanley Donen for the first time. We discussed what the scene was all about, and we rehearsed it a couple of times. He then blocked the scene for both the cameraman and me. We rehearsed it a couple more times, they checked my hair, wardrobe, makeup and we were off and running. He shot a master shot of the complete scene and several close-ups from different angles. Stanley was very easy going and didn't give me a lot of direction.

He went along with how I felt about the scene and asked if I was comfortable and satisfied. If I wasn't happy about something and thought I could do it better we could shoot it over. I told him I felt okay about everything and asked him how he felt about my performance. He said I did well. I thanked him, the cameraman, hairdresser and the makeup man and was on my way.

Unbeknownst to me, Al Trescony had also watched the test and congratulated me for doing a good job. He said he'd call me at the end of the week. Later that day I called Tommy Dorsey to tell him about the test and he was pleased to hear Stanley Donen took such good care of me. I closed our conversation by telling him I would call him next week and should have the results of my test. I busied myself by reading and attending an acting workshop in Hollywood, supervised by Jeff Corey, a well-respected character actor/coach for many years. The week went pretty fast and before I knew it, I was on the phone with Al.

My timing was perfect, he had just gotten word from Dore Schary's secretary that he liked the test and they were putting me under a seven-year contract. He told me I was to report to Al's office on Monday to finalize the deal. I immediately thanked him and told the Cummings the good news, Tommy Dorsey, and my family in Stamford, Connecticut. I thanked the Lord for his continuous guidance toward my transition from my unpredictable baseball career to a promising acting career. It was a wonderful feeling to know so many people were rooting for my success.

My dad told me a number of years ago when I left to play professional baseball, that for every one person that wanted me to succeed, there were ten that didn't. I never forgot those words of wisdom and used it to guide me in that vast forest of wasteland called Hollywood.

It didn't take long to discover that Dad's words were right on the money: Hollywood was indeed loaded with envy and jealousy, because I had so much to offer. I always allowed my strong family and athletic background to guide me toward my objective.

That Monday I arrived at Al's office at 10:30 a.m. and the contract was ready and waiting. I sat down with Al and he gave me the phone number of the singing coach, Maestro Cepero, speech teacher, Ms. Gertrude Fogler and acting coach, Ms. Lillian Burns. He told me to call their respective offices and arrange a schedule to meet with them. That was the studios policy for all contract players. I took a brief look at the contract, and it was a standard seven-year studio contract, which I happily signed. He handed me a copy of the contract and the list of the phone numbers. He shook my hand, congratulated me and said he was looking forward to working with me. He also said to stop by the office anytime, if I had a problem or just to come by to say hello. I did just as he said and made arrangements to work with each one of the coaches at least twice a week. I learned something each time I met with each and every one of them.

They had a lot to offer, it was all there for the taking. The Maestro and I knew that I wasn't going to have a singing career, but I still enjoyed working with him. Working with my speech teacher, Ms. Fogler was such a joy. She was a soft-spoken, elderly woman, who worked with every big star on and off the lot. She was always in demand and said I had a good speaking voice. However, my diction needed a lot of work and in a short period of time thanks to her, I was articulating so much better and having fun doing it. Likewise with acting coach Ms. Lillian Burns, a middle-aged woman who was married to fine movie director, George Sidney. I had the pleasure of meeting George and worked for him in a film he directed starring Kim Novak entitled *Rain*. As soon as I got acclimated I began to visit some of the sets and meeting a lot of the actors and actresses working there. About the second or third week while under contract, I received a call from the publicity department, and I was instructed to bring my baseball glove to the studio. I was going to take a publicity picture with Grace Kelly signing my glove.

A representative from the publicity department escorted me to the set of *High Society* starring Grace Kelly with Frank Sinatra, Bing Crosby and Louis Armstrong. It doesn't get much bigger than that. When I arrived on the set, they called Miss Kelly from her dressing room to take a picture with me, autographing my glove. She was so beautiful, charming, gracious and unpretentious and was so kind. She invited me to stay and watch her work and said that anytime I wanted to visit the set, I was more than welcome. I saw her a few times after that and made it a point to say hello. It made my day when she nodded and smiled back. Who knew then what an incredible and tragic path her life would eventually take.

The same day Grace Kelly autographed my leather glove, I had the pleasure of meeting Louis Armstrong. I told him I was a big fan of his. Although we spoke briefly, he was impressed with some of the great jazz musicians I admired and rattled off names such as Lester Young, Charlie Parker, Dizzy Gillespie, Art Tatum, Charlie Ventura, Bill Bradley, Joe Jones, Thelonious Monk, Paul Desmond, Oscar Peterson and Joe Morello. They all had to get back to work, but I made a point to visit the set to talk to him a from time to time. Louis liked to sit outside the big soundstage door when they opened it to bring in the fresh air. I stopped to see him only when he was sitting outside. I thoroughly enjoyed our brief conversations about jazz with such a legend.

He always had a white handkerchief in his hand and occasionally wiped his brow. It was vintage Louis Armstrong. Many years later I was invited to participate in a telethon hosted by singer John Gary in New Orleans, Louisiana. The hotel where we were staying was not very far from the Louis Armstrong Park. He had passed away a few years before. I had some time off and it was a beautiful day, so I decided to take a walk in Louis' park to pay my respects, remembering our enjoyable conversations. The park had his namesake along with benches and shady trees. It was so serene. Frank Sinatra was not working that day on the set, but about two weeks later I invited four players from the PCL Hollywood Stars baseball team to watch the filming of *High Society* thanks to producer Jack Cumming's invitation.

He arranged for us to meet Frank and the opportunity to chat with him and take a group picture. We were all impressed at how warm and friendly Frank was. During our conversation with him we learned he was a big baseball fan. As a matter of fact, several years later, when the Brooklyn Dodgers moved to Los Angeles, Frank purchased season box seats at Dodger Stadium. He and manager Tommy Lasorda became close friends and socialized for many years.

The players that thoroughly enjoyed our day together were outfielder Lee Walls, outfielder Bobby Del Greco, pitcher George O'Donnell and pitcher Nelson King with his new bride. Frank teased Nelson and told him he better be nice to her, or else. He was in a good mood and was charming as anyone could possibly be. We were all big fans of his before we got there, so you can imagine how we felt after we left. All four of the players went on to play in the major leagues within two years.

I met Frank Brahoda, Clark Gable's makeup man, in the commissary one afternoon. During our conversation he mentioned he knew I was a former professional baseball player and it was as

Members of the Pacific Coast League Hollywood Stars baseball team visiting Frank Sinatra on the set of High Society. *Front row: Me, pitcher Nelson King with wife. Back row: Outfielder Lee Walls, Frank Sinatra, outfielder Bobby Del Greco, Producer Jack Cummings and pitcher George O'Donnell.*

if I knew him all my life. We talked baseball for a while and said how much he and Clark loved the sport. He extended an invitation for me to come on the set of *Betrayed*, where I could meet Gable who was about to do some pick up and publicity still shots with his co-stars Lana Turner and Victor Mature. It turned out to be his last picture under contract to MGM.

I didn't get a chance to visit the set, but the next day I was having lunch in the commissary with another contract player when Frank came in and walked directly to where I was sitting. He said to me, "Come to the set around 4:45 p.m. Clark never works beyond five o'clock and have a drink with us afterwards. I talked to him about you and he would like to meet you and talk baseball." I couldn't believe it! I finished my voice lesson with Ms. Fogler around 4:30, and I ran over to the set. They were shooting a close-up of Clark Gable at the time.

I could see everything from my vantage point behind the camera when suddenly, an African American man dressed in a tuxedo tapped me on the shoulder and said Mr. Gable and Mr. Brahoda were expecting me in Gables' dressing room after 5 o'clock. In the meantime, I watched Gable work and he certainly was the ultimate professional, no doubt the "King." They called it a wrap and I waited about ten minutes and greeted again at the door by his butler, who ushered me inside.

Visiting with the gorgeous Lana Turner.

The dressing room was in a giant trailer parked inside the soundstage and had a beautifully decorated living room, a wet bar and everything that a good-sized apartment would have to offer. It was fantastic! He and Frank treated me like an old friend, and immediately offered me a drink. I sat down to a table full of hors d'oeuvres and we talked baseball for the next two hours. In between our conversation, he called his wife to tell her he was going to be a little late getting home. I was in awe. He was married to actress Kay Williams Spreckels Gable at the time and they lived in Encino.

It was a most memorable two hours. Both men made me feel at home and told me I was always welcome on their set. They wished me good luck with my new career and looked forward to seeing me around the studio lot. I left feeling so fortunate being in the presence of two bigger than life, ultra talented people. Those moments made me even more determined to work hard to succeed.

As time went by, I began to meet lots of actors, actresses, producers, directors and composers that were under contract to the studio. One day I was working out hitting a punching bag on one of the soundstages. It was equipped with weights and several other kinds of equipment for anyone under contract to use. I was working up a good sweat on the heavy bag. I then heard a distinctive voice behind me.

"Good, very good," he said. I turned around and it was Marlon Brando, who was preparing for his next movie, *The Teahouse of the August Moon*. I met him about a week before at Gertrude Fogler's bungalow.

At that time he was working with her to develop an Okinawan accent for his role of Sakini. I could tell right away that he liked boxing. He picked up a pair of training gloves and said he would like to spar around using the big glove, which looks like catcher's mitt. We both enjoyed the workout and then talked a bit. He spoke above a whisper and was surprisingly personable.

That same week, the Cummings hosted a dinner party at their home. I was invited along with actor Gilbert Roland and his wife, director Rouben Mamoulian and his wife Azadia, Marlon Brando and attractive Greek actress Irene Pappas, who were an item at the time. I was seated next to Mrs. Mamoulian and to her left was Gilbert Roland. About midway through the dinner Azadia was speaking with me while other conversations carried on throughout the table. I wasn't aware of it, but her husband, Rouben was in a heated exchange with Gilbert. She and I were talking and suddenly she excused herself to me and turned to her left and slapped Gilbert in the face.

"Don't you talk to my husband like that!" she scolded him. Everyone stopped talking and was in shock, especially Gilbert. His face on the one side was all red. He stood up, looked at her and the hosts. He excused himself and his wife got up and they left the table. Gilbert handled himself with self-control. The atmosphere in the room became uncomfortable. Mrs. Mamoulian was a slight, thin woman, but obviously very protective of her husband. Nothing more was said about the incident.

I eventually moved from the Cummings guest apartment above the garage and found a one room furnished apartment on Castle Heights Avenue about ten minutes from MGM. The rent was a $100 a month. It was a compact apartment with a living room, kitchen, bedroom, bathroom and a little dining area. It could not have been better for the price. It was all I could afford because my contract was for $200 a week for the next six months.

The studio had the option to resign me after the first six months, and thereafter for the next six-and-a-half years. It was a standard seven-year studio contract. I had just finished working with Ms. Burns, my drama coach and walked out of her office to the main street on the lot, not far from the commissary and the main entrance gate, where Joe Hollywood's booth stood.

Sporting a white knit alpaca sweater bought at Layton's in New York while filming Somebody Up There Likes Me.

There in the center of the street talking were Cummings and director Daniel Mann. At the same time, coming through the main gate was Marlon Brando. He no doubt saw the two men in the center of the street, but walked directly to me to the left of where they were standing to say hello. I really thought he had a purpose for keeping Jack and Daniel waiting. I was aware of the move and as I learned later, he was already over an hour late for lunch with them.

I quickly walked into the direction of Jack and Daniel said hello and made my exit. I wasn't about to be a party to keeping them waiting any longer. It was obviously an important preparation meeting between the producer, director and the star of *The Teahouse of the August Moon*. Coincidentally, a couple of days later I received a call from an actress friend of mine, Lisa, to go with her to have dinner at Brando's house. She was a good friend of Wally Cox, star of the successful TV comedy show *Mr. Peepers*. He was one of Marlon's best friends and always stayed at his home when he came to California. Lisa and Wally knew each other from New York. I told Lisa I would like to accompany her because I knew Marlon slightly from meeting and seeing him from time to time on the MGM lot and our brief boxing session.

I picked her up in my beautiful brand new little black beetle Volkswagen with whitewall tires and drove up to the top of Mulholland Drive overlooking the Valley, where Brando lived for many years until he passed away. That little car of mine was noisy, but I still got my 30 miles on a gallon of gas and filled up my ten-gallon tank for three dollars.

We arrived and it was easy to tell that Wally and Lisa were good friends, and even better, Marlon remembered me. We had a delicious dinner cooked and served by Marlon's wife Movita. Lisa and I found it strange that she didn't sit down for dinner with us. Wally and Marlon both had a terrific sense of humor and shared several funny stories. Movita didn't say much, but she had a lovely charismatic quality about her and was warm and humble. We lounged around after dinner still being entertained by Wally and Marlon, telling more funny stories. It was a beautiful balmy night and we all decided to take a swim in the pool. I never saw Wally Cox again, but did see Marlon at the studio. During this same time frame, Academy award-winning director Bob Wise was finishing directing a Western entitled *Tribute To A Bad Man* starring James Cagney, Irene Pappas and Steve McNally.

I just finished lunch in the commissary and was headed down to the soundstage where they were shooting interiors. I've always been a big fan of Cagney and was looking forward to watching him work with Pappas and McNally. I was halfway there when I looked to my left, and in my peripheral vision, I could see someone was riding a bicycle and moving about the same pace as I was walking. I recognized his voice immediately.

"Hi son, where 'ya headin'?" I turned and it was Mr. Cagney. I downplayed my shock and played it cool.

"I was going to watch you and Irene Pappas work," I replied. He said, "You're certainly welcome any time. I saw you in the commissary a couple times. Are you one of the contract players here?" I told him yes and by that time we reached the soundstage.

He parked his bike near the door and I went in to say hello to Irene. I watched them do a couple of scenes before I left. It was such a joy because I went back in time to when I was a youngster, seeing every film Cagney ever made. I met a lot of my idols at a rapid pace, and it was a very special time in my life.

The studio lot was full of activity. And again there was that buzz that permeated, an energy coming and going in every direction. It was so electrifying! I had just finished working with acting coach Lillian Burns and again ran into director Daniel Mann and producer Jack Cummings. They had just finished lunch and were walking toward Jack's office in the main building and I met them head on. Just about that time, the beautiful, talented actress Greer Garson was walking toward us and stopped to say hello to Danny and Jack. They introduced me to her. She had the most beautiful porcelain skin, a gorgeous face and a lovely figure. She mentioned the lawn party she was giving at her home. Jack and his wife were already invited and cordially invited Danny and me. She asked for our phone numbers and told us her secretary would be in touch with us to send an invitation. That area between Joe Hollywood's security booth and the commissary was the main runway where I ran into many stars, directors and producers. The next day I received a phone call from her secretary and a few days later I received a beautiful invitation to attend her lawn party at her Bel Air home.

The next day I was headed to the studio to prepare with Ms. Fogler, my speech coach. I got in my Beetle and turned on the radio. It was Tommy Dorsey's theme song, "I'm Getting Sentimental Over You." I just caught the last few bars of the number and the disc jockey talked in past tense about Tommy's career. He mentioned Tommy had passed away at his home in Greenwich, Connecticut. When I heard the news, I pulled the car to the side of the road and cried. Tommy was like family to me.

I pulled myself together and drove to the MGM parking lot. I tried to gather my thoughts about

On location in New York City filming Somebody Up There Likes Me. *Left to right: Paul Newman, Steve Mc Queen, Sal Mineo and me. What a cast!*

the terrible news. I managed to get through my appointments the rest of the day, seemingly in a fog. When I got home I called Tommy's residence in Greenwich. I also called Tommy's manager and my friend Tino Barzie. Tino told me the whole story of how he passed away.

Tommy was watching a baseball game on television alone in his den and ordered a veal takeout dinner from an nearby restaurant. Tino said that he took a sleeping pill; fell asleep and choked on the veal. It took me quite a while to get over his death. I cannot put into words what Tommy did for me. Without him, I wouldn't be writing this book. He gave me the opportunity to pursue my second career and I will be forever grateful to him. He was a special man and I was proud to call him my friend.

About a week, later I chauffeured myself to Greer Garson's lawn party, on a beautiful sunny afternoon in Bel Air, an exclusive section of Los Angeles. There were several expensive cars in front of me and I pulled up behind them in my little Beetle. The attendants were hustling, opening the doors for the guests and then jumping inside to park the cars down the road. It was the making of an interesting and glamorous afternoon. I got out of my car and began walking down the pathway with beautiful flowers on the left and right on both sides of a rock-bedded stream that ran through the side of the house where beautiful tables with white linen cloth dressed the tops and flowing to the ground with gorgeous flowers for centerpieces. I was a long way from home and it was like a part in a magical movie.

Before I got to the end of the walkway a butler dressed in a tuxedo was holding a tray of champagne to offer. I took a glass and walked several paces toward the beautiful Greer Garson and her handsome husband, Buddy E.E. Fogelson, who personally greeted everyone as they meandered into the house.

I walked around imbibing the atmosphere and got a chance to speak with Gene Kelly, Howard Keel and Fred Astaire for a while. The head of the hairdressing department, Sidney Guilaroff, composer, conductor, songwriter Johnny Green, conductor, composer, musician Andre Previn, and actress Elaine Stewart arrived. The music was perfect for the atmosphere, and the guests were incredible. I didn't know it at the time, but this would be the beginning of the end of the glamorous Hollywood that once was so special.

I talked with the Cummings and Danny Mann, and they introduced me to some of the most talented and prominent people in the business throughout the afternoon. The food was exquisite and everyone seemed familiar with each other enjoying a great Saturday afternoon with the family. Bob Wise was preparing to do the life story of Rocky Graziano, starring Paul Newman, entitled *Somebody Up There Likes Me*. There was a script available to read in the casting office. I read it and discovered there was a role I could play, 'Shorty the Greek.' He was one of Rocky's buddies in the youth sequences of his life story. Not a big part, but a good start for me to get my feet wet. And besides, the picture locations would take place in New York City, which was only one hour away from my hometown.

It was like something in one of my dreams and it was all coming true.

20

The Actor's Life

I went to Bob Wise's office and told him I was a contract player and asked if he would consider me for the part of 'Shorty the Greek.' A week or two later I heard from the casting office that I had the part. It was my first real job in the film industry. Before I knew it, I was called to the wardrobe department to get fitted for my wardrobe and then to the casting department for my transportation reservations to and from New York City. I got those particulars all squared away and I was on my way to the Big Apple, filled with wonder and excitement.

The whole company stayed at the historic Warwick Hotel, located right in the heart of the city. The famous hotel was popular for housing actors and production personnel for most of the movie companies that worked in New York City. What a treat that my first picture was an East Coast location just an hour from my hometown of Stamford, Connecticut, and walking distance from many of the finest restaurants, theaters and clothing stores. I loved to walk and window shop and I was looking forward to dining at all the popular restaurants like Sardi's, Danny's Hideaway, Vesuvio's, Stage Deli, Lindy's and The Carnegie Deli.

My favorite clothing store was located in the heart of Broadway called Laytons. When I was a teenager, I bought a couple of very expensive alpaca sport shirts with the tip money I saved from caddying all summer long at the Hubbard Heights golf club in Stamford. My dad always said I had good taste in clothing, but expensive. I spent $100 for those two shirts. That was a lot of money in those days for a grown up, let alone a teenager. As soon as I arrived at the hotel I called my folks to let them know where I was staying. The first day of shooting was a half hour from the hotel. I had an 8 a.m. call for makeup and was told to be out in front of the hotel an hour before under the canopy for the limousine to pick me up. I arrived in front ten minutes before seven and it was raining so hard I could barely see across the street.

I was standing underneath the canopy when a motorcycle pulled up and stopped right in front of me. The operator was soaking wet from top to bottom. He was wearing a light jacket and cap on his head. No rain gear whatsoever. I mean, he didn't have a dry spot on his clothing.

Speaking above his engine noise, he asked me if I knew where the MGM movie company was filming *Somebody Up There Likes Me*.

He then said he was working with the company and was told to meet here to get a ride to the location. I told him he was in luck, because the limousine would be coming any minute to pick me up and take me to the location. Just about that time the limousine driver pulled up, but he declined the ride. The rain never let up and traffic was moving slowly. I kept looking through the back window from time to time to see if he was still following. We arrived at the location and the driver dropped me off at my dressing room. It was small with basic amenities. It was just for a wardrobe change and a place to relax when not working. Just as I was putting on my wardrobe the motorcycle driver entered, soaked to the skin.

He put out his hand and said, "I'm Steve McQueen. I guess we're sharing this dressing room." We shook hands and the water was dripping from his clothing so much, in no time the floor was all wet. I told Steve he could have my towel to dry himself off. The rain continued throughout the day so Steve and I did not work, but the following day was sunny and clear, perfect for filming.

The sequence we were shooting the second day consisted of Paul Newman, Sal Mineo, Steve and me robbing fur coats from the back of a truck. We shot on the east side of town with several hundred spectators roped off behind the camera observing. Sal, Steve and I were supposed to hop on the back of the truck after Paul steps in front of the truck to make the driver stop briefly, so we could steal the furs. Yes, yours truly, the athlete, was the last to jump off. It was a little scary getting off last when the truck reached twenty five miles an hour.

The shot was set up with the camera located on the driver's side of the truck. As he came down the street, Paul entered the shot on the passenger side of the front of the truck to make the driver stop. When the driver halted, he put his head out of the side window and said, "What's the matter with you, are you crazy?" Paul answered him, "No, I just wanted to see whether your brakes worked." That was our cue to run behind the truck, jump on and throw the furs onto the street. Steve and I were on the left side near a huge brick wall and Sal was by himself, not far from us but towards the back of the truck. There was a whole flock of pigeons where Steve and I were waiting to enter the shot. Steve was fascinated by the birds and wasn't paying attention to the truck.

This was an old vehicle and I noticed it was coming down the street on an angle. The front end without a doubt was out of line. I didn't like the looks of the truck and I never diverted my eyes from it while it was in motion. We rehearsed the scene with the truck moving at about 20 miles an hour. Director Robert Wise instructed the driver, who was an actor, to go 25 miles an hour for the take. The camera was located about three feet to the left of the truck's front tire. It was a huge Mitchell camera mounted on a dolly and secured on the dolly by a 2 x 6 plank that overlapped the dolly by about three feet. For some reason, no one sawed off the three feet of plank overlapping the dolly. In addition, behind the camera there were about 300 spectators roped off watching the scene.

We were all in our starting positions when the director called "action." The actor driving the truck put the stick shift in first gear then second and then into the third gear getting up to the speed the director wanted. My full attention was on that truck and Paul Newman. Steve had his back turned to the action watching the pigeons. The driver got the truck up to the proper speed and as he approached his mark near the camera, he applied his brakes when he saw Paul stepping in front of the truck.

He stepped on his brakes and all you could hear was a distinct sound…thump, thump, thump… hitting the floor; his brakes were gone.

The driver turned the truck away from the camera and spectators, but unfortunately he hit that three foot plank that overlapped the dolly. The camera operator went straight up into the air and his assistant was thrown from the dolly at the same time. The truck just missed Paul and was heading toward Steve and me. I turned and grabbed him, who was still not paying attention and pulled him toward me as the truck struck a lamppost in front of us. I ran around to the driver's side, who was in shock yelling, "I hit them…I hit them," thinking he hit the camera crew and the spectators. I opened the door and shook him and kept telling him everyone's okay. Within a few seconds, first aid and all concerned surrounded the truck to try to comfort the driver who was in shock. An ambulance arrived shortly and took him and the camera operator to the hospital.

Fortunately, both were not seriously injured. Mr. Wise stopped production for the day and said we would shoot the sequence again when the actor was ready and when they had another working truck available. It was one hell of an experience for all of us, and thank God no one was hurt.

Steve thanked me for pulling him away from the oncoming truck, but several years later, he failed to repay the favor. In the mid-to-late '60s I was working quite a bit in television and motion pictures. My timing was just right to make that jump to the next level in my career when I met with producer Phil D'Antoni, director Peter Yates and executive producer Robert E. Relyea, who were working with Steve on the classic movie *Bullitt*. They saw *The Desilu Playhouse* show I did with Rory Calhoun, entitled *The Killer Instinct* and liked my performance every much. Phil verbally gave me the part to play Steve's cop partner, Delgetti. I was invited to have lunch the next day at the Warner Bros. commissary and Phil said Steve would join us later on. The meeting went well and McQueen arrived about a half hour late. I had forgotten about Steve's complex regarding height. Seems the bigger Steve grew in stature, the more he wanted his costars to physically shrink. He wanted no competition on the screen whatsoever, and did whatever he could to control the situation.

When we finished lunch and got up to leave, I made a monumental mistake: I stood up before Steve did and in front of him as well. Being taller than him, he looked up at me and said in his cool jargon, "Whoa…hey man. What did 'ya do? Get taller since I saw you last?" When I heard Steve say that, it was like a knife going through my heart. I instinctively knew I was out of the picture. I got in my car and left the lot and thought about all the strange and sometimes negative things about our business.

About an hour after I arrived home, I got a phone call from Relyea, informing me that Steve would not work with anyone taller than him. That, of course, meant me. A good actor, Don Gordon (and Steve's close friend) later got the part. I was on a roll, going from one project to another. This role would have given me more of the impetus I needed to further my career at the time because it was a good part and a hugely successful movie. I could've sued the studio because I had a verbal commitment, but then I probably would've never worked again in Hollywood. I liked Steve and he was a terrific actor, but it took me a long time to get over that one.

After the first week of shooting I invited my mother, father, three sisters and brother to dine at Vesuvio, one of New York's finest Italian restaurants. We enjoyed a wonderful dinner and just when we were about to order an after dinner drink, the captain came to me and said, "Mr. Carmine DiSapio would like to buy you and your family an after dinner drink." DiSapio said he was a good friend of Steve Barry's. I met Steve the second day of shooting on the set of *Somebody Up There Likes Me*. We struck up an instant friendship. He was in public relations and knew everyone in show business and politics in New York at the time.

Steve was supposed to join us for dinner but couldn't make it. He said he would like me to meet Mr. DiSapio when I spoke with him earlier that day. The captain handed me a note that read, "Mr. DiSapio would like you to join him and his friends upstairs in the private dining room after you've finish dinner." I left my family briefly to meet Mr. DiSapio and his friends upstairs, who were just finishing their dinner. After meeting him, he introduced me to his friends and told them I was a young actor working in New York in the movie *Somebody Up There Likes Me*, the life story of Rocky Graziano.

They were all handsomely dressed in suits and ties and were gracious and kind to wish me all the good things I wished for myself. Steve told him all about me, and it was unfortunate that he was unable to be there that evening. The next day I called Steve to thank him and tell him what took place the night before. Mr. DiSapio handed me his card and said, "Anything you might need while you are in New York, please call." I thanked him and said goodnight to everyone. Mr. DiSapio and his friends were the political machine in New York at that time, better known as Tammany Hall.

Steve Barry didn't stop there. He introduced me to all the publishers of all the fan magazines, Wanda Hale, Kay Gardella both of the *Daily News* and two restaurant owners, Danny Stradella the owner of Danny's Hideaway and Vincent Sardi the owner of the famous Sardi's Restaurant. I went to Danny's Hideaway quite often. The food and ambience was outstanding and catered to the show business crowd. Danny was one of the most generous guys I have ever known. One night he introduced me and sat me down to have dinner with Gabby Hayes and Keefe Brasselle.

I grew up watching and loving all the Westerns Gabby did with Roy Rogers and all of my other favorite cowboys. After we finished dinner, Danny invited us to the Copacabana, the famous nightclub, to see the show. Guy Lombardo was the headliner that night and a friend of Danny's. I had a wonderful time conversing with Gabby and Keefe throughout the entire evening. It's hard to put into words how much I enjoyed being with Gabby, for he brought a great deal of joy to my life when I was growing up. A year or two later I was saddened when I heard he passed away. I was blessed to have spent time with this wonderful talented and colorful character.

One night I invited one of my best friends, Remo Cipri, an ex-professional boxer and a talented artist from my hometown, to join me for dinner at Vesuvio's and to see a play, *Damn Yankees*, starring Jayne Mansfield and Tab Hunter. He had never seen a Broadway play before. The dinner was excellent and we got to the theatre just before curtain. Remo and I grew up with a lot of street humor and about halfway through the first act something struck him so funny and I found it funny too, particularly because he was enjoying it so much. We couldn't stop laughing.

Unfortunately we were the only ones laughing at that moment. A woman sitting behind us didn't like it. This theater snob tapped Remo on the shoulder and told him to keep it down. Remo turned around and said, "Lady, why don't you find a job? Everybody's talking about you." Everyone within hearing distance began laughing hysterically. I'm sure the people that heard what he said, never, ever heard anything like that before. She never said another word after that. I was fortunate to experience so many exciting things working in my first job on location in New York City.

After a few days of filming, I got to know Paul Newman a little better and he invited Steve and me to have a beer with him after work. Paul loved beer and he could drink a lot of it, but never put on any weight. He was interesting to be around and loved to talk about racing cars. Steve loved motorcycles, so you can imagine the conversation that transpired. I had a box seat right in the middle of these two talented guys talking about their other passion, machines with engines.

I've always thought the best work Paul ever did was in *Somebody Up There Likes Me* because it was such a departure from most of his other roles. The character he played, Rocky Graziano, was Italian and Paul was as ethnic as a glass of milk. He really had to stretch and I thought he did a fantastic job. His characterization was believable and the fight sequences were terrific.

Speaking of Graziano, he came to the set while we were shooting a couple of times and he was hysterical. He possessed a terrific sense of humor and was a unique guy, not to mention a great champion. I saw every one of his televised fights and he was truly something special. We all idolized him and Rocky Marciano growing up and to think one day, I would get to meet and know both of them. I didn't get to see Graziano again until one day I ran into him having lunch at the famous Nate and Al's Delicatessen in Beverly Hills.

We had a couple of laughs and I asked him whatever happened to the real Shorty the Greek? He said he was killed in an automobile accident while he was riding on the back of a truck.

That was the last time I ever saw Rocky. In 1990 he passed away at the age of seventy one from cardiopulmonary failure. To me, he will always be "The Champ."

21

Back For More

We completed all location shooting for *Somebody Up There Likes Me* in New York and returned to the studio in Los Angeles for the interior scenes. I only had a few days left to complete my work in the film. I enjoyed every minute working with such talented people, and I learned quite a bit in a short period of time. Robert Wise was such a talented director and I could not have asked for a better start.

Shortly after I finished my work in the picture, I went back to my routine on the lot working with the drama coach, speech teacher and the voice Maestro. I finished lunch one day at the commissary and ran into Daniel Mann, who was talking with Arthur Schwartz, the award-winning composer, songwriter partnered with lyricist Howard Dietz. They wrote classic songs such as: "You and the Night and the Music," "I Guess I'll Have to Change My Plans," "That's Entertainment" and "What a Wonderful World." He just finished his contract with the studio and was moving back to New York in a few weeks with his family to write and produce a Broadway play. I met Arthur once before on the lot and he was warm and charming. He invited me to his going away party at his home in Beverly Hills. He asked for my number and said his secretary would call me with all the details. Being under contract was like being a member of the family.

Just about that time the studio began filming *Raintree County* starring Elizabeth Taylor, Montgomery Clift, Eva Marie Saint, Lee Marvin, Rod Taylor. The lot had an ambience of excitement, reeling with all the expectations of this film with hopes of another *Gone With The Wind*. Elizabeth Taylor and Monty Clift were close friends and looked forward to working with each other on this well-crafted screenplay written by Millard Kaufman and directed by Edward Dmytryk. I got a call from the casting office to play a very small part in the beginning of the picture. This would be my second and last job while under contract to MGM.

Despite my small part, I had the opportunity to meet Elizabeth Taylor, Monty Clift, Lee Marvin and Rod Taylor, who was under contract to MGM at the time. As the years went by, Rod and I became good pals. We had many laughs and fun throughout our careers. There were two or three other contract players, who also had small parts in the race sequence between Monty Clift and Lee Marvin. I felt truly blessed to once again be amongst Hollywood's finest.

Of course, being able to look at Elizabeth Taylor every day, gave us all something special to look forward to during the shoot. She had the most beautiful eyes I've ever seen on a woman and was drop dead gorgeous. During the filming of *Raintree County*, Montgomery Clift was injured in a serious automobile accident and it dramatically changed his appearance.

73

Even with all the makeup expertise, you could see that there was a definite change in his looks. Monty had a problem with alcohol and it was said that the accident occurred after a night of drinking. The studio had to shoot around him until the swelling and the healing took place. When he reported back to work, you could see that there was some permanent damage to his profile. Sadly, his face never looked the same after that accident.

That same year, I went home to spend the holidays with my family in Stamford, Connecticut. It was Christmas Eve when I stopped by the corner store on Stillwater Avenue on the west side of town where I grew up. I wanted to say a quick hello and wish the owner, my friend, Joe Girardi, a Merry Christmas. I stepped aside when the door with a bell on it rang out and a guy walked in and ordered several bottles of booze. It was Montgomery Clift. He was so thin and frail looking. It was cold outside and he only had a sport coat on. He appeared to be cold and his posture was not good. I simply observed and didn't say anything because I didn't want to put Monty in an embarrassing position. It was obvious that he already had a couple of drinks. Whenever he was in the area, he stayed with singer/actress Libby Holman, who had a nice home in Stamford. I'll always remember it as a vignette out of some sad storybook. Monty was another fine actor and a troubled man who left the cinema world, much too soon at the ripe old age of forty six. Show business was not for the faint of heart.

When I got back to LA, I received a call from Arthur Schwartz's secretary giving me the details of their going away party. It was a lovely house just off Sunset Boulevard. I was a bachelor at the time and so I went stag. It was an elegant affair. All the tables were located outside on a large beautiful lawn with live music floating through the air on this gorgeous balmy evening at dusk. The party began to fill up with all the producers, directors and stars under contract to MGM.

Some of the luminaries in attendance were Ava Garner, Lana Turner, Greer Garson, Howard Keel, Delores Gray, Johnny Green, Arthur Freed, Joe Pasternak, Gene Kelly, Tania Elg, Elaine Stewart, Howard Dietz, Bronislau Kaper, Jack Cummings, and André Previn to name but a few. Believe it or not, I sat at a table with three other people that came alone, Josephine Baker, Fred Astaire and the brilliant songwriter Johnny Mercer. This evening was the first time Fred socialized since his wife passed away one year prior. He was such an elegant gentleman. The talented Josephine Baker, who resided in Paris, France, was visiting for a short period of time.

Josephine shared with us the story about the orphans she brought into her home, and cared for them like they were her own. She was so interesting and alive with stories of her youth and career. I found her just as fascinating as Johnny Mercer, who after a few drinks, exchanged stories about people and anecdotes that took place throughout his life. I was the rookie on the team absorbing everything that was being said, and could not believe I was in the company of these larger than life people.

They were also good listeners and were interested in hearing what I had to say about my journey to Hollywood. I shared with everyone my short lived baseball career and having the good fortune of meeting Tommy Dorsey. They all knew Tommy well and had a great deal of respect for him.

No one moved from that table the whole night except to go to the bathroom. Arthur and his beautiful wife were well aware that we had not left the table all evening. Believe it or not, we sat down at around 6:30 that evening and left around 2 a.m.. We were one of the last to leave. Of the three people, Fred was the only resident. I came to know his son, Fred Jr., and beautiful daughter, Ava, and was invited to their home to shoot a round of pool. They were warm and friendly, unpretentious people. Josephine Baker went home to Paris, and Johnny Mercer left for his home in the south. Unfortunately I never got to see any of them again.

Two days later I walked into the MGM commissary and Lana Turner was having lunch with her makeup artist Del Armstrong. I walked to the table to say hello and they invited me to have lunch with them. Lana wanted to know what was going on with my career and asked me if I had an agent and a public relations person. I said I couldn't afford a PR person, but I was looking for an agent. Before we finished lunch, we exchanged phone numbers and she said she wanted me to meet Glenn Rose, her PR person. I left saying that I would call her and make arrangements to have lunch and meet Glenn.

Television was beginning to gain more and more momentum, but MGM did not believe television would last very long and certainly not capable of competing with motion pictures. Other studios began to take television seriously, but foolishly MGM didn't pay much attention to its enormous potential and was reluctant to follow suit. Louis B. Mayer, the head of the studio was not on top of his game, and Dore Schary had taken over the reins of the studio with a different philosophy for making movies. The handwriting was on the wall, even before Mr. Schary arrived. The studio was not renewing contracts for the people they had under contract for years. That included big stars such as Clark Gable, Lana Turner, Greer Garson, Ava Gardner, Delores Gray, Rod Taylor, Howard Keel, Eleanor Powell, Vic Damone, Syd Charisse, Debbie Reynolds, Gene Kelly, Elaine Stewart and a host of others. For the most part, musicals, as we knew them would unfortunately become something of the past. Other contract players like me didn't expect their options to be picked up. We knew what the answer would be, when our contract dates arrived. I called Lana and made arrangements to have lunch with her and her press agent Glenn Rose. I told them I knew what the situation was at the studio and that they most likely were not going to renew my contract. Lana and Glenn were well aware of what was going on at MGM with all of the people under contract.

Lana had read and enjoyed a paperback book entitled *Handsome* and was interested in making it into a movie with her recently formed company. During the luncheon they both suggested I should change my name to something that would sound good and looked good on the marquee.

My name was Ralph Vitti, which was the same last name identical to the great Italian actress Monica Vitti. They suggested I seriously consider the suggestion and not make a decision until it sounded right and looked right for me. I agreed and thought about it constantly. I knew this was important and I had to be patient before I made a final decision about the change. My instincts told me that the opportunity would present itself in the near future. Before we finished our lunch Lana gave me the book *Handsome* to read and the picture of the young man on the cover resembled me a great deal.

It was a solid love story and I'm sure if it ever got made, it would've been captivating. It could've been made affordably and had a lot of PR potential. I read the book and there was a perfect part for me to play. Unfortunately, Lana did a couple of pictures back-to-back and her own project got sidetracked. In the meantime, I saw Lana socially and we had dinner several times. She had a lovely home on the corner of Sunset and Mapleton with a swimming pool and a beautiful garden area. I met her mother, Mildred, who was living with her at the time and Lana's daughter, Cheryl. Her mother was so sweet and a true grandmother to Cheryl. She adored Cheryl, and was loving and protective of her.

I enjoyed seeing Mildred and speaking with her from time to time. She was down to earth and enjoyed hearing stories about my family. Lana was invited to the opening night of comedian Don Rickles at the Slate Brothers nightclub on La Cienega Boulevard. She asked me if I would escort her that evening. I picked her up at her home and joined the many celebrities at the opening. Don was a rising star at the time, and his controversial style of humor was the talk of Hollywood.

If you've ever heard or seen Rickles' comedy act, you know that he loved to attack people, particularly celebrities in the audience. That night he took shots at Burt Lancaster and, of course, Lana, as well as several other luminaries in attendance. He was hysterical. His humor was edgy, but funny. Lana and I both met Don that night for the first time and became friends over the years. He too loved baseball. A few years later he played on the softball team I managed and played shortstop for in The Entertainers League. Don played first base and was a pretty good athlete. During the games he was extremely entertaining. He found a way to keep us all loose and laughing from the beginning to the end. Some of the players who played in the Entertainers League were James Garner, Bobby Darin, John Cassevettes, Shecky Greene, Seymour Cassell, Michael Parks, Bruce Dern, John Beradino, James Caan, Mickey Callan, Harvey Lembeck, Tom Sellek, Robert Donner, Norm Alden, Larry Pennell and me. I benched Don Rickles one game and I never heard the end of it. To this day, I still hear about it when I see him!

Leaving MGM

My option date on my contract was about to expire and I was called into Al Trescony's office. The studio was no longer interested in developing and keeping various potential stars and established stars under contract any longer, and that meant I was out the door. I believe at the time they were the first studio to unload contract players, and those in other creative areas as well. It was a sad sign of the changing times.

Lana finished the picture she was working on and wanted to get out of town for some much needed rest. She asked me if I would like to spend a few days in the Palm Springs area at her friend, actor Willard Parker and his lovely actress wife's hotel/spa in Palm Desert, California. Willard appeared in quite a few motion pictures, namely *The Fighting Guardsman, Calamity Jane and Sam Bass, Apache Drums, Lone Texan, Young Jesse James and Kiss Me Kate,* and co-starred with his wife Virginia Field in *The Earth Dies Screaming.*

He was probably known more for his successful TV series entitled *Tales of the Texas Rangers.* Virginia was a fine actress and enjoyed a long and successful career as well. They both retired from show business and sold real estate in the Palm Springs area, along with acquiring a small, charming hotel/spa in Palm Desert. It was located about two blocks above El Paseo and just East of Portola, as we know it today. In the late 1950s, there wasn't very much real estate at all in Palm Desert. So, the Parker Hotel was a quaint little romantic hideaway for Hollywood. We arrived to a warm reception. It was obvious that the Parkers loved Lana and she adored them. They greeted me with open arms. After a brief chat and a cold drink, we went to our rooms, but not before Willard and Virginia invited us to take a swim, and enjoy some cocktails and a barbecue dinner at poolside as soon as we got settled.

I had my own private room, which was decorated with a lot of Hollywood motion picture posters. They were creatively arranged with many of the stars that both Willard and Virginia worked with over the years. Willard liked to barbecue, and for the next couple of nights we dined under the beautiful desert sky. There was millions of twinkling stars and a gentle warm breeze to go with it. Willard and Virginia were such hospitable hosts; they made us breakfast and lunch. We enjoyed cocktails and conversation before and after dinner. I wasn't much of a drinker, enjoyed a beer or two at most. Lana enjoyed vodka and like most people during that period, smoked quite a lot. The Parkers were full of wonderful stories about their youth and how they got started in show business and the many interesting people they worked with over the years. They were very intelligent and talented people with a good sense of humor and were glued to every word about my background and how I got started in the business. Both of them were baseball fans and followed the sport. This made me different from any of Lana's ex-husbands or boyfriends and I really enjoyed sharing every moment of our stay with them.

My character Henry Anthrobus with two cast members from the play, The Skin of Our Teeth.

Time flew by and on the last day before departing, Lana's daughter Cheryl and one of her classmates from school, joined us for the day. We all drove back home to Los Angeles together. Of course, this was all prearranged with Lana and Cheryl before we left. I didn't know Cheryl very well but I did know she wasn't a happy child. She attended a private school, which meant spending a lot of time away from her mother.

When I returned to my apartment, I received several phone calls to audition for a play at the Pacific Palisades Theater, entitled *The Skin of Our Teeth* and written by Thornton Wilder. I was familiar with the play, but I had not read it in quite some time, so I jumped in my Beetle and drove to the Samuel French book store on Sunset Boulevard to pick up a copy. I read it that same night and knew I was right for the part of Henry Anthrobus. It was the same part that Montgomery Clift played on Broadway to rave reviews. The next day I called the production office at the theater and set up an appointment to audition.

There were a lot of actors and actresses trying out for various parts. The atmosphere was full of energy and enthusiasm. I read a couple times and returned for a callback a third time and eventually got the part. For the next couple of weeks I was focused on learning my dialogue along with rehearsing with the rest of the cast at the theater.

Henry sets the mood. Each member of the cast with their facial expressions and body language in their reactions to me are classic.

We were only giving three performances on Friday, Saturday and a matinee on Sunday. This would be my first performance on stage with other professional actors. I really felt good about the play and the challenge to bring to life the character Henry Anthrobus. I was full of energy and anticipation every day of our rehearsals and could not wait until opening night to hear the reaction of a live audience. Like everyone else in the cast, I was nervous as hell opening night but felt more relaxed before the Saturday night and Sunday matinee performances. I was fortunate that Steven "Solly" Biano, head of the talent department at Warner Bros., was in the audience on Saturday. He came backstage to give me his card. He asked if my agent or I would call his office on Monday. I arranged for an appointment to talk with him about doing a screen test at Warner Bros. That Sunday matinee brought a couple of agents to the play, they came backstage afterwards to give me their cards and to contact them the beginning of the week to talk about representation.

Everything was falling into place at a rapid pace. My timing was perfect and in Hollywood, luck is equal if not better than having talent.

23

Contractual Obligations

Monday morning could not come fast enough. I called Solly Biano's office at Warner Bros. and he invited me to the studio the following day to have lunch with him and talk about a screen test. Warner Bros. Studios had a different kind of excitement at this time. It looked similar to the MGM Studios lot with production buildings and sound stages and lots of people busily going here and there. But, because of the rapid growth of television in the film industry, the studio was busy hiring a lot of people to create, write, produce and film television shows. Unlike MGM, they embraced the medium of television.

We had a productive meeting and Solly brought me up to speed on the studio, and what its future looked like with the fast moving success of their television programming. He said he was in the process of arranging for another actor to do a screen test and perhaps we could kill two birds with one stone and do it together. I told him that was fine with me. Solly immediately arranged for us to get together and pick out a scene we mutually liked and start rehearsing as soon as possible. We were to report to his office as soon as we both thought the scene was ready. A few days later I called and told him we were ready to go. He told us to report to one of the soundstages with our own wardrobe and props. The actor I did the screen test with was Peter Brown. We did a scene from Arthur Miller's award winning play *Death of a Salesman*. We chose one of the best scenes involving the two brothers Happy and Biff. It could not have gone better. We both felt very comfortable and positive. We gave it all we had and the results were there on the screen when we saw the test two days later.

We also did our own personality test, which consisted of questions they asked us about our background, family, education, likes and dislikes very much like the screen test I did at MGM. That too was successful and looked good up on the screen. Prior to the test, we were asked to sign a letter of commitment. In return they would pay us a salary of $250 a week for the first year, with options of automatic increases for the next six years. It was a standard seven-year studio contract. The final contract was spelled out in much more detail. As soon as those contracts were made up, we were to sign the official contract and be available for work. Well, it so happened, they didn't give me that letter of commitment prior to taking the test. For some reason the casting department didn't give me those papers to sign. So when it came time to sign my official contract I refused to unless I got $275 a week to start. I did it all myself, without the help of an agent. The head of casting had no alternative but to unwillingly give me an extra $25 a week because Jack Warner and Bill Orr had already approved my test and wanted me signed immediately. The head of casting never forgave me for that and I was in his little black book from that point on. But that extra $25 a week in those days sure came in handy and went a long way.

Under contract at Warner Bros. Studios.

Date Night with Connie Stevens. Warner Bros. and all the studios at the time made sure that the arranged dates for their movie premieres were with the new, rising stars. We were oh-so-young and good looking.

For the period of time I spent there, he ignored me as much as he could. He was a real narrow-minded schmuck with no sense of humor whatsoever. Warner Bros. was becoming the busiest lot in the business. One television series after another was developed starting with *Cheyenne* starring Clint Walker, *Maverick* starring James Garner and Jack Kelly, *Colt 45* starring Wayde Preston, *Sugarfoot* starring Will Hutchins, *Lawman* starring John Russell and Peter Brown, *Hawaiian Eye* starring Robert Conrad and Connie Stevens, *Bronco* starring Ty Hardin, *77 Sunset Strip* starring Efrem Zimbalist, Roger Smith and Edd "Kookie" Byrnes. Warner Bros. at one time had ten and a half hours of primetime television on the air. No other studio compared with the success of their television department.

In time, I became one of the busiest actors in the business. I did get a chance to tell Lana about the contract at Warner Bros. and she of course couldn't be happier for me. She asked if I had chosen a professional name yet. I said no, but that I was going to have to make a decision soon. About that same time Johnny Stompanato began dating and romancing Lana Turner. I knew that our relationship wasn't going anywhere but we certainly would always remain friends.

For the first few months I began doing quite a few episodes of all their Western series; *Cheyenne, Maverick, Lawman, Sugarfoot, Colt 45* and when I wasn't filming I was in the sound room dubbing kids voices, middle age and older characters on a regular basis. The studio took advantage of my ability to do those things, and I thoroughly enjoyed the challenge. They certainly got their money's worth with me. I got a call from the casting department to pick up some sides to test for the other Maverick brother in the series. I remember it like it was yesterday when Stuart Whitman and I tested for the part that same day with James Garner, feeding us dialogue on the other side of the camera. The test was being directed by one of the best directors in the business, Budd Boetticher, who was deemed a young John Ford. This became one of the most important days of my career. We had a lot of fun working together and we've all been friends ever since. Budd was so talented and made everything interesting, along with his great sense of humor.

Despite the test and all the good vibes, Stu and I did not get the part. I eventually learned it went to Jack Kelly, who was different looking than James Garner. He was much better suited for the part than Stu or me because we looked too much like Garner, so they said. The series became a big hit and lasted several years in their time slot until James Garner left the series and the studio because the legal department neglected to pickup his option before it ran out. That was a costly mistake for Warner Brothers. James went on to enjoy a huge motion picture and successful television career for five decades. It couldn't have happened to a nicer guy.

The following day I got a call from casting to come and pick up the script that would star Randolph Scott, Virginia Mayo and Karen Steele, which was being produced by Henry Blanke and directed by Budd Boetticher. The day before Budd directed me for the other *Maverick* character, he later told me he made up his mind then and there that he wanted me to play the one-armed character, Rod in his western *Westbound.* It turned out to be a life changing moment.

24

Westbound

***Westbound* was my first starring role** in a motion picture. It was a terrific challenge to play a one-armed soldier coming back from war to the beautiful Karen Steele, left to run a farm with a major disability. I could hardly describe how I felt when Budd told me I had the part. I learned later that the studio wanted to cast one of their two hot young stars they had under contract at that time – Tab Hunter and Troy Donahue. They were immensely popular and getting tons of fan mail on a daily basis and Jack Warner wanted either one to play the part of Rod. Budd did not want them and told Mr. Warner that if I didn't play the part then he could get another director. After reading the script and realizing what an incredible opportunity it was for me, I met with Budd and told him how grateful I was.

Before I left Budd's office, I asked if he could clear with the prop department my taking home a lever action Winchester for the weekend. I wanted to start working with the prop I chose to use in the film so I could be comfortable and accurate with it, using only one arm.

I worked with the rifle diligently cranking it up with one hand balancing it to pull the trigger, then putting my fingers in the lever to crank it up again and repeat the action. As an athlete I enjoyed the challenge to balance and coordinate the timing needed to make it look easy. This was not written in the script but it was my creative contribution to the role. Little did I know how important this was in the development of my character and the overall story. The moment I arrived on the set I called Budd aside to show him what I had perfected with the Winchester. I put on a little exhibition and Budd was really impressed. It was unfortunate for Randy because it was the first scene of the day when he was trying to encourage me that there are a lot of things you could do with one arm on a farm.

Budd inserted the rifle in this part of the story, whereby Randy would demonstrate to me how to crank a Winchester with one hand. Randy did not have a weekend to work on the timing and coordination needed to make it look easy. In the scene, Randy was to teach me to crank the Winchester with one hand. Unfortunately, Randy was not as coordinated as I was. His hand and fingers got all cut up. The first aid and makeup man had to cover him with band aids and heavy makeup so it wouldn't show in the shot.

It took about thirty takes to get the shot right. The front office came down on Budd real hard because he hadn't printed a shot all day. This was so important to the picture that Budd said, "We will get this shot, however long it takes or you can get another director." Randy finally got the shot, and all was forgiven. If you see the film *Westbound*, you'll know precisely what I'm talking about. Several years after *Westbound* was released, I received a phone call from a critic in television syndication stating the five greatest performances played by an actor portraying a one-arm character. They were Spencer Tracy for *Bad Day at Black Rock,* Tom Tryon in *Three Violent Men,* Chill Wills in *The Man from the Alamo,* Bill Raisch in *The Fugitive,* and my performance in *Westbound.* I was by far the youngest and there were no special affects to assist in our performances in those days. I was certainly proud to be in that company. It was such a pleasure working with the talents of Randolph Scott, Virginia Mayo, Karen Steele, and my favorite director of all time, the talented Budd Boetticher. During the filming of *Westbound,* Budd and Karen were an item. Karen was not only beautiful but a talented actress. Unfortunately she left us too early at the age of 56 in 1988.

Budd was a talented storyteller, on and off the screen. His association and the stories he told about his two close friends, two of Mexico's greatest bullfighters, Carlos Arruza and Luis Dominguin were so interesting. Budd was one of a few Americans studying and practicing the art of becoming a bullfighter. I believe directing was his first love, and bullfighting was a close second. On two separate occasions, Carlos and his retinue and Luis and his compadres came to visit Budd on the set of *Westbound* at the Warner Bros. lot in Burbank during our filming. You knew immediately when they saw and greeted each other they were close amigos. We all had the pleasure of meeting Carlos and Luis, as well.

As Rod, a one-arm soldier boy in Westbound. *It was my first starring role in a feature film.*

Both men had a distinct presence about them, and terrific smiles to go along with their continuous sense of humor. They stayed about an hour on the set to watch us work and then we all went to lunch together. On two separate occasions, Randy, Virginia, Karen and I met and shared some laughs with these two great artists. About a year later, a few of my friends and I went to see Carlos Arruza on a beautiful Sunday afternoon perform in the bull ring in Tijuana, Mexico and he was fantastic! He survived over 100 bullfights in the ring and tragically died in a car wreck on May 20, 1966 at the age of 46.

About a couple weeks into filming, Randy, Virginia, and I were waiting for another set up when Randy mentioned to us that in the future Americans would be purchasing groceries, gasoline, transportation, buying automobiles, you name it, with credit cards. Virginia and I looked at each other and could not quite make out what he was talking about, but Randy was so far ahead of most people in the world about business. We all knew that he was a smart and wealthy businessman. He mentioned a few things that were happening in the stock market world. Then suddenly he asked me, "Michael, do you have $10,000?" I looked at Randy straight away and told him that I had just purchased a house in Encino and put $10,000 down and only had $5,000 left to buy furnishings. He called the prop man over to fetch a pad and pencil to give to me.

"Michael, I want you to write these three stocks on that notepad," he said. "In a couple of years, you won't have to worry about your agent having to get you a job as soon as possible." He said this is what he wanted me to do. I said, "Randy, I don't know anything about stocks. Just a year ago I invested $3,000 in a stock I knew nothing about, but an actress friend of mine talked me into buying Cataract Mining in Canada. Well, I lost $1,500 in one week but I was fortunate to get half of my money back and swore I would never buy another stock again." He said, "Now write this down, IBM, Xerox, Polaroid, and if any one of those falter, substitute with Eastman Kodak." He encouraged me to keep it there and do not sell any of it; just let it ride and I'd be worth a lot of money in a few years. About ten years ago my brother and I calculated approximately what those stocks were worth over the years, if I just sat back and let it ride. About $5 million.

We had about a week to go to finish the picture and were sitting in our chairs talking about Dodger baseball. They were new to the city and it was the talk of the sports world. Randy and his attractive wife Mary had two adopted sons, and during our conversation I asked Randy if his sons had ever been to a Dodger baseball game. He said they hadn't and he wasn't much of a baseball fan, but a golfer and a good one.

I offered to take his boys to one of the games because I knew the general manager Al Campanis and some of the players. The next day, Randy said the boys would like to go, so I made arrangements to attend one of the games. We went to one of the night games on the weekend and had a lot of fun. We sat with Al Campanis in his private box and had dinner with him. Later we went to the dugout to meet some of the players and scrounge up a couple baseballs and baseball caps. The boys couldn't be happier. We saw a good game and they got a chance to meet some of the players and the manager, Walter Alston. When I brought the boys home and we were met at the door by Randy and Mary. They thanked me and just before we said good night, Randy took one step into the house and then turned around cracking a small smile said, "Did you?" He was referring to whether I had purchased the stocks he gave me. I sheepishly shook my head indicating 'no' and off I went. The next day, and for the rest of the filming, nothing was ever said about purchasing those stocks again.

Just before we finished the picture I got a call from the casting department and they said that Jack Warner wanted to see me right away. I had no idea what it was all about. I thought possibly I did something wrong, when the head of the studio wants to see a $275 a week contract player in

You know you have it made in Hollywood when you get your own director's chair with your name emblazoned on the back. That's me with Virginia Mayo and Randolph Scott during a break on the set of Westbound.

his office. Indeed something was not right. I went to see him and his secretary ushered me right in.

"Come on in, young man," Jack said. He was kind of rough, but to the point. He said, "You're doing a great job in the picture *Westbound*. You will be receiving costar billing along with Karen Steele, but you have to change your name. People are calling the publicity department and asking to do an interview with actor Ralph Bitti, Mitti and Sitti and no one knows who the hell they're calling about. Write down some names on the paper in front of you and see how they look, then take a look at some of these names I wrote down as well. Remember, the first name you choose should be long and the second name short or the first name short and the second name long."

We went over several names and we mutually liked Michael Brady. He seemed to favor that name but said to go home and over the weekend think of some other names and come back to his office at ten o'clock on Monday morning with some more choices. I went home and thought about it all weekend and came up with one of my relative's name, Dante and proceeded to write Michael before Dante. It looked and sounded good and so did Michael Brady. Monday morning I arrived at Jack's office at ten o'clock and wrote the two names—Michael Dante and Michael Brady—on a large piece of paper and handed it to him. He pronounced each name aloud. He paused for several moments and repeated the name, "Michael Dante...Michael Dante...I like it, that's you! Now go down to casting and the publicity department and tell them that will be your name up on the screen. Okay, now get out of here."

I was happy he liked Michael Dante because I didn't want to change my Italian heritage. Everyone that I spoke to and shared my choice with, agreed it was a great name and that it was

With Randolph Scott on location at Warner Ranch filming Westbound.

Acting does have its perks, including meeting beautiful women and interesting people. Here I'm hanging out with co-star Karen Steele and famous bullfighter Carlos Arraza, who visited us on the set of Westbound.

'me,' including Budd, Virginia, Randy and Karen. I called Lana and Glenn Rose and they liked it as well. I never forgot that tack room scene from the movie *The Rainmaker* with Burt Lancaster and Katharine Hepburn when the rainmaker said to Maggie, "Maggie, the name you choose for yourself is more your own name than the name you was born with."

It was with mixed emotions when we finished the film. We all had an enjoyable time working together and knew we had a good picture. It was time to thank everyone and say so long until we would see each other again and hopefully work together in the near future. When actors work for any length of time on a film, they become 'family' during and for all the years down the road. Even if you had not seen or spent much time together afterwards, that bond is still there. The next time you see each other, it's as if no time had passed at all. It's so special, because in order for the project you are mutually working on to become a success, the talent and love has to be shared and that same bonding applies to professional baseball. It's all teamwork and the energy and love that is put into the making of a film or a good ballclub is very powerful and long lasting.

Immediately upon finishing the picture, I got a disappointing call from casting to appear in one of the *Cheyenne* episodes. It was such a small part. I just finished costarring in a major motion picture and now I found myself cast in a television show and it wasn't even a decent role. Talk about a serious letdown.

I couldn't understand their thinking; where was the respect for my advancement and concern for my moving up the latter after having done a terrific job and having had co-star billing in a good movie? This all seemed a step backward in my eyes and I let that schmuck in casting know exactly how I felt. His answer was, "Do you have script approval in your contract?" Of course I didn't have script approval. He was giving me another shot in the gut, and it hurt like hell.

He was getting even with me whenever he could for not signing that commitment sheet prior to taking my screen test. I certainly wasn't his favorite actor under contract, and he certainly was not my favorite person at the studio and we were jabbing at each other. I had no choice but to do the role and to do whatever they assigned me to do or go on suspension, which meant that I would not receive my weekly paycheck.

Evidently something I said resonated with him because from then on all the parts were much better. He couldn't ignore me because I did a good job with everything they asked me to do. I kept hoping they would not put me in a series because I didn't want to do one at the time. In those days, if you did a series and it was not successful, it was difficult to get work afterwards. With the money they were paying and if it was successful, you were stuck with a studio contract with only small increases in salary regardless of how successful that series was. The studio would be making all the money and by the time taxes and agent fees were taken from our paychecks, and then not paying overtime and residuals, there wasn't much left. I was fortunate they didn't put me in a series and kept me busy going from one show to another at least once, twice and in some cases three times on each show. I thoroughly enjoyed it because it gave me the opportunity to play all kinds of different characters in each episode.

I wanted to be known as a versatile actor; a leading man who had the ability to adapt to the material and not have the material written for him, but to be able to go into character. That was my goal in order to sustain and survive in show business—versatility. Accomplishing that objective was my salvation in the business. But there were still many bumps and bruises ahead of me before I got to that point.

'WB' Movies and TV

I immediately got called back to work to do another *Cheyenne* with Clint Walker; *Maverick* with Jack Kelly and *Sugarfoot* with Will Hutchins. They were one-hour series that grew more popular with each week. The ratings for those shows and many shows Warner Brother had in prime time were at the top. So these series were undoubtedly going to be picked up for the following season. Warner Bros. couldn't be happier for they were riding high in the saddle.

I certainly enjoyed working with Clint, Jack and Will. They were all good actors who were comfortable with the characters they had to play on a weekly basis, which eliminated all the pressure to finish a show on schedule. The pressure was always on to finish on time. Jack Kelly was always good for a few laughs. We had respect for each other's work and became friends until he passed away, much too soon. Will was one of the nicest people you'd want to meet; he was different, had a unique quality, a naïve innocence about him that made his character so much different than any Western show on television. There was no one else like him on the air.

Clint, on the other hand, was more of a serious type, a rugged guy, a gentleman, but somewhat rigid, finding his way with *Cheyenne* and his sudden growth to stardom. I thought Warner Bros. made a big mistake not doing more western films with him. They should've never let him get away because he could've been another John Wayne. He had the size, looks, charisma, strength, and ability, everything needed to set him apart from any other actor in that genre of filmmaking. Clint went on to do several more films after he left Warner Bros., but I think things could have been much better for both of them with the assistance and power of Warner Bros behind them. What I learned while working with these fine actors was they were vastly under paid. The money the studio was making from the sponsors of each show compared to the salary they were earning was a joke. The studio should have given them raises immediately and kept them happy. They were not happy campers!

Warner Bros. commenced filming a contemporary Western at the studio entitled *Born Reckless* starring Mamie Van Doren, Jeff Richards, Carol Ohmart and Arthur Hunnicut, one of my favorite character actors of all time. I had the pleasure of working with him in *Winterhawk*.

Born Reckless was directed by Howard W. Koch, a veteran TV director with a lot of credits to his name and as a producer as well. Howard was best known for producing *Airplane! The Manchurian Candidate, The Odd Couple* and *Airplane II: The Sequel*. For television, just a few of the well-known shows he directed, *The Untouchables, Hawaiian Eye* and *Maverick* and the list goes on. He was a good communicator and it was obvious he enjoyed his work. He knew what he was doing and did it well with ease and with a smile. I got a call from casting to come in to pick up the script and while it was not

Mamie Van Doren is ageless and is as beautiful and lovely today as she was the first time I met her in the 1950s.

a big part, it was a nice cameo. Again, the studio was taking advantage with all of my exposure on television, and particularly the release of *Westbound* as well as all the publicity I was getting from the fan magazines.

The character was described as a handsome cowboy dude on the make for Mamie Van Doren. It was a fun sequence dancing and romancing the beautiful, voluptuous, sexy Mamie. She was a joy to work with; uninhibited with a great smile and a flirtatious quality. We had more laughs working together and it permeated throughout the set. We became fast friends and to this day my wife Mary Jane and I see

Mamie and her husband, Thomas, when we get a chance to spend a few days in the Newport Beach, California, area. Mamie looks as beautiful as ever.

I met Maria Cooper, daughter of Academy Award winning actor Gary Cooper, at a social event in 1959 and saw her again on the Warner Bros. lot. We talked briefly. She was such a beautiful, elegant young lady. Maria asked me if I would like to attend a studio screening of the film, *The Hanging Tree,* a Western her father had just finished for Warner Bros. The movie costarred Maria Schell, George C. Scott and Karl Malden, directed by one of my favorites, Delmer Daves. That evening I met Mr. Cooper and his wife Veronica, her close friends called her "Rocky." The four of us walked the red carpet to the theater on the Warner Bros. lot. When we were leaving the screening room Mr. Cooper said hello and spoke briefly with Maria Schell (sister of actor Maximilian Schell) about the movie. They introduced me to her and I noticed she had the most beautiful blue eyes. As we continued our exit, Mr. Cooper asked me what I thought of the movie in a slow and shy manner. I told him I thought it was good and added that I liked everything he'd ever done. He could do no wrong in my eyes. He was not in the best of health and didn't look his best on the screen, but he was still Gary Cooper!

The picture didn't do much business at the box office but he was still in high demand. He did a couple more movies before he passed away of cancer in 1961 at the age of 60. It was another one of those rare evenings I had the pleasure of enjoying with talented, interesting and larger than life people. Maria and her mom moved back east to live there permanently. Maria later married the talented classical pianist Byron Janis.

The studio was preparing to do a Western with Clint Walker and Virginia Mayo entitled *Fort Dobbs,* directed by Gordon Douglas. They were testing young boys from the ages of 10-12 to play a key role in the picture. The casting department called me to report to Gordon Douglas to cue the youngsters who were going to be testing for the part. They gave me a couple of pages of dialogue that would be used in the scene. I looked at the call sheet to see what stage they were shooting the tests and I reported to Gordon, eight o'clock the next morning. Quite a few kids tested for the part and I enjoyed assisting them, and working with director Gordon Douglas. Gordon had directed countless television shows and motion pictures such as *Them!, Robin and the Seven Hoods, In Like Flint* and *The Little Rascals,* just to name a few. As a youngster living in New York, he dreamed of working as an actor.

He wasn't successful, so he focused on working behind the camera. Gordon eventually graduated to assistant director and became an in-demand director for many years. He was colorful, spoke with a heavy New York accent and possessed a good sense of humor. It was another new experience that was a part of the things I was called upon to do while under contract. Gordon thought I did a nice job and said he had a part in the picture for me. It wasn't a big role, but he wanted me in the picture because we got along so well and he liked baseball. Even though it was a small part, I received costar billing because the studio was taking advantage of my fine performance, reviews and billing from *Westbound*. The first day of work began on location in Kanab, Utah, where many Westerns were filmed over the years. We lucked out, the weather was perfect and we all enjoyed the beautiful surroundings for the next few weeks. The low, rocky mountain formations with rolling hills, red clay dirt and just a few trees around the landscape set the stage for the perfect scenery for the film. Kanab was sparsely populated at the time and it really hasn't changed much over the years. During the filming of the picture, it was nice to see, talk and work with Virginia Mayo again, however brief. She looked beautiful as usual and was the consummate professional. There really wasn't much to do in Kanab except work, eat and sleep, so some of the cast and crew brought their guitars and entertained every night out on the patio area of the Parry Lodge, located in the center of town. I had a terrific time singing along with everyone and learning many of the well-known country western songs. To this day I am a big fan of country and western music.

I finished my work on *Fort Dobbs* and got a call from casting to guest star in a segment of *Lawman*. It featured Edgar Buchanan, a wonderful character actor, and was directed by Abner Bibberman. Abner was a character actor for many years and later became a busy television director. He directed quite a few shows during Warner Bros. reign in primetime. I read the script and liked the character I was to portray and was looking forward to working with Abner.

John Russell didn't have much to do in this segment and Peter Brown, John's deputy, was featured in this episode. This was the first time Peter and I worked together since we did our screen test. I was always a big fan of Edgar Buchanan. I wished that someday we could work together. I got my wish and I was so looking forward to hearing that gravel voice of his. I enjoyed every minute of working with Edgar and Peter along with the director, Abner Bibberman. Like all good things, it always went too fast.

My next assignment was a TV pilot for a series entitled *Public Enemy*. I had a leading role playing a gangster. It was an adaptation from the motion picture that James Cagney starred in for Warner Bros. The studio had an option on Frank Gifford, the sensational running back for the New York Giants, to play the lead detective. Frank had no acting training and since I knew him, the studio asked me if I would coach and work with him. I did the best I could to get Frank ready, but he just didn't have enough experience to play the lead character in a series. The pilot didn't sell and I know it was a big disappointment for the actor who was going to play that James Cagney role. He looked like Cagney and sounded like him, too. I met Frank several years before while he was playing with the Giants. Andy Robustelli, the defensive end and defensive coach for the New York Giants, later became a Hall of Famer, introduced me to Frank when the Giants came to play against the Los Angeles Rams at the Los Angeles Coliseum. Andy was born and raised in Stamford, Connecticut, like me. He was like an older brother to me. As a matter of fact, when I got married to Mary Jane, Andy was in my wedding party. He and his wife Jeannie flew to California to be in our wedding. I lost two of my best friends in the same year because in 2011, Andy and Jeannie both passed away. The pilot did not sell, but Frank went back to playing great football for the New York Giants and was later inducted into the National Football Hall of Fame in 1971.

Like Frank, I too had something to fall back on – the hometown premiere of *Westbound*.

26
Westbound Hometown Premiere

Westbound was being released throughout the country in 1959. I got a call from one of my best friends I grew up with back east, Canio Carlucci, a successful construction contractor. He and three other friends of mine, Andy Robustelli, Francis "Chico" Vejar and Robert "Buddy" Vanderheyden saw the coming attractions of *Westbound* at the Ridgeway Theater in Stamford, Connecticut, and took a meeting with the owner to buy out the theater for the opening night. Chico became a successful and popular professional boxer in the lightweight and middleweight division. He had over 100 fights and once fought Chuck Davey for the world lightweight championship. Andy played for the Los Angeles Rams for five years and then was traded to the New York Giants were he played for nine more years. He was the Giants defensive end and coach for many years and was inducted into the National Football League Hall of Fame in 1971. Buddy was an outstanding running back for the Stamford Golden Bears, a professional local football team. He played and managed the Sacred Hearts baseball team in the Twilight League in Stamford. Buddy respected my accomplishments so much that he named one of his sons after me, Michael Dante Vanderheyden.

The four of them formed a committee and went to the Ridgeway Theater owner and bought the theater for the opening night of *Westbound*. They succeeded and wanted to make it a local premiere event, bringing a bit of Hollywood to Stamford. The committee sold out all of the tickets within a week. My mom, dad, three sisters, brother and I were their guests.

It was an exciting evening with several of my relatives, friends and the people I grew up with in attendance. What made it so special was that I was the first person born and raised in Stamford, Connecticut, to have a successful career in Hollywood and coming home to share my first co-starring role in the theater with my family and hometown friends. It was quite emotional for me. What a warm and beautiful reception they gave me. It was done in exquisite taste, red carpet and all. It was as professional as any Hollywood premiere that I can attest to. After the event, Canio Carlucci invited my family and closest friends for food and drinks at his home. I could see it on their faces and heard in their voices that they all really liked the film and loved my performance. There was some money left over from all the tickets that were sold and graciously gave it to me for my expenses. As long as I live I will never forget how wonderful everyone treated my family and me that special evening. The great author, Thomas Wolfe, wrote the book, *You Can't Go Home Again*, but I can say that I never left. I knew that I could always go home and feel welcome. It's still that way, even today.

Telegram sent to the Ridgeway Theater from Steve Allen congratulating me on the Stamford premiere of Westbound.

27

Fan Magazines

I was still under contract to Warner Bros. and had to get back to work. They only allowed me a few days off for the Stamford event. I just got back in time to settle in for a day and got a call to do a *Motion Picture* magazine layout with the 'Beach Nuts.'

The 'Beach Nuts' were a group of actors and actresses coupled; Van and Vicki Williams, John Ashley and his wife Debbie Wally, Connie Stevens and me. Connie and I did a number of magazine layouts together. I had the opportunity to meet her parents and the rest of her family and they practically adopted me. They were the nicest people you'd ever want to meet. Connie's dad, Teddy, was a standup bass player and her brother, Chuck, was an excellent drummer. It was a busy and happy household full of a lot of love, delicious food and beautiful music. I was privileged to always be welcome into their home. To this day I treasure those days and Connie's friendship.

Pat Campbell, the editor of *Motion Picture* magazine, genuinely had fun with the gang. She came along to supervise this layout and had as much fun as we did. This was a longer trip than some of our other layout excursions. It took place at the Erawan Garden Hotel in Indian Wells, California, about 20 miles east of Palm Springs on Highway 111. It was the opening of a posh Oriental designed hotel. It had several pagoda style buildings with a beautiful oriental garden, swimming pool and a large rickshaw that was part of the landscape. The guys took turns pulling the rickshaw while the gals were laughing on the ride as our pictures where being taken. We got there on Friday and left Sunday after taking lots of pictures as well as enjoying the music, dancing, swimming, food and atmosphere. I never ate so much Chinese food in my life. We had more fun than anyone ever had during any Chinese New Year, that's for sure! Warner's publicity department was inundated with writers and fan magazine editors calling to interview the stars of the various series and other actors like myself under contract to the studio. In those days, there were countless movie and television fan magazines on every newsstand, but the two most popular were *Photoplay* and *Motion Picture* magazine. I had just finished guest starring in an episode of *Hawaiian Eye* starring Robert Conrad and Connie Stevens. The name of this segment was called "Go Steady with Danger," directed by Dick Benedict. Dick was also an ex-actor who turned to directing later on in his career.

We all got along well and enjoyed ourselves during the shooting of the segment. Again, we were all a part of the Warner Bros. family working together to succeed as well as building a career to climb the ladder to do bigger and better things as actors.

About a week after I finished the show, I got a call from the publicity department to do another picture layout for *Motion Picture* magazine at Walt Disney's Golden Oak Ranch. Actor John

Ashley and his wife Debbie Wally, Van Williams and his wife Vicki, Tony Young with his girlfriend Madeline Rue and Connie Stevens joined yours truly again. We rode horses, paddled canoes, went swimming and had a terrific lunch together. The photographer took a lot of pictures while we were genuinely having a real low-down, hoe-down.

Our exposure in those fan magazines was really an important part of building a career. Everyone read *Photoplay* and *Motion Picture* in barbershops, salon's, waiting rooms, hotel lobbies, you name it. They all wanted to read about their favorite stars in the television, motion picture business, and also about the new rising stars, just like today. So whenever I received a call to do a magazine layout, I made myself available.

Beyond *People* magazine and with the exception of a few, it's a totally different world and market today. It seems to me like the stars today spend an awful lot of money for their press agents to keep them *out* of those magazines, to keep their private lives private as possible. Go figure.

28

My New Car

Another interesting call came from the publicity department at the request of the proprietor of a Pasadena drive-in theater in Pasadena, California who wanted me to make a personal appearance on the opening night showing of *Westbound*. He asked if I would autograph 100 photos of me as my character Rod, two hours before the screening. The studio would supply the pictures and a representative from the Warner Bros. publicity department would accompany me to the event. They said they had three automobile sponsors that promoted their agency before every screening and if I were interested in purchasing a car, they would give it to me at cost. I was looking to buy another car at the time because the noise of the Beetle engine was finally getting to me. I saw a beautiful Italian sports car in a showcase window on Wilshire Boulevard, a black two door sports coupe convertible, a Lancia Vignali. I went in to price the car and much to my surprise

My first new car was a dandy – a Lancia Vignali – a very rare Italian sports car.

it wasn't that expensive. It was the only car I was interested in buying. Wouldn't you know it, one of the sponsors only sold Maserati, Lamborghini and Lancia automobiles. Now, what were the odds of that happening? I told him I would come out to look at the car I was interested in purchasing. I drove to Pasadena in nothing flat and took even less time to buy it.

They only had one color of the Vignali on the lot and it was red. I told them if they would paint it black, we would have a deal. They agreed. This was the beginning of the week and *Westbound* was premiering on Friday, so they had enough time to publicize my appearance. My thumbs were a little sore from autographing, but I got the job done. I picked up my Lancia after they painted it. Thanks to an actor friend of mine, Johnny Melfi who mentioned it more than once, whenever I wanted to sell my Beetle, he would buy it. It was in mint condition, and he knew I treated it like a Rolls Royce. The price of the Volkswagen had doubled since I bought the car. I sold it to him for the blue book price, which was exactly what I paid for the car three years before. That $1,200 was my down payment on the new car. The total price with tax and license came to about $4,000.

I made arrangements to make monthly payments for the remaining $2,800. I knew I was getting a good deal because I compared the price of the car with that of the agency on Wilshire Boulevard. I learned there were only four two-door Lancia Vignali cars in all of Southern California. Little did I know that the movie business, I discovered, had many fringe benefits.

29
Warner's Western Fare

I was cast to do another episode of *Maverick* with James Garner who was a good guy and a lot of fun to work with. Jim had a great sense of humor. He always had a bunch of jokes to tell because the crew and other actors loved sharing their stories with him. Appearing on *Maverick, Cheyenne, Sugarfoot* and *Lawman* gave me good exposure as an actor, because they were all highly rated shows with huge audience participation. What made this show extra special was working with the beautiful Angie Dickinson. Angie is a good actress with an earthy personality. She guest starred in several of the series at Warner Bros. and was well liked by everyone. I saw her on the studio lot several times. She was warm, friendly and we always enjoyed a nice chat. Angie went on to appear in many motion pictures with all of the top stars in the business. Her guest appearances on television were many and she also starred in her own successful television series entitled *Police Woman* with Earl Holliman later in her career. The last time I saw Angie I gave her a big hug at the Frank Sinatra Celebrity Golf Classic in Palm Springs. She still looks beautiful.

Shortly thereafter, I was called to do another *Sugarfoot* segment with Will Hutchins and Ruta Lee, who was the show's guest star. Ruta literally did more guest appearances on all of their TV series than any other actress. She went from one show to another. She was a beautiful blonde, a perfect contrast to most of the dark-haired male stars in each of the series. Ruta was born and raised in Canada, and had a bundle of talent; she was a singer, dancer and actress performing in every media. She went on to appear in countless television shows, stage and motion pictures including a successful celebrity talk show, *Talk of the Town* that she hosted with another beautiful blonde, Toni Holt Kramer. Throughout the years in Hollywood and Palm Springs, my wife and I have developed a friendship with Ruta and her husband Webster B. Lowe Jr. Toni and Bob Kramer have become two of our dearest friends.

During filming, a middle-aged woman introduced herself as the manager of a young actress working in the show. Her name was Angie Vitt, a personable lady. During our conversation, she asked me if I was of Italian descent and I answered yes. She said she was as well. We immediately started talking about Italian food and I told her cooking Italian food was one of my favorite hobbies. She said she was hosting a dinner party that weekend and invited me to attend. Before the assistant director called me into the next shot, we exchanged numbers. She lived in an attractive home on Riverside Drive in the San Fernando Valley. Little did I know, accepting that invitation would change the course of my career and life.

I arrived to a welcoming reception and the aroma that permeated throughout the house was Angie's delicious Italian sauce brewing in the kitchen. I could hardly wait for the food to be served. That evening I met actress Wanda Hendrix, ex-wife of actor Audie Murphy and Mabel Smith, the oldest living astrologist in California at the time. Mabel entertained everyone by doing a brief astrological reading of each person present. When she did my numbers, she became so animated, because she saw a long successful career and life in my future. Mabel was so energetic, along with an ingratiating personality. She was the type of person you fell in love with the moment you met her. I grew to know and love 'Smithy,' we called her, until she passed away several years later.

Wanda was my dinner partner that evening and sat opposite me at the table. She had a lovely face and a great laugh. I was attracted to her the first time I saw her and she seemingly to me. During our conversation I told her I was under contract to Warner Bros. and I suddenly realized that I had been at the studio almost a year. The option on my contract was due in a few days and I didn't know if they were going to extend it for another year or let me go. Wanda then asked me who my agent was and I said I didn't have one. She was shocked and said, "You have to talk to my agent, Sy Marsh at the William Morris Agency because he's the best. Whether Warner Bros. picks up your option for another year or not, you have to have good representation." She said she would call Sy on Monday and arrange for the three of us to have lunch.

Wanda arranged for us to meet at the other location of the famous Brown Derby restaurant, this one on the corner of Rodeo Drive and Wilshire Boulevard in Beverly Hills, two blocks from the William Morris Agency. Wanda was right. Sy and I had a lot in common and our communication was positive. He said I had all the attributes to be a leading man and star. After a delicious lunch, we went straight to his office and I signed with the agency. He thanked Wanda for bringing me to him, because he said, "There weren't many young actors with Michael's potential in the business." He would be my contact at the agency and look after me personally. My timing to make the move could not have been more perfect.

Wanda and I began to see each other as much as our schedules would allow. When I got home I searched my file cabinet for the Warner Bros. contract and there it was; it was up in three days. Believe it or not, I got a call from Hoyt Bower in casting the next day telling me that the studio was not picking up my option. I thanked him and hung up the phone. I was so happy and relieved because I didn't have to worry about the studio putting me in a series. Now, I was free to pick and choose as much as I could about the work I wanted to do in the future as a freelance actor.

I was fortunate and grateful for the opportunity of being under contract to Warner Bros. and being able to do 13 television shows and three films in one year, particularly co-starring in my first film, *Westbound* to great reviews. I truly learned my craft working in front of the camera while I was there. I wouldn't trade that for anything. Years later, I saw William T. Orr, the executive producer of television at Warner Bros., socially from time to time. After leaving the studio, it was known among my peers and executives that I had done a lot of good work for them. William looked at me with a big smile and said, "How the hell did you get away from us?" I casually replied, "Ask that schmuck who's running your casting office." He knew exactly who I was talking about.

I called Wanda and told her about leaving Warner Bros. and I would call Sy to tell him I was now available for work. He was happy to hear that I was no longer under contract because there was no doubt in his mind he could get me a lot more work and money than I was making at

Warner Bros. That was nice to hear because I had a mortgage and those monthly payments on my new Lancia. This was an awfully busy time in my life, everything was happening so fast. There was so much going on with me and in Hollywood at the time.

The demand for screenwriters, producers, directors and actors was awesome, and I was proud to be a part of the "Golden Age of Television" when it began to flourish. I received a phone call from Los Angeles restaurateur Nicky Blair who I met at the MGM commissary with a singer/actor Vic Damone awhile back. He invited me to his bachelor party at his Hollywood Hills home off Laurel Canyon. He said he was serving pasta, salad, chicken and dessert. I didn't mention it to Nicky at the time that one of my hobbies was cooking gourmet Italian food. It was taking place on a weekend night and I was looking forward to a good meal and meeting new friends.

I arrived with a bottle of wine under my arm and made my grand entrance. Everyone arrived before I got there and Nicky greeted me like family. He introduced me to his pals Tony Curtis, Huntz Hall and Perry Lopez, three well-known actors. They all knew each other and were interested in meeting me, where I met Nicky, and how I got to Hollywood. Their ears really perked when I told them I started out as a professional baseball player with the Washington Senators. Baseball was always an immediate entrée for me because a lot of actors were actually frustrated ballplayers. Tony was already a big star and we all loved Huntz when we were growing up.

I had a lot in common with Perry, because at one time he was under contract to Warner Bros. studios just like me. We shared interesting stories in and out of Hollywood, especially about the women, food, wine and company. It couldn't have gone better and we all remained good friends for years.

During the evening Huntz told me about a Hollywood Stars softball team he was playing for, which played their games around town for charity. They were thinking about going on tour to places like Las Vegas, Phoenix, Scottsdale and Tucson, Arizona. He said they had several stars like Forrest Tucker (captain of the team), John Agar, Jack LaRue, John Beradino, Frank Faylen and 'Slapsie Maxie' Rosenblum.

The evening was over but never forgotten, I was convinced that Nicky Blair did know everyone in Hollywood. I'm sorry to say that Nicky, Tony, Huntz and Perry are now in heaven, no doubt sitting around and having another Nicky Blair bachelor party.

I spoke with Lana Turner who was busy doing a film entitled *The Lady Takes a Flyer* with Jeff Chandler at Columbia Studios. She invited me to visit her on the set and I showed up the next day. I was also looking forward to saying hello to Jeff because I had met him one night at La Scala restaurant. As a matter of fact, another ex-professional baseball player/actor John Beradino and I talked baseball with Jeff that night for two hours. He was one hell of a guy and a big New York Giants fan. Every year he joined the Giants at their spring training camp in Phoenix, Arizona. They were still located in New York, but soon to be relocated to San Francisco. In between setups and shots we took up right where we left off talking about baseball. I later saw him several times at La Scala and our conversation was always about baseball. He loved the game and the Giants. It was a sad day for all of Hollywood when Jeff passed away in 1961 at the age of 42. When there was a break in the action and everyone moved from one set to another, Lana's hairdresser/makeup artist Del Armstrong and I headed to her dressing room. We all got caught up with each other's lives and professional careers and shortly thereafter, Johnny Stompanato, whom Lana was dating at the time, arrived.

He was all smiles and very charming. He made it a point to single me out and said, "I heard a lot of nice things about you." We talked for a while and it was time for Lana to go back to work.

We all said our goodbyes and I was on my way. I had no idea I was shaking hands with the man who was Mickey Cohen's bodyguard and enforcer, who aimed a gun at Sean Connery on a movie set in a fit of rage and whose eventual death would make headlines around the world. I take a big gulp when I say I'm glad he liked me.

30

Hollywood Stars Celebrity Softball

Sometime after Nicky Blair's bachelor party, I received a phone call from actor Forrest Tucker. Forrest did hundreds of motion pictures and television guest appearances. Later in his career starred in the highly successful TV series for Warner Bros. called *F Troop*. He told me that Huntz Hall had called to tell him I was interested in playing softball with the Hollywood Stars Celebrity Team. He informed me they practiced on Saturdays at a Burbank public park near the airport. He said they had new uniforms and would bring them to distribute to the players according to their size.

I arrived at the appointed time and place with my spikes and glove ready for action. I met everyone and we were all looking forward to our first inter-squad game. It was a whole lot of fun from the start. Former light heavyweight boxing champion 'Slapsy' Maxie Rosenblum was our pitcher. Slapsy might have had a killer punch but he couldn't throw hard enough to break a pane of glass. In order to get anybody out he had to be deceptive, like gyrating his arms in all directions before throwing the ball. His windup was all over the place but surprisingly effective, throwing one changeup after another, keeping everyone off balance and keeping us laughing the whole time. Playing shortstop I had to be ready for a lot of hard hit balls or get myself killed and this was just a practice!

We had a team meeting afterwards and Forest told us we were going to play our first out of town game in Phoenix, Arizona. He would let us know the date as soon as he got a confirmation from our opponents. We left anticipating his phone call and the day of our next practice.

About a week later Forrest called to ask me to join him for lunch at Bob's restaurant near his home in Toluca Lake in the San Fernando Valley. He was a hell of a character, smoked and drank too much, but it never interfered with his work. His reputation followed him, he could drink while he worked and never missed a line of dialogue. Forrest wanted to know if I was free to play for the next two weekends in Arizona. I told him I had no plans, and was really looking forward to the trip. He said he would call as soon as he had a confirmation from Phoenix.

Five days later the call came from Captain Tucker and the team met at the Burbank public park. Everyone showed up on time and hopped on the bus heading for Phoenix, but not without water, soft drinks, beer, booze, cigars and cigarettes. By the time the bus got underway it was filled with cigarette and cigar smoke. It didn't make any difference whether you smoked or not you were inhaling secondhand smoke. In those days, most of the actors and actresses smoked and drank. It was an enjoyable ride, because actors are interesting people and always have a lot to share with their colleagues. Slapsy as usual, had some funny stories to tell even if the joke wasn't

Hollywood Stars Celebrity Softball Team visiting Phoenix, Arizona.
Left to right: John Agar, Maxie Rosenbloom, myself and Forrest Tucker.

very funny. His interpretation was usually more hilarious than the joke. We made one whistle stop during the five-hour trip and before we knew it, we were unpacking our bags out of the bus and registering at the front desk of the hotel. It was an old well-kept hotel with high ceilings, carved wood throughout, giving it a nice, warm feeling. Tucker gathered everyone and said we were all to meet on the mezzanine floor in one hour.

In order to save money we were assigned two to a room. Huntz Hall and I teamed up, grabbed our bags, went to our room to freshen up and get a little rest before our team meeting.

We all gathered on the mezzanine floor to hear what Tucker had to say. It wasn't very good news. He told us the promoter that he was dealing with left town with the $5,000 guarantee.

"There are two options," Tucker said. "We could pack our bags turn around and go home or play the game." There was some promotion on the radio, television and in the papers, but we had no idea how many tickets were sold. We decided that we should take a show of hands, who wanted to stay and those opposed. Everyone raised their hands to play the game. We all believed the show must go on.

Huntz Hall provided as many laughs off the field as he did on camera, and could always be counted on to give the Hollywood Stars a little comic relief.

As we were all talking and making our plans to play ball a stranger over six feet and weighing about 230 pounds, interrupted our meeting and said, "Who in the hell do you actors think you are, making all this noise?" Out of nowhere, Jack La Rue leapt at this guy's throat and had him bent over the railing before he knew it. We all pulled Jack away just in time otherwise, that guy was going over the railing.

I learned later from Tucker that he had known Jack for many years, and Tucker said, "I'd rather fight a bear than mess with Jack La Rue." Tucker said there was still time to do some important promotions on radio and television. He had previously spoken with a few radio and television stations from Los Angeles and laid the groundwork.

He asked Huntz and me to do an interview on the television sports segment of their five o'clock local news program. We had a seven o'clock game, so there still was time for some last minute promotion. We jumped into a cab, got there in plenty of time and the interview could not have gone better. Huntz was still extremely popular and known all over the world. The guys at the station were no exceptions, Huntz was a big hit and we plugged the game for at least five minutes, a lot of time on the air. We got back in a cab and headed right for the ballpark. We were surprised to see there were quite a few fans in the park and many of them still making their entrance.

We went right to the locker room to suit up and report the good news. I got ready and went right out on the ball field and started to warm up playing catch with Johnny Beradino. He became the star of the long running daytime series "General Hospital" as the character of Dr. Hardy for over thirty years, thanks to me. I was offered the role first, but didn't want to do a soap opera series at the time. A pretty young lady standing at the railing to my left, called me to autograph her magazine. I went over and looked at the book and it was the *Motion Picture* magazine. Inside was the layout I did a few months before.

"I've seen several of your television appearances on the Warner Bros. western series," she said. "But my favorite was your performance in *Westbound* playing the one-armed soldier coming back from the war."

She stepped up front and said her name was Sandy and would like to spend more time with me after the game. She was awfully cute and I told her we'd meet here after the game, but to give me some time to shower afterwards.

We were fortunate to have about 400 or 500 people in attendance and everyone had a hilarious time. Slapsy was so much fun; everybody got such a kick out of all his antics and moon balls he threw up at the plate. We managed to hang in there, but came out on the short end of a 10 to 8 score. Beradino and I did everything we could to keep it close. Before leaving the locker room Tucker asked all of us to meet in his suite for drinks and a buffet of deli food. He told us he had some things he wanted to share with us. I met Sandy afterwards and told her I had to attend a meeting at the hotel, but didn't know exactly what time I would finish. I would say around 10:30 or eleven o'clock.

Huntz and I went to the meeting, enjoyed a soft drink and some good Jewish deli. All the guys were there having a great time drinking, eating, smoking, and reminiscing about the game. Tucker took center stage and told us the rooms, the bus, bus driver and food was on him. He apologized and felt responsible for not having the promoter put the $5,000 guarantee into escrow until we got there. The money would have been enough to cover expenses and all of us to share equally whatever money that was left. He added the bus was leaving at eleven o'clock in the morning, but not before he told us how proud he was to be with such troopers. Huntz and I were not drinkers, although he had imbibed pretty good in his younger days, but didn't touch it for the rest of his life. It was about eleven o'clock, when we headed to the room.

I looked at the time when we arrived, and thought it might have gotten too late for Sandy. I was halfway taking my clothes off when the phone rang and it was Sandy. Before I could explain she was on her way up.

I told Huntz, "You have to help me out, she's coming to the room." He didn't want to get dressed and leave, so we decided he would hide and wait in the bathtub. I got three pillows and quickly placed them neatly in the tub. I tucked him in and closed the curtain tightly from one end to the other so he could not be seen if she went to the bathroom. The timing was perfect, I heard a soft knock at the door opened it and there was Sandy looking so lovely. I closed the door behind her and we immediately began kissing very passionately.

It all happened spontaneously. One thing led to another and we were in the throes of a romance. We

Group photo of The Dead End Kids.

talked for a while afterwards, and I apologized telling her she had to leave because my roommate was expected any minute. She went to the bathroom to freshen up and never saw Huntz in the tub. We said goodbye and she left.

I raced to the bathroom to see how Huntz was doing in the tub. I opened the curtain gently and he was sound asleep. I called out, "Huntz!" He jumped up and asked, "Did she leave yet?" I helped him out of the tub and he shook his head and said, "I'm known all over the world and would you believe I slept in a bathtub while my roommate was romancing a pretty lady the night away?" We didn't get much sleep because we laughed about it half the night. The next morning we hopped on the bus and Huntz couldn't wait to tell all the guys. Needless to say, they laughed their heads off. John Agar said, "There is no way in the world anyone could make up a story like that. It's one-of-a-kind, a classic!"

The trip home was the same, lots to drink and lots of smoke. Getting to know all of those talented and fun guys better was a treat! My life was much richer for having shared that precious time together. I'm the last remaining member of that great team. A joyful, warm smile comes to my face whenever I think of them.

31

Dinner Dates and Friends

Lita and Rory Calhoun hosted a huge dinner party at their Beverly Hills home in 1959. I was invited and my dinner date that evening was Debbie Reynolds. She came alone and Lita and Rory wanted me to meet her. It was a lovely evening that included several actresses, actors, producers and directors. Debbie couldn't have been sweeter. We talked, had a few laughs, and that was it.

That same evening I met two of the nicest people I've ever met in my life, Mary Lou and her husband screenwriter, director and producer, Delmer Daves. We talked during the evening and exchanged phone numbers before we left. Delmer wrote, directed and produced approximately 60 motion pictures. Some of his biggest films included *Destination Tokyo*, *Broken Arrow*, *310 to Yuma* and *An Affair to Remember*.

He was without a doubt one of the most prolific and talented filmmakers in Hollywood. It wasn't long after we met that I received an invitation to the Daves' dinner party. This was the first of several dinner parties they hosted where I was invited. There were never more than ten people, so everyone got a chance to communicate with one another throughout the evening. Mary Lou and Elmer often invited their unmarried friends, seating them opposite one another for the evening.

The first time I attended, my dinner date that evening was the lovely actress Anne Baxter. She was recently divorced from her husband after living in Australia for a few years. We really got along well; she had a good sense of humor and possessed a down to earth personality. I saw Anne again after that evening and we had dinner a couple of times together. The last time I spoke with her she was off to New York on business and would be back shortly. Unfortunately, while in New York she suffered a stroke and passed away. She was such a special lady and a wonderful actress.

I recall on two other occasions I was the dinner partner to Donna Reed and Maureen O'Hara. They were two absolutely gorgeous, interesting and intelligent women. Delmer and Mary Lou were the perfect hosts; the food, people and conversation was always interesting and stimulating. Delmer was an etymologist. He would select one of his guests name and research the history, derivative of that name and what it meant. He would write it all out in his excellent penmanship and give it to that person afterward. He was so bright, talented, articulate and entertaining at the same time. I always looked forward to spending an evening with them. They treated me like family. Delmer paid me one of the nicest compliments of my life. "I retired a year or two too soon," he said. "I would have loved to have made a film with you." I will always remember how gracious he and Mary Lou were to me. I felt like I lost a member of my family when he passed away.

Around the same time, there was the Pre-National Football League Pro Bowl game at the Los Angeles Memorial Coliseum. One of my closest friends from my home town, Andy Robustelli, was selected to play in the Pro Bowl game, along with three other members from the New York Giants team; running back Frank Gifford, quarterback Chuck Conerly and linebacker Sam Huff. The players selected had a fun time during the two weeks preparation for the Pro Bowl game because it was designed more for the fans. Several other Giants players had been to my house previously, when they played against the Rams a couple of years before. They enjoyed the food from their last visit and requested the same menu. The chef, yours truly, made a huge antipasto salad and pasta ragu for the main course. I had everything there to drink to complement the meal.

Andy made several trips to the west coast playing in quite a few Pro Bowl games at the Los Angeles Memorial Coliseum. The games were played there before the league decided to move the event to Hawaii. Andy enjoyed coming to the West Coast because he had fond memories of starting his career with the Los Angeles Rams and being a part of that National Football League Championship team in 1951. He also had a cousin by the name of Vince Robustelli who lived and owned a used car business in Los Angeles. As soon as he arrived in town, Vince loaned him a car for the duration of his stay. That made it possible for Andy to get to and from the practice field without the expense of cab fares. I had a three-bedroom house in Encino and several times when Andy and his wife Jeannie accompanied him, they would stay with me. I recall one year when Andy came out and I was still living in my apartment on Castle Heights Avenue in 1958, not far from the MGM studios. I invited Andy and Huntz Hall for dinner and we were enjoying our conversation over a cup of coffee when the phone rang. It was about nine o'clock.

I picked up the phone and it was Johnny Stompanato on the other end. He asked what I was doing and I told him I was having coffee and dessert with Huntz Hall and Andy Robustelli. He asked if he and a beautiful red-haired lady could come by to say hello. I gave him the directions and they were on their way.

He arrived with Claire Kelly, the ex-wife of my friend Perry Lopez and a cold bottle of champagne. I heard he and Lana were not getting along at the time and Johnny began dating Claire. We had a fascinating evening of conversation, laughter and storytelling until three o'clock in the morning. I don't know how Andy was able to practice the next day, but he did. It was the last time I saw Johnny Stompanato. Shortly thereafter, he and Lana got back together again, but unfortunately their relationship was stormy and that lead to the terrible tragedy of Johnny's death, which changed Lana and Cheryl's lives forever. It was another Hollywood story about relationships ending in tragedy. Sadly, all of the people that were there with me that evening have since passed away.

With Debbie Reynolds and Rory Calhoun at his birthday party in his Beverly Hills, California, home.

32

Free Agent

I called my agent Sy Marsh as soon as I returned to LA. He didn't waste any time calling some of the producers and casting agents for me to see about doing one of their shows.

The first show I did after I left Warner Bros. was *Tales of the Texas Rangers* shortly thereafter, *Rescue 8* and *The Adventures of Rin Tin Tin*, playing the part of a bullfighter. I had a lot of fun fantasizing the likes of Carlos Arruza and Luis Dominguin, whom I had the pleasure of meeting when I was filming *Westbound* at Warner Bros. I never forgot watching Carlos fighting the bulls in Tijuana, Mexico. He was simply sensational. The next show I did was *Death Valley Days* costarring with Caesar Romero. These were all different parts, just as my agent and I had planned for me to do when I joined the agency and he had me moving in the right direction. In between these shows I got a call from an editor for *Movie TV Secrets* magazine to participate in another publicity layout.

The theme of this layout was we were headed for stardom and having an enjoyable time on the way. The lineup included James Franciscus with Cathy Case, Burt Reynolds with Lori Nelson, Nina Shipman and me.

It was an athletic day as we played tennis, badminton, piggyback games in the pool and finished everything off with a hardy luncheon. What I liked most about doing these magazine layouts was getting to know each other on a fun and social basis. This was a way to relax, communicate and share our personal lives with each other. I always looked forward to the next invitation to do a magazine layout because we went to new places and it was with different actors and actresses most of the time.

I continued to see Wanda Hendrix as much as I could between jobs, until it became apparent that she had a serious drinking problem. When she was out with me she would order just one drink but by the time we finished dinner she was curiously tipsy. I was acutely aware that she was going to the restroom often and the only thing I could figure out was that she must have had a flask of booze in her handbag and nipped on it when she went to the ladies room. I took her home one evening and her mother laced into me about giving her too much to drink. I told her it wasn't true.

"You must know something I don't know," I replied. I felt disappointed that Wanda was in no condition to defend me. The next morning I called Mabel Smith and Angie Vitt and told them what had occurred. They were both aware of her problem and thought that she was staying away from drinking and apologized for not telling me up front. They knew that I was not a drinker and hoped I could influence her to stay sober. Both agreed that her mother was a part of the problem. We all cared about her and tried to help but to no avail. The only one who could help Wanda was Wanda. It was so sad because she was a lovely lady, a good actress and above all, a beautiful human being.

Around this time I got a call from my agent, Marty Dubow, who was assigned to cover the Desilu Studios for television at the William Morris Agency. I was told to go to the Desilu Studios to meet with producer Victor Orsatti about a Westinghouse *Desilu Playhouse* episode that he was producing entitled *The Killer Instinct*. It was the true story about a boxer by the name of Joey Barnum, a welterweight from Chicago, Illinois who fought 72 professional fights during his boxing career.

I met with Vic and we got along royally. After we discussed the script and the character Angel, I noticed a picture he had on his desk of two players in St. Louis Cardinals baseball uniforms. He told me that was he and his brother, Ernie Orsatti.

He was impressed with the fact that I knew Ernie was a great ballplayer, a member of the Cardinals famous 'Gas House Gang.' I didn't tell Vic I was an ex-professional ballplayer because I was working to get rid of that association at the time. I wanted to have the reputation of being a fine, versatile actor rather than an ex-jock who was trying to become a professional actor. My agent made sure that was perceived upon meeting Vic. I went home to read the script and returned the next day to read for Vic and the director Lamont Johnson.

I had a good understanding of the character and gave it my best. Angel was from an extremely poor background in Mexico who wanted to go to Los Angeles to become a professional fighter. Vic Orsatti and partner Rory Calhoun of the successful series, *The Texan*, had already signed Rory to play the character Joey Barnum, who finds Angel fighting in a makeshift boxing ring in Mexico. Joey studies him and recognizes he has the killer instinct to become a champion and takes him to Los Angeles to teach him the art of boxing.

They were reading other actors for the part, so they asked me to come back and read again the next day. I was happy about that because it gave me more time to work on the Spanish accent.

I worked hard and went back the next day to read again and did the best reading. I was totally prepared, so I was awarded the part co-starring with Rory Calhoun and Janice Rule. Rory and I performed all the fight sequences ourselves without any doubles.

We enjoyed a good relationship on and off the screen. Rory was the most unselfish actor I ever worked with. He would say to our director, "Keep the camera on Michael and go in close on him, he's doing a terrific job." Until the day he passed away we remained good friends.

We had a successful show and the reviews were excellent. The *Desilu Playhouse* was a popular television show with a tremendous following. The whole town and country, for that matter, looked forward to watching the show every week. As a result of my performance in that show, the direction of my career and life was to change for the better. Vic and Rory were already talking about me being nominated for an Emmy Award for Best Supporting Actor in 1960. Unfortunately, that was the only year they combined the Best Supporting Actor and Best Actor nominations instead of having nominations. There were only five nominations for the combination of the two awards. Lawrence Olivier won the Emmy Award that year for his outstanding performance in *Moon and Sixpence*. It was a bad break for me and simply was not meant to be.

Just a few days after I finished shooting *The Killer Instinct*, I received a call from Sy Marsh to say that the same producers of the show, Vic Orsatti and Rory Calhoun, wanted me to guest star in four episodes of *The Texan* to be shot back to back with Rory. I didn't have to audition, just pick up the scripts at Vic's office. They had viewed a rough cut of *The Killer Instinct* and really liked what they saw. I was delighted to be working again with Rory and the same crew.

The Killer Instinct was scheduled to air just about the time I finished the four episodes of *The Texan*. The Westinghouse *Desilu Playhouse* shows were filmed about three weeks in advance of a play date to complete all of the post-production work. *The Killer Instinct* played on prime time to a huge Nielsen Ratings. Sy called early the next morning and in less than 24 hours I had two contract offers waiting for me to sign. Marty Dubow met me at the Desilu Studios to meet with producer Quinn Martin, who was producing a new series called, *The Untouchables*. He had already locked in Robert Stack to star in 13 shows and wanted me to star in the other 13. Bob and I would alternate shows, which was appealing because it would have given me more time to memorize and work on each script. We would be co-leads on the show, which was a new concept at the time. I was totally up front with Quinn and told him what I had waiting for me at 20th Century-Fox. It was a five picture deal, one a year for five years, pay or play beginning with *Seven Thieves* starring Edward G. Robinson, Rod Steiger, Joan Collins, Eli Wallach, Berry Kroeger and Alexander Scourby.

At this juncture, Quinn asked me to leave the room so he could speak privately with my agent. I returned to the meeting to learn a good size raise in salary was now in the offing. At this point, it wasn't about money, I wanted to do films and 20th Century-Fox was offering just that. I was always concerned if a series were not successful, then it would be hard in those days to get work afterwards because of the association with a flop. I asked him if it were possible to do both.

I wanted to shoot *Seven Thieves* first because it was starting soon but unfortunately, *The Untouchables* was starting at the same time. I asked him if it were possible for Stack to do eight shows consecutively and then I could catch up after I finished *Seven Thieves*. I would then work something out with Fox to give them a picture a year for the next four remaining years. The conflict in shooting schedules made it impossible to make a deal. Sy and I left to meet with producer/writer Sydney Boehm to sign the five picture deal with Fox. The meeting went extremely well and Sydney said how much he liked my performance in *The Killer Instinct*. I left the room and they talked about money. They went back and forth, and I finally got the salary that I wanted. I picked up my script and left as one happy actor. From that day forward Sydney and his wife Ellen became very close friends of mine, including my mom and dad.

The following week, a good friend of Rory's by the name of Patricia Smart gave a dinner party for Rory and his wife, Lita. Patricia and her friend, Cliff visited *The Killer Instinct* set when we were filming and I met them there for the first time. I received a phone call from Cliff inviting me to the party and if I was coming alone they had a beautiful lady they would like me to meet. It all sounded nice to me because I was not dating anyone at the time. They were absolutely right, that night I met a beautiful tall red-haired lady, a socialite who recently moved to Beverly Hills from Long Island, New York. Her name was Fern Gimbel. We were attracted to each other the moment we met and dated for the next two years. Fern had two adorable children, Robin and Thomas. Our relationship immediately grew into a romantic one and we were inseparable during the two years we were devoted to each other. We spent as much time as we could together and it wasn't easy for Fern, because she had to give a lot of attention to her two children. She adored them and they were well-behaved and a joy to be around.

I wish I could've spent more time with them, but unfortunately I was in full pursuit of my career when I wasn't working. Fern was very understanding, supportive and generous. The more time we spent together our romance blossomed.

A little over a year after we were seeing each other her mother, father, aunt and uncle came to visit. They were from a long line of socialites from Southampton on Long Island, New York, and seemed to be nice, intelligent people. That said, it was also clear to me they all had a serious drinking problem, and that made it difficult for me to be around them. I became concerned and uncomfortable because, again, I wasn't a drinker so communicating with them socially was awkward. We were from two different backgrounds and worlds apart regarding social behavior. Fern wasn't a drinker and I wondered how she was able to tolerate their lifestyle all those years. It was a situation I certainly would not be happy to be around for the rest of my life.

After spending several evenings with Fern's parents, I didn't think they were too happy about their daughter being seriously involved with an actor. I allowed my sensitivity to go to work for me and sensed they thought she should get involved with someone back east with a lot more financial security to offer. I was used to the warmth and the love of family. Unfortunately, they made me feel uncomfortable to be around. I'm not insinuating my way of life was right and theirs was wrong, but for me, it wasn't right. Fern was well aware of the heavy-duty drinking but there wasn't much she could do about it. We spent a lot of happy times together and socialized with a lot of the actors, actresses, directors and producers I worked with.

It was time to make a decision to get serious about getting married. Fern decided to go back east, to tell her family that we decided to make plans to get married. She was gone for a couple of weeks, and when she got back, she decided to move back to New York. Our marriage plans were canceled and she packed her belongings. There wasn't anything I could do or would do to prevent her from leaving. That slight doubt about my decision to marry her was now magnified in my heart and mind. It was difficult in the beginning, but I knew it was the right thing for both of us. I said this before and I'll say it again, "You never lose anything you never really had." I eventually learned that she got married and was divorced within a couple of years.

Whatever the reasons for her decision, she was a good human being and deserved to do whatever it was that made her happy. And the same applied to me.

33

20ᵗʰ Century-Fox

We started filming *Seven Thieves* on the 20th Century-Fox lot, and I was excited about working with Eddie G. Robinson, Rod Steiger and Joan Collins. Eddie was a family favorite of ours and my dad loved his films. The first day I met Eddie we shook hands and I said to him, "Mr. Robinson, you've been one of my favorite actors for many years and I'm delighted to be working with you." He said, "Michael, if your work wasn't on the par with the rest of us, you wouldn't be working in this picture. I'm looking forward to working with you as well." You could have knocked me over with a feather. He was such a gentleman and made me feel right at home.

I met Henry Hathaway, one of the best dramatic directors in the business, along with the rest of the cast: Rod Steiger, Joan Collins, Eli Wallach, Beery Kroeger and Alexander Scourby to make up the seven thieves. Our writer and producer Sydney Boehm was not only talented but one of the nicest people I ever met in Hollywood. About the second week of shooting Rod and I had to climb out of the window of the Monte Carlo Casino set onto a four-inch ledge of the building, cautiously taking it step by step to another window that was to be opened by Joan Collins from the inside. Below us was a simulation of a drop to the cliff's edge and ocean about 200 feet below.

The sequence was shot on the soundstage, but we were actually 20 feet above the mattresses that were placed below us in the event that one of us would fall. I laughed and looked at Rod before the shot and said, "Be sure we don't fall because that mattress is almost as hard as the cement floor below it." To make the scene more dramatic, it was dark and my character Louis was afraid of heights. Fortunately for us the scene went perfectly, but Rod and I were holding on for dear life until we got inside that window. It was really touch and go for a while.

More caution is taken today with scenes like this, with lots of soft cushions and boxes put in place in case someone does fall.

Some conflict took place on the set during the filming between director Henry Hathaway, Rod Steiger and Joan Collins. Joan and Warren Beatty were romantically involved at the time and he was working on the next soundstage as one of the students in the series *Doby Gillis*. Henry would call for a rehearsal and Joan was nowhere to be found. When they finally got a hold of her, four letter words were spewed across the set. When it happened more than once, Rod got into the act and in no uncertain terms let Joan and Henry know exactly how he felt. It really got hot and heavy when all three unloaded on each other, and there was nothing we could do but watch it unfold.

On one occasion Eddie and I were sitting in our chairs outside of his dressing room and he leaned over to me and said, "Michael, don't ever behave that way, it's so unprofessional." I took his

What wasn't there to enjoy about Louis Antonizzi, a handsome lover boy and safecracker in Seven Thieves?

advice and made it a point to never have an argument or heated disagreement with a director or an actor throughout my career.

We had an off day and Eddie invited me to lunch at his home in Beverly Hills to see his famous art collection and to meet his wife Jane and his butler, who was a big Dodger fan. I promised his butler I would get him an autographed Dodgers baseball the next time I went to the ballpark. After we enjoyed a delicious lunch, I was given a tour of all the artwork throughout his beautiful home in Beverly Hills. When we finished looking at all the talented artists works by Auguste Renoir, Georges Seurat, Paul Gaugin, Edgar Degas, Vincent Van Gogh, Hinri de Toulouse-Lautrec, Henri Matisse, Pablo Picasso, Cezanne, Camille Corot Eugine Delacroix, Jean Baptiste and two American painters, Grant Wood and Yasuo Kuniyoshi, we sat down to talk over a cup coffee. Jane asked me, "What painting did you like best of all the paintings in the house?" I was sitting opposite Eddie in the breakfast nook and behind him was a huge magnificent still life with no name attached to it.

I said to Mrs. Robinson, "You're not going to believe this, but of all the paintings that I've seen, the one that excites me the most is that still life on the wall behind Eddie."

"You see Eddie, Michael is the second person who thinks that still life is the best painting in the house," she said. Jane proudly announced that Eddie painted it. I heard he was a painter, but this was beyond good, it was magnificent. Eddie told me that when he divorced his first wife Gladys, a painter, 60 additional paintings of his collection were sold to collector Stavros Niarchos, known as the "Golden Greek" shipping tycoon, in the divorce settlement.

I called Al Campanis, the general manager and vice president in charge of player personnel for the Los Angeles Dodgers, who I met a couple months prior to visit with him and see the Dodgers play on the weekend. I sat with Al in his private box and had a good baseball conversation as well as a perfect view of the game. I went down to the dugout after the game to say hello to Tommy

Casing the joint, the Monte Carlo Casino, with Rod Steiger and Joan Collins before our daring heist. This film was Joan's favorite role.

Pleasantly greeting the Monte Carlo officials. Little did they know…

Lasorda, the third base coach at the time and got an autographed ball for Eddie's butler. I invited Tommy and Al to visit me on the set of the *Seven Thieves* at 20th Century-Fox studios. This was all new to both of them. I introduced Tommy and Al to the director, producer and the cast, but they were over the moon with joy when meeting and talking with Eddie G. Robinson, a longtime favorite actor of theirs.

In between setups, Eddie and I were sitting and relaxing when I asked him if he ever saw a major league baseball game. He said he never had. I asked him if he would like to go to see a Dodgers game one evening and I would pick him up and we'd sit with Al Campanis in his private box seats at the game. I called Al and told him we would like to come out to the ballpark and he said he would like us to join him for dinner in his private box as well. I picked up Eddie and took him by the arm like father and son to join Al for dinner prior to the game. Al was so gracious and had an autographed ball and a Dodgers baseball cap waiting for Eddie when we arrived. Eddie was like a little kid seeing everything for the first time. I'll never forget the wide-eyed, childlike look on his face imbibing all the nuances and excitement of the game. Mr. O'Malley, the owner of the Dodgers came by during the ballgame to meet Eddie. They were also big fans of his and extended an open invitation to sit with Mr. O'Malley in his private box seats at any game he wished to attend. Believe it or not, Mr. O'Malley sent his limousine for Eddie to join him at the ballpark during the rest of the season. When Eddie got home, he presented the autographed baseball to his butler.

Exterior shot of the casino ledge with me and Rod Steiger.

According to Eddie, the food and service around the house was so much better after he received the treasured baseball.

I was really having a good time working with such an outstanding cast, particularly with Rod during our one-on-one scenes together. We interacted well together, especially when we had the opportunity to improvise. Rod was a dedicated and intelligent actor. I learned an awful lot working with him. I also enjoyed our friendship and had fun visiting him at his beach house in Malibu for lunch and dinners many times. He was always so interesting and intense about what he felt and believed. He was a competitor, as he displayed on the tennis court with me and actor Jack Warden and some of the other showbiz residents in the Malibu Colony. The last time I saw Rod, my wife, Mary Jane and I went to interview him on my radio show in Malibu, but this time his home was on the other side of the highway. He sold his beach house and bought another house on the high side of the Pacific Coast Highway. We had a joyful time and reminisced about our work together in *Seven Thieves*. His last words to me were "When am I going to see you again to do Part Two?" About two years later, Rod passed away. There are a lot of people you'll always remember, but very few you *never* forget.

On the set of *Seven Thieves* I got a call from Jack Leonard, Nat King Cole's manager, asking if I would like to play in a celebrity softball game against the sports writers and sports announcers prior to one of the Dodgers baseball games. I told him I would be delighted as long as the game took place on the weekend. He knew I was an ex-professional ballplayer and shared that Nat took the game seriously. We had lunch and talked about the actors and entertainers that had athletic ability. I immediately came up with two ex-major league ballplayers, Chuck Connors and Johnny Beradino.

Nat and Jack had already lined up the following players: Dean Martin, Olympic champion Rafer Johnson, Pat Boone, Vince Edwards, Phil Crosby, Nick Adams, Sugar Ray Robinson, Ricky Nelson, Dennis Weaver, William Tallman, Joan Staley, and Soupy Sales for some entertainment.

Rod Steiger and me packing the stolen casino money into wheelchair in Seven Thieves.

Profile shot as Louis Antonizzi casing the inside of the casino.

Ernest Borgnine coached at another ballgame a year later. It became an annual event for the fans and the invited stars for many years.

Jack and Nat respected my opinion and they invited me to a meeting over lunch. Nat announced he was resigning as the playing manager of our celebrity stars baseball team. He said there were too many players added to the roster, most of them couldn't play a lick, and it became a comedy event. That did not sit well with Nat, who was surprisingly competitive. I couldn't agree with him more. Nat believed a comedic situation should never occur on purpose during a game and felt it was best left for clowns. I've never known two people who loved and respected the game of baseball more than Tommy Dorsey and Nat King Cole. By the way, they both played first base.

The ballgames continued for many years, organized by agents and played for laughs. Nat was right – it became a circus! I not only thought Nat King Cole was one of the most talented entertainers that ever lived, but one of the most outstanding people I've ever had the opportunity to know in my lifetime.

During this time period, the editor of *TV Film Stars* magazine called to ask if I would like to do a layout with several other TV stars. He said he would like to do it on the weekend and asked if I had an idea about a good location and subject matter.

I told him I just finished painting every room in my house, but the kitchen and I was planning to get started painting it on the weekend. Well, he laughed and said, "That's what we are all going to do, paint your kitchen." I greeted all the beautiful and talented people early that Saturday morning.

Valerie Allen, June Blair, Dick Sargent and Adam Stewart arrived at my home in Encino and I put them all to work. I had the coffee, paint, rollers and brushes ready to go. I cracked the whip and the only time we took a break was for lunch, which I prepared earlier that morning.

I had music blaring the whole time and before the end of the day, we finished the job. Our

Ernest Borgnine, who had just won an Academy Award for his brilliant role in Marty, *is kidding around and having a lot of fun at the annual Sportswriters and Sports Announcers Celebrity Baseball Game at Dodger Stadium. Every year we all had a blast.*

bodies were full of white paint and I got cleaned up before I made an Italian salad and pasta for dinner. We had plenty of wine, beer and soft drinks. I can't tell you how happy I was when we finished. I was dreading to have to do that job myself. You can imagine how grateful I was to have all that help and they did a terrific job. The writer and the photographer enjoyed the shoot as much as we did. I invited them to stay for dinner, but they had to run off so the six of us ate like a bunch of wolves that evening. We sat around, sharing stories with each other until about ten o'clock that evening. Only in Hollywood could such an arduous chore turn into a photo layout.

My mom arrived in Los Angeles to visit and stay through the Christmas and New Year's

Valerie Allen, June Blair, Adam Stewart and Dick Sargent hard at work, painting my kitchen with me, as a freebie, for a TV Film Stars *magazine layout. How lucky can a guy be?*

holiday. It would be her first trip to the West Coast and initial opportunity to see me work, so you can imagine how excited we were to share that experience.

I am an immigrant's son, as my dad was born in the town of Settefratte, Italy, about an hour and a half south of Rome near the town of Casino. He came to America at the age of nine, assimilated and learned to speak English fluently and never spoke with an accent. My mom was born in New York City on the west side, not far from Hell's Kitchen. Both their parents moved to Stamford, Connecticut, where Mom and Dad met and were married. I have three sisters who still live in Connecticut and one brother who practiced law and lives in Newport Beach, California. My parents were hard working people and gave us everything they had. We were so blessed to be raised in a happy, patriotic, American household. My dad was in the wholesale produce business, selling packages of produce to the small and large local stores. His job kept him busy, seven days a week and he didn't have much time for vacations until he brought in a partner in later years.

Mom was so dedicated; cooking, baking and taking care of five children. We were so fortunate and blessed to be brought into this world by our mom, dad and God. Now she had a chance to see her son and appreciate what I had accomplished since leaving home. I know how proud she was of me and how proud I was to introduce her to everyone.

Introducing my mother Philomena and girlfriend Fern Gimbel to Joan Collins and Rod Steiger on the set of Seven Thieves.

Fern Gimbel and I were still going together and she brought my mother to the set of *Seven Thieves*. Fern and my mother got along royally. I was delighted to introduce both of them to the cast, director and the writer, producer, Sydney Boehm. Sydney felt the warmth and humble, earthy quality that Mom possessed and we quickly became like family. We finished the film and it will always be one of my favorite movies. In fact, upon release of the film, Joan Collins was on *The Johnny Carson Show* and said the role of the exotic dancer in *Seven Thieves* was her favorite role in all of her films, as well. Still going strong in 2013, *Seven Thieves* premiered on the Turner Classic Movie channel to rave reviews.

Christmas and the New Year were at hand and my dad was going to join us for the holidays. It would be one of a few vacations in his lifetime and his first trip to California. Mom, Dad, Fern and I were invited to Sydney Boehm's annual New Year's Eve party at his home in Beverly Hills.

There were quite a few celebrities there with their wives, Edward G. Robinson, Charlton Heston, Jack Palance, Milburn Stone, and Rod Steiger. Dad didn't recognize anyone except Edward G. Robinson, who was his favorite. I introduced them and they began to talk about Italy and how much Eddie enjoyed the country and working with the Italian people.

I could see they were having a friendly chat and then Dad went to get a drink where Sydney was playing bartender and talking to Charlton Heston. I approached the bar at the same time and introduced my dad to "Chuck," Charlton's nickname to his friends. I played tennis with him several times and knew that he was quite a gentleman. My father didn't know who Chuck was and to start a conversation he asked him, "Are you in show business?" Well, Sydney thought that was so hysterical. Chuck got a big kick out of it when Sydney said, "That ought to tame your ego." Chuck was such a good sport and said to my father, "Can I buy you a drink, John?" We all had a good laugh, especially Sydney.

Dad became the hit of the party and every time we got together in the ensuing years, Syd would bring up that scenario and we would break up laughing. It was a special evening and one that Mom and Dad never forgot. Sydney and his wife, Ellen, where the perfect hosts and we all loved each other like family throughout the coming years.

For all the knocks that Hollywood gets, back then it was a place where dreams did come true.

34

Softball Game With the Mob

Before the tragedy occurred I received a phone call about twelve o'clock one night from a friend of Johnny Stompanato's, telling me Mickey Cohen would like to suit up against my celebrity softball team. If I could arrange it he would supply all the bats, new balls, umpires, food and beverages afterward. He said that he knew my work as an actor and explained that Johnny told him I played professionally. Mickey was also aware I played on a few celebrity softball teams around town. The caller said they would arrange to play the game in the park across from the 20th Century-Fox studios, which I was familiar with. I told him I didn't have my own softball team, but I would put one together.

"Call me back in a few days and I'll see what I can do," I said.

I was half asleep and when I hung up the phone, and after a split-second I realized the caller was talking about, Mickey Cohen, the infamous gangster. The man who called was one of his bodyguards.

What the hell am I getting myself into? I wondered.

When I asked some of the celebrities what they thought, they laughed and felt it would be a hoot. I gathered a celebrity team together and coordinated a time and place.

Somehow the word got out and we had a good number of people show up to watch the game. Everyone had a hilarious time teasing Mickey and his team of "goodfellas." Turned out Mickey was the pitcher for their team and we clobbered them 25 to 3. The mob played like they were wearing cement shoes, but even more surprising, we lived to see the next day.

After the game we enjoyed a huge buffet with soft drinks and all the ice cream we could eat. Mickey owned an ice cream parlor on San Vicente Boulevard in Brentwood and was generous in defeat. He even invited people in the stands to join us eat and drink. I must say it was *hilarious* and we all had an enjoyable time. There was enough food and soft drinks for an army.

The bodyguard who first approached me held out his hand and said, "Thank you for doing such a good job putting all this together. If there's anything we can do for you, just let me know." It was a generous offer but one that I didn't necessarily ever want to take him up on.

35

Ms. Fontaine

The following week I got a call to do a segment of *Bourbon Street Beat* and directly after that, I was cast in a period piece entitled *The Story of Judith and Holofernes*, playing opposite Academy Award winning actress, Joan Fontaine.

It was a *General Electric Theater* segment for Universal Studios. At the time, I was in my mid-to-late twenties and had to be aged to play the character Holofernes by curling and graying my hair and beard every morning before we started filming.

The first day of work I had a 6 a.m. call for makeup, followed by the hairstylist. Joan and I were sitting in our chairs at the end of the makeup department on opposite sides of a center floor plan. From the other end of the department we could hear an over-trained Assistant Director marching down the hallway and calling out loud as he approached each makeup room on his left and right. "Joan Fontaine… Michael Dante," he said as he approached the room, "Joan Fontaine…Michael Dante," all the way down the hall and finally getting to the last two rooms where we were getting made up. He unfortunately ducked into Joan's room first, and she ripped into this rookie and let him have it.

"Listen to me you asshole," Joan said through clenched teeth. "Don't you ever address Mr. Dante by calling him Michael Dante; it's 'Mr. Dante' to you and don't you ever again address me as Joan Fontaine! It's 'Ms. Fontaine' to you! Do you understand that? If you don't, I'm going to kick you right in the balls! Now get the hell out of here!"

Like a wounded animal, the Assistant Director popped his head in my room and said gently, "Mr. Dante, whenever you are ready they're waiting for a rehearsal on the set." Well, the makeup man and I had to bite our lips until he got out of earshot, so we could let out a huge laugh. We didn't want to embarrass him anymore than he already was.

I'll never forget that morning of work as long as I live. Joan was so professional and knew her craft extremely well. I enjoyed working with her and several months later I worked with her again at Universal Studios in a segment of the successful series entitled *Checkmate*, starring a good pal of mine, Doug McClure. Joan was without a doubt the consummate professional but, I never, ever wanted to get on her bad side.

I had to gray my hair so I looked older than my 25 years, to play opposite Academy Award winning actress Ms. Joan Fontaine.

36

Foxes and Thieves

The post-production work on *Seven Thieves* had just been completed when I received a phone call from producer Sydney Boehm to come to his office.

"I'm sending you and Joan Collins to New York to meet with Charlie Einefield, the head of distribution for 20th Century-Fox, to promote the release of *Seven Thieves*," he said. Mr. Einefield was arranging a press junket with film critics and fan magazines and appearances on *The Tonight Show with Johnny Carson* as well as *The Mike Douglas Show* in Philadelphia.

I was put up at the Warwick Hotel, the same place I stayed when filming *Somebody Up There Likes Me* while under contract to MGM. Joan was staying at the Blackstone Hotel. She and Warren Beatty were in the midst of a torrid love affair at the time, so he tagged along with her and we were to contact Mr. Einefield's office at ten o'clock the next morning. I promptly called Mr. Einefield's office at the appointed time and his secretary informed me that he was in a meeting and would get back to me before noon. I went and had breakfast, picked up a paper and hung around my room until noontime. I was just about to leave when the phone rang and it was Joan, asking if I heard from Charlie.

"I'm going to give them a call as soon as I hang up to find out what's going on and then I'm going to have lunch at Sardi's Restaurant. If he answers my call I will call you right back," I said. I spoke with the secretary and she said, "Mr. Einefield wants to meet with both of you and he will definitely call around five o'clock today." I rang Joan right back to tell her the news and she ripped off some language about Mr. Einefield that he would not have liked to hear about himself. I told her that we would talk one way or another at five bells. I left the hotel to have lunch at Sardi's with my friend Steve Barry, a fine press agent who I befriended on *Somebody Up There Likes Me*.

I did my usual window shopping on the way. I noticed there was a life-size cardboard figure of Pat Boone outside a theater in Times Square advertising the motion picture *Journey to the Center of the Earth*. It was a Fox made film and seemingly getting a lot of action with people standing in line to buy tickets.

Our lunch was good and I enjoyed my visit with Steve, telling him the whole story. We both agreed something was wrong and unprofessional. I said I would keep him abreast of what was going on with Mr. Eienfield before we parted.

I made my way back to the hotel, but not before stopping at Layton's, my favorite clothing store in New York, to buy a shirt. I arrived back at the hotel and checked if I had any messages just in case Charlie may have called before the scheduled five o'clock call.

I waited until 5:30 and still no call, so I called his office to check in. His secretary said he was in an important meeting and would get back to me the first thing in the morning. I spoke with Joan and she hadn't heard anything either. We both agreed there was something wrong. That night, I went to see my friend Danny Stradella, had dinner at his restaurant, and chatted with him for a couple of hours. The next morning I received a call, but it was from California. It was Sydney Boehm asking me how everything was going. When I told him I hadn't spoken to Mr. Einefield since I arrived, he went through the roof.

"Don't leave. I'll call you back in 20 minutes," he said. He told me the studio was broke and they were having a very difficult time deciding which picture to release at this time. They only had money for prints and advertising for one film.

Since *Journey to the Center of the Earth* was doing so well in the one theater on Times Square, indicating they might have a big hit on their hands, they decided to put what money they had into the distribution of that film instead of ours. Syd was fit to be tied. He told me to come by the studio to see him upon my return. "Everything is taken care of, so have a good time and enjoy yourself," he said. Sydney said he would call Joan and tell her the bad news.

I would have been interested to hear her reaction, which I'm positive wasn't pleasant. That extra day gave me the opportunity to visit with two of my favorite writers, Wanda Hale and Kay Gardella of the *New York Daily News*. They had seen a press screening of *Seven Thieves* and had high expectations for me as a result of my performance. Three days later I was sitting in Syd's office at 20th Century-Fox. We were all disappointed at the turn of events.

"The exposure would have done you a world of good, Michael," he said. "It would have given your career quite a boost because you did such a terrific job in the film." To add insult to injury, an actor's strike was beckoning and it was up in the air when the picture would see a timely release.

Syd said he had a book that he wanted to option and write the screenplay adaptation, starring Sidney Poitier and me. He also wanted his friend Richard Brooks to direct. Unfortunately, the actors went on strike for six months and all studio contracts were null and void. Since Fox was out of money, everyone under contract was let go. Prior to the strike, I was one of the hottest young actors in the business. When we went on strike, things changed, making me one of the last of the contract players. Once again, "Timing is not important, it's everything!"

Syd never did option the book and Fox did not renew his contract. As tantalizing as show business could be, it was equally heartbreaking at times.

37

Actor's Strike

During the actor's strike of 1960-61, I made the best of a bad situation. I played a lot of tennis to stay in shape and spent many evenings at Dodger Stadium watching baseball and visited with Al Campanis when the Dodgers were hosting.

I was becoming a bit disillusioned with the industry at the time. Drugs were floating around freely and the glamour was vanishing quite rapidly. I didn't indulge or associate with any of that crowd, so I spent a lot of time watching big league baseball, the game I love and owe so much to.

Al Campanis was one of the smartest baseball executives and nicest human beings I ever met. We became close friends and I was invited to his home in Fullerton many times when his wife and his mother were still alive. I also attended the weddings of his two sons, Jimmy and George. Many years later, I was heartbroken when Al lost his job with the Dodgers after that controversial interview with Ted Koppel. I knew Al well and sat with him in his executive box on and off at the ballpark for approximately 25 years. I never heard one adverse comment from him about anyone's race, color or religion. As a matter of fact, Al was more of a minority than anyone I knew in baseball. At the time he was the only major league baseball executive born in another country, Greece. His mother brought him from the island of Coss in Greece to live in America.

They settled in New York City and Al became an outstanding athlete, playing football and baseball for Columbia University. He signed a professional baseball contract with the Dodgers upon graduation and moved quickly through the ranks. Unfortunately, he met with a terrible accident when an opposing player slid into second base that he was covering, cutting the tendons in his throwing hand. His future as a promising shortstop for the Brooklyn Dodgers came to an abrupt end, but owner Branch Rickey recognized the leadership quality of this special athlete and guided him into the executive side of the Dodgers organization.

It didn't take long for Al to move up the ladder on the executive side of the game and the rest is history. I will always be grateful for his generosity and friendship.

I was playing tennis well enough to be invited to play in most of the celebrity charity tournaments throughout the country. It began with stars like Charlton Heston, Lloyd Bridges, Chris Connelly, James Franciscus, Ron Ely, Ed Ames, Ben Murphy, Lyle Waggoner and me playing tennis in a competitive environment with people who paid to play with and against us to raise money for various charitable causes.

Quite a few tournaments were played in Los Angeles and in various cities throughout the country such as Pebble Beach, Santa Barbara, San Jose, San Francisco, Santa Cruz, Phoenix, Arizona and Toronto, Canada.

I think the best tennis tournament I ever played in, for all the right reasons, was hosted by Clint Eastwood and Merv Griffin. It was a celebrity tennis tournament that took place for four days, July 1-4 in Pebble Beach, California, at the Del Monte Lodge and Tennis Resort. Most of us stayed in private homes or in guesthouses surrounding the golf course and tennis facilities. A special dinner and entertainment took place outside in the open air every night after the tennis matches. Clint and Merv were the perfect hosts for several years until a conflict occurred with the resident tennis pro, Don Hamilton and the Del Monte Lodge management. Don was a close friend of Clint's, so Clint took his side of the disagreement. That pretty much ended the tournament.

We had a lot of fun along the way, but unfortunately were not able to consistently raise enough money for our efforts to meet our expectations and sufficiently help the charities. Over the years we learned with the exception of a few, that tennis players as a rule were health conscious people, but not the most generous participants in their sports events at that time.

Some of the celebrities, who were able to play golf as well, learned that golfers and associated sponsors were much more generous. Celebrity golf tournaments raised more money than celebrity tennis tournaments and as a result the idea of raising money for charity through a celebrity tennis tournament faded away into the sunset. Fortunately, tennis has made a huge resurgence with the professional players and fan-based tennis events for charity. I was proud to be part of that original celebrity group in both tennis and golf. Today, both sports tournaments have raised millions of dollars for various charitable organizations throughout the globe.

Just after the strike ended, I guest starred as "The Champ" in an episode of *The Detectives,* a riveting series starring Robert Taylor. It was a dramatic story about a boxing champion and once again my athletic ability and having played this kind of a role before with Rory Calhoun in *The Killer Instinct* gave me an advantage to play this character. The many hours I spent as a youngster developing my athletic skills paid off for me many times over in pursuit of my acting career.

Robert Taylor was one of my favorite actors when I was a teenager. He always played the handsome leading man that wound up with the beautiful girl. Now who knew, approximately 20 years later, I would be guest starring on his television series. It was all a bit surreal.

This was Taylor's first crack at television after years of being a major movie star. He owned 50 percent of the show, but unfortunately, the series was cancelled in the midst of the third season. Robert was such a professional and a gentleman, he knew more about the business in front and behind the camera than any one I ever worked with. The only two bad habits Robert had was drinking black coffee and smoking cigarettes – he did both all day long. The only time I ever saw him without a cigarette or a cup of black coffee in his hand was when he was on camera.

From the first to the last day of work, it was such a joy to be in his presence and I was looking forward to hopefully working with him again. Several years later I got my wish. Robert was the last host of the long running and popular western television series, *Death Valley Days.* Stanley Andrews, the 'Old Ranger' was the first host of the show followed by Ronald Reagan and Robert Taylor. This was the last acting job before Ronald Reagan went into politics and one of the last shows Robert ever hosted.

At this point in time, Bob Stabler was the producer of the show. It was so interesting and unique how we were transported to location for this show. Taylor and I flew commercially to Las Vegas from LAX and met Stabler, who was also a pilot. He flew us to Moab, Utah, in his privately owned twin engine plane. Along the way it was hard not to notice Robert's deep cough.

"How long have you had that cold?" I asked. He said he had it for a couple of weeks and hadn't been able to shake it. As a matter of fact, he said he was going to see a doctor right after we finished the show. We were halfway there when Robert asked Bob if he could take over flying the plane. He was already sitting in the co-pilot seat and was a pilot instructor in World War II. Robert was familiar with the plane and appeared to be comfortable behind the controls. As we approached the landing area which was situated atop of a mesa, the cross winds were blowing pretty good, but he handled the controls with ease and brought the plane down as smooth as anyone could.

We had dinner together that night at the lodge where we were staying and he continued to smoke, drink black coffee and occasionally coughed at the table. We both ordered fresh trout almandine and talked about the script briefly, when he called the waitress over to fill his huge thermos with black coffee. He didn't eat much of his dinner. The waitress brought him his beloved coffee and he excused himself to work on the script. He smiled and said, "This script is a little different than the last one we did together. Everything is taken care of, you're my guest; I'll see you in the morning." As he left the table with his thermos underneath his arm, I could hear that cough once more. I went to sleep that night, thinking how blessed I was to have so many of my dreams and fantasies become a reality in my life to date. Robert and I had an early call the next morning to work inside the Fort.

The director and I were both aware of Robert's chain smoking, so whenever he put a cigarette down during rehearsal or in between shots, one of us would pick it up and toss it in the fireplace nearby. This went on for three days because it was a half hour show and Robert never complained. He just reached inside his coat pocket and lit up another one.

Every once in a while I would hear that familiar deep cough, which was getting to sound like more than just a cold. We had a well written script and a director that knew what he was doing. Like Rory Calhoun, Robert Taylor was also one of the most unselfish actors I worked with. When the director asked or wanted to block a scene, Robert would say, "Forget the two shot, go in and get a big close up of Michael, he's doing a great job." That gesture was certainly not the norm for most of the television series stars.

The director and I tried our best to cut down Robert's cigarette smoking, but to no avail. I had the feeling he knew what we were doing all along but never let on. Bob Stabler picked us up again in his twin engine plane after finishing the show and we left Moab for Las Vegas. Robert took the controls again and flew us into Vegas like a true professional. He and I then boarded a commercial flight back to Los Angeles.

"Rory Calhoun, Clark Gable and I are going deer hunting as soon as the hunting season opens," Robert said, inviting me to come along. I told him I knew Rory well and met Clark when I was under contract to MGM. We exchanged phone numbers and said he'd be in touch. We went our separate ways and I heard that dreadful deep cough once more. Just before hunting season, I received a call from his beautiful actress wife Ursula Thiess. She was calling off the trip. I spoke with Rory over the phone and he said Robert was not well. He didn't have to tell me how this was going to end. Robert Taylor died on June 8, 1969, of lung cancer at the age of 57. It was those damn cigarettes. The industry and the world lost a special talent and person. How fortunate I was to know him and work with him before he left us.

38

Good and Bad
After the Strike

In 1961 my agent contact at the William Morris Agency, Sy Marsh, left the heralded firm to become a partner/producer with Sammy Davis Jr. I certainly wasn't happy about his decision to leave because Sy was one of the best in the business.

The agency was still keeping me busy, doing some episodic television. Two of the shows that I was excited about doing were *Cain's Hundred* and *87th Precinct*. In *Cain's Hundred*, I played the son of character actor Sam Jaffe. I'll never forget his terrific performance in the Academy Award winning movie *Gunga Din,* one of the greatest black and white films of all time. He was a soft spoken and gentle man. I enjoyed working with him and developing the warm father and son relationship the story required. It was the only time I worked with him and never had the pleasure of seeing him again. It was another rare experience with a fine actor.

In *87th Precinct,* I was cast as a character named Larry Brooks, a professional baseball player at home in the off season. I really had a lot of fun because I had the opportunity to work with a lot of youngster's on the ballfield as part of the story. I had to demonstrate to them the proper way to throw, catch, hit and slide into a base.

I never thought I would land the part because I had a strange experience with a producer who was doing a baseball story two months before. I was up for the role of a ballplayer in the script. Ultimately, I didn't get the part.

"Sorry kid, but you just don't look like a ballplayer," he said. I was floored but politely informed him that I had played professionally for two and a half years. He then switched gears and told me he thought I was too good looking for the part. I just got up and left. Hollywood breeds some of the best silver-tongued devils I have ever come to know.

39

Kid Galahad, EP and Me

As far as I was concerned, my next job, a 1962 movie entitled *Kid Galahad* opposite Elvis Presley, felt like I hit a home run. I played the part of Joie Shakes, a boxing champion. It was only by the insistence of casting agent Lynn Stalmaster that I got the part. He saw me a while back in the television show *The Killer Instinct* with Rory Calhoun and brought the film to director Phil Karlson to see. Phil was thinking of casting another type for the part, but after he ran my film, he liked what he saw and I got the part. They had a good cast lined up for this movie; Gig Young, Lola Albright, Joan Blackman, Charles Bronson and a host of fine character actors.

The movie location was filmed in Idyllwild, California, a small, quaint town up in the mountains, about one hour from where I live today near Palm Springs. Elvis and I did all the fight scenes ourselves, we didn't have to use stuntmen. One day during a boxing sequence, Elvis threw an extra punch at the end of the routine just as I was slipping my mouthpiece out. The blow caused me to cut my mouth and it started bleeding. Elvis was really upset and must have apologized ten times. I assured him that I was all right and had been hit before. "Please don't worry about it," I said.

Elvis was such a gentleman. He was polite, well mannered, never late, always knew his dialogue, a good athlete, soulful singer and an underrated actor. He didn't keep a very good diet though. He loved to eat cheeseburgers and drank a lot of Pepsi Cola.

I never sang in a motion picture or television show before. As the story goes, Elvis enters the training camp and for a five dollar fee, he spars with me and knocks me out to the surprise of everyone. After I shake the ringing sound in my ears, Elvis and I become friends. That same evening, all the other fighters, trainers, and me are enjoying singing on the steps outside the lodge. Would you believe, in my first singing role, I asked and convinced Elvis to sing with us! The name of the song was "This Is Living."

I enjoyed every minute of it and so did everyone else. But it was my first and last singing role. Do you think they were trying to tell me something?

Elvis was appreciative of the work we were doing together and he asked with a slight stammer, "I rented a bunch of rooms at the Howard Manor Hotel in Palm Springs. I happened to look at the schedule and we're finishing early on Friday and not working Saturday." We worked six days a week while on location, so we had the weekend to get away for a change of atmosphere. The Howard Manor was one of the best hotels in Palm Springs at the time. Elvis said he rented quite a few rooms and would like for me to be his guest. He also invited Gig Young, Gig's wife, Liz Montgomery and Charlie Bronson, along with Elvis' retinue.

This photo was quickly taken behind Colonel Parker's back by my friend Joe Esposito on the set of Kid Galahad.

There wasn't much to do in Idyllwild so that weekend getaway sounded awfully good. Elvis asked me if I wanted to drive down with him in the limousine or take my own car. I decided to ride with him so we could talk and leave the driving around those treacherous turns down Highway 74 to his driver. I got in the car with Elvis, as he had two limousines.

We went driving down Highway 74 and just before we started descending down a winding road to the valley, on the right was an A-frame real estate office building. It was set off to the right side of the road about 50 yards back with a huge parking area. It was called Alpine Real Estate.

We were driving slowly and I could see about a quarter to a half-mile down the road. I spotted someone who looked vaguely familiar. "EP, I think I know that gray-haired guy standing on the side of the road talking to that woman," I said. "I don't remember his last name but his first name is Tommy, a part time actor and bartender, and God knows what he's doing here." As we got closer I could see Tommy talking to an attractive lady there. I asked Elvis if he would mind stopping the car, because I'd like to say hello to him. Elvis didn't mind, so we stopped.

I introduced Elvis to Tommy and he introduced the lady to us. I thought she was going to have a heart attack. She was a huge Elvis Presley fan. She couldn't believe it was Elvis Presley and that here she was in the middle of Highway 74, out in the boonies talking to my friend Tommy about purchasing the lot across the street. She totally lost her poise and could hardly speak when I introduced Elvis to her. He was polite and charming. I asked Tom what he was selling.

He told me he was selling one acre lots across the street and that the road in front would eventually lead to Palm Springs on the other end when it's finished. I asked him how much the lots were selling for. He said, "$7,400" I looked across the street and I couldn't believe the only lot sign standing read "Unit One, Lot 637."

I turned to Tom and said, "I'll buy that lot." He said with a smile, "What took you so long?" The address of the house I grew up in Stamford, Connecticut, was 637 Fairfield Avenue. I thought it was a good omen. This all took place in about 10 minutes.

We got back in the limo, said goodbye to the lady and meeting Elvis made her the happiest woman in the whole world. I slid back into my seat when Elvis asked me, "What did you do?" I told him the whole story why I bought the lot and I would make arrangements to pay for it after I finished the picture. Elvis offered to pay for it and then pay him back whenever I could. I told him I couldn't do that, but I thanked him for his kind offer. I bought the lot and throughout the years the road leading from the property to Palm Springs was never built. So I finally sold it seven years ago for $10,000 making a profit of $2,600. The lot is gone but the memories of that special experience will stay with me forever.

Landing a good left hook against Elvis Presley.

I enjoyed the weekend at the Howard Manor. We did a lot of swimming, listening to music, dancing with the ladies, and relaxing around the pool having a good time with EP and the gang. Elvis loved to play football. Every time we had the chance we would throw the football back and forth until it was time to go back to work. It was close to the holidays when we finished shooting on location in Idyllwild. Elvis wanted to be able to spend Christmas at his home in Memphis and he got his wish.

Before he left he called me aside and gave me two wrapped gifts, several of his albums and a clock radio, which I still have at my bedside today. He was very thoughtful, generous and a good human being.

After the holidays, Elvis returned to Los Angeles to finish the interior work at the studio. On the weekend Elvis and his buddies along with a couple of stuntmen; Red West, Nick Dimitri and Louis Elias had a running touch football game every Sunday at a public park near the fire station on Coldwater Canyon in Beverly Hills. I joined them several times. When the word got out, we were playing before quite a few spectators.

The game lasted as long as Elvis remained in town. I had a lot of fun and enjoyed the camaraderie while it lasted. Even after all these years, I find it difficult to believe he's gone but will always have many fond memories of the time I spent with Elvis.

40

Housewarming Party

The money I made on *Kid Galahad* went toward putting the finishing touches on furnishing the rest of my house. I took my time and made sure everything was just right. It was around that time I received a call from the editor of *TV Picture Life* to do a fan magazine layout. During our conversation I told him that I had just finished furnishing my house. He immediately suggested I throw a housewarming party with certain actors and actresses he had in mind. I told him that it was a good idea and said, "Let's make it happen."

I had a shake roof house in Encino with a wall on three sides, a breezeway separating a two car garage, a circular drive up front and a bunch of fruit trees in the backyard. I didn't have a pool. It was all located in a spaciously arranged cul-de-sac. Several days later, I greeted Cathy Case, James Franciscus, Lori Nelson, Burt Reynolds and Nina Shipman. I had a shady patio in the back of my house with a green lawn between the patio and the back wall. I had pear, nectarine, orange, lemon, pomegranate, apple, kumquat and persimmon trees in my orchard. We had fun picking

Housewarming party at my Encino, California, home. Left to right: Cathy Case, James Franciscus, Lori Nelson, Burt Reynolds, Nina Shipman and me.

whatever fruit was in season and made it a part of our lunch, which I served outside on the patio with a variety of cold drinks.

I had super jazz music playing in the background, the likes of Dave Brubeck, Paul Desmond, Charlie Parker, Lester Young, Count Basie and always, my dear friend Tommy Dorsey. I made a big spinach salad with oil, vinegar and blue cheese, along with several cold cuts; prosciutto, mozzarella cheese, salami, sliced turkey and Swiss cheese, served with wheat and rye bread rolls.

The photographer took lots of pictures of us enjoying our luncheon while we were yacking away and hanging out. It was another cool afternoon with everyone getting to know each other just a little bit better. These layouts we participated in over the years were to be remembered for the rest of our lives as truly 'Hollywood' at its finest and a whole lot of fun.

41

Operation Bikini

Operation Bikini was a low budget picture produced by American International Pictures, noted for its exploitation films. They were fortunate to have quite a few good actors cast in this movie, namely, Scott Brady, Tab Hunter, Jim Backus, Frankie Avalon, Gary Crosby and yours truly playing the lieutenant, second in command of the submarine involved in the story.

With Scott Brady and Tab Hunter looking on, telling the crew a Japanese cruiser is moving in… fast.

My first military role playing an executive officer, Bill Fourtney. Nothing wrong with starting at the top!

Listening to the scary sound of an approaching enemy cruiser above us, hoping we don't get hit.

Urgently, we came up with a plan of action to submerge and avoid the depth charges.

Veteran actors Scott Brady and Jim Backus kept everybody loose on the set with jokes and Jim's famous Mr. Magoo character, which he often performed off camera. I know they made a lot of money with this picture because we shot it in two weeks and no one was overpaid by any stretch of the imagination. As far as we were all concerned, it was work. The contributions the cast made in making this film were far greater than the story.

I'm certain this movie made its money back in distribution in a couple of weeks and has been playing for years in national and international television syndication. The story was about dropping the bomb on the Bikini Atoll, not about beautiful ladies in bikini bathing suits. We were all recognizable and working actors at the time. They knew how to exploit that with the title name. A.I.P. was extremely successful in making these types of films, and even more successful keeping the money in *their* pockets.

42

The Naked Kiss

Speaking of low budget pictures, the next film I did, *The Naked Kiss,* was with a talented and popular director who could do more with less money than anyone in the history of show business. His name was Sammy Fuller.

Sammy wrote, directed, and in some cases, produced many fine motion pictures. Some of his films include *Shock Corridor, Steel Helmet, I Shot Jesse James, Run of the Arrow, Merrill's Marauders, The Big Red One* and *The Naked Kiss.* He was one of the greatest storytellers on and off the screen. He reminded me a great deal of my favorite director, Budd Boetticher.

Sammy was a true joy to work with, always energetic, enthusiastic, with a rugged visual style. Sammy brought so many creative ideas to work on a daily basis. He truly loved his work and it permeated throughout the soundstage, cast and crew. He loved actors and loved working with them. Every actor in the business wanted to work with him too. *The Naked Kiss* was one of Fuller's best and most controversial scripts. He told me in our first meeting, the picture would not be a commercial hit until many years later. He said that we were about thirty years ahead of our time, with regard to audience exposure to that subject matter. I played the first pedophile in the history of American films.

Sammy loved to surprise his audiences, for there was always a red herring in many of his stories. The character was tall, dark and handsome, athletic, a war hero, wealthy and a humanitarian who falls in love with an ex-prostitute. The storyline gives no indication there is a problem with Grant, the character I play, until the latter part of the film. He is everything a woman loves in a man until accidentally she discovers his secret. Those moments in the film are extremely surprising and storytelling. It was Fuller at his best.

The morning of the important discovery scene, Sammy came to work with a big smile on his face and full of energy.

"Michael, you're going to shoot your own close up today. We're going to put a plank just behind the lens that will be fastened to the camera," he said. By the way, it was a huge Mitchell camera. "It will be on a dolly and you'll push the camera with your shoulders pressed tightly against the plank. You will have to take very small even steps, because the camera is so tight on your face. You have to maintain even and steady small steps so you don't go out of frame." It was quite a challenge and one of the most innovative camera shots in my career. Sammy was famous for inventing so many interesting, creative ideas.

Many directors in Hollywood learned so much observing Fuller's work. Award winning director Martin Scorsese said the greatest opening sequence he had ever seen was in *The Naked*

As Grant with Constance Towers in Sammy Fuller's film noir classic, The Naked Kiss.

Kiss. Curtis Hansen said the two films that inspired him to become a director were *The Man Who Shot Liberty Valance* and *The Naked Kiss*.

Every year the Restoration of Film Committee honors a director at the William Wyler Theater in Westwood, California to speak after the screening of a film that most inspired that person to

Sammy Fuller, the award winning director of The Naked Kiss.

become a director. Hansen chose *The Naked Kiss*. Constance Towers and I were invited to the event and to be a part of the symposium that took place afterwards. Every seat in the house was taken and I was not surprised to still hear raves about the film. Fuller was right when he said the movie would bring much more awareness and exposure about the subject matter down the road. Prior to this event, The Palm Springs Film Festival chose the film, now Fuller's cult classic, as its Directors Choice landmark film. The following year, *The Naked Kiss* highlighted the festival and honored me.

Sammy once called to tell me how proud he was of that experience. Ditto for me.

43
Audie Murphy and Me

The thought of working with America's most decorated World War II soldier and actor Audie Murphy was something beyond my comprehension. I have never seen anyone in my lifetime with more medals on their uniform than Audie Murphy. He was awarded with a medal from every Allied country in World War II including the highest award, The Congressional Medal of Honor. General Alexander M. Patch, 7th Army Commander pinned the Medal of Honor and the Legion of Merit decoration on Audie Murphy on June 2, 1945, near Salzburg, Austria, for continuous bravery in volunteering for dangerous missions from January 1944 to February 1945. Audie chose to accept the honors on the field, rather than back in Washington, D.C.

The first film I co-starred in with Audie Murphy was a 1964 western entitled *Apache Rifles* for 20th Century-Fox, produced by Grant Wytock and directed by one of Hollywood's finest of the Western genre, Mr. William Witney. The two other co-stars stars were Linda Lawson, who was so pretty and a good actress and character actor L.Q. Jones, who I later worked with in *Winterhawk*.

Most of the scenes were done in the Mojave Desert where the everyday temperature hovered around 117 degrees. We only used our dressing rooms to dress and undress; we didn't dare spend any time inside any longer than we had to because of the contrast in temperature. Audie and I sat outside, underneath a canopy between shots and roughed through it. Of course, when we rode our horses and moved around in our heavy wardrobe our body heat was much more than the outside temperature so you can imagine at the end of the day, we were dehydrated and worn out.

We stayed in a motel not far from our location and the first night I got to sleep fairly early. In the middle of the night I heard a train and a strong white light was shining through the window. The sound of the train was getting louder and louder and coming directly toward my room. I was half asleep and I thought that train was coming right into my room to run over me.

I was never so scared in all my life. I got the assistant director out of bed and made him move my room to the back of the motel. I told Audie that story the next day at breakfast and he got the biggest laugh out of it.

The assistant director and a still photographer approached us while we were sitting under the canopy outside of our dressing rooms to take a couple of publicity shots. As usual, it was hotter than hell and he snapped a couple of shots, but he wanted a few more of us smiling. We stood up and he said, "Smile guys" and Audie with his sense of humor, slid his hand down on the top of my gun resting in the holster. I never felt a thing until the photographer said smile and then Audie pressed down on the gun and we both smiled to get the shot he wanted. When you see the photo, you'll know exactly what I'm talking about.

Red Hawk knows his future is on the reservation but stands tall with dignity and pride for himself and his tribe.

Ready to attack the miners who were stealing gold from his land, Red Hawk was never afraid to defend what was his.

Audie had a good sense of humor, polite, sensitive, soft spoken, and didn't talk much. He was a very private person. I had a lot of respect for him as an actor and as a person. We had a nice conversation one day, and he told me his family were sharecroppers from Kingston, Texas. Growing up, they went through some rough times financially and moved around quite a bit. He said he would take his .22 rifle and go hunting for rabbits so they could have a cooked meal once in a while. He became a fine marksman at a young age. I've never seen anyone handle a colt .45 with such finesse. So many people have asked me what kind of a person Audie Murphy was. I would say that he's the only person I knew that I could describe in one word, 'feline.' He had the grace and the moves of a cat. I can understand how he survived many close calls during the war, because he moved so quietly and smoothly. He was the epitome of the adage 'less is more.'

About a year later, I co-starred with Audie in another western film entitled *Arizona Raiders*, directed by the same director, William Witney and again produced by Grant Whytock for Columbia Pictures. They both liked what I did in *Apache Rifles* and wanted me to play the role of Brady, a certifiable bad ass character.

The film would be shot on location in Apache Junction and Old Tucson, Arizona. Two good veteran character actors and a leading lady were cast in the film, former Olympic swimming champion Buster Crabbe, Ben Cooper and Gloria Talbot.

Apache Junction with the beautiful Superstition Mountain in the background were perfect for long chases and Old Tucson with all its adobe buildings and a beautiful church were exactly what was needed for the exterior locations. The company stayed in a southwestern-style motel in Tucson with an Olympic-sized swimming pool in the center of a horseshoe-designed compound, which I could easily see from my first floor room window. I slept with the window open, and every morning since the first day of principal photography at 6 a.m. sharp, I could hear Buster Crabbe diving into the water and swimming laps like a fish for a half hour, getting his morning exercise. Audie was in a first floor room as well and we knew we didn't have to ask the operator at the hotel to wake us up after the first day because Buster's morning routine got us up whether we liked it or not. He was our wakeup call!

Arizona was the perfect place to film a western in those days; cactus all around and you could ride for miles without seeing a house or a telephone pole. We all had the best time working together and the results were up on the screen. The only problem was, it went too fast, it was one of the last conventional westerns made.

I was honored in 2011 at Apache Junction where they embedded my cowboy boot prints in cement at the Superstition Mountain Museum. It's hard to describe how proud I was to have my prints up on the wall at the Museum with the likes of John Wayne, Gene Autry, Roy Rogers; the list goes on and on. It was such a pleasure to be amongst some of the most friendly people and supportive fans and enjoy a terrific country western music concert under the stars by Rollie Stevens and his band. They made us feel right at home. Needless to say, that event will always be one of the highlights of my career.

A few years after *Arizona Raiders* was released, I received a phone call from a writer I met on the picture by the name of Rod Piffath.

He said he wrote a western script specifically for Audie and me because we worked so well together. Two days later Rod gave me the script over lunch and I read it that night. The title was *The Perfect Target*. It was about a corporal in the Salvation Army, the character Audie would play. The story begins in St. Louis, Missouri in the 1800's. The character inherits a fortune from his deceased uncle in the fictitious town of Minerva, Arizona and must journey there to claim the

Co-starring as Brady in Arizona Raiders, *my second film with Audie Murphy.*

As Brady, ready for action. There was never a dull moment on the set of an Audie Murphy movie.

Audie was a very humble man with a great sense of humor. Here he has his hand on my gun to make us smile for the photo.

will. Along the way, my character and Audie meet. In the middle of nowhere he saves my life from a bunch of renegades. I choose to tag along until I return the favor. When we arrived in Minerva, he learned his uncle had a mistress and a son out of wedlock, and they felt they should inherit his uncle's fortune. That's when the conflict and fireworks began. The evil forces go to work to destroy Audie's character, they fail to succeed and he defeats them in a non-violent way. When a member of a citadel inherits a large sum of money, the Salvation Army allows that missionary to build his own citadel. He converts this decadent town into a religious and law-abiding community.

It was quite a departure for Audie, for no one in a million years would think of him in this role except Rod Piffath and me. I brought the script to Audie at his home in Toluca Lake, California. He read it and loved it.

We both agreed it was excellent script and we would work hard to get it done. I met with him a second time and he said he was going out of town for a couple of weeks. He said we'd get together when he returned. Unfortunately, I never saw or spoke to Audie again. He was killed in a plane crash in the Brush Mountains of Virginia about 12 miles outside of Roanoke on May 23, 1971. This great American hero and underrated actor left us far too soon in a most unexpected way.

Rod Piffath moved to the Philippines to work on a special project he was involved with, making cigarette lighters at a very economical price. He asked me if I could get the script made or sell it because he was going to be gone for a long time. He was an exceptionally intelligent and talented man. I couldn't get it made but I was able to sell it to Disney Studios to a producer friend of mine by the name of Christopher Hibler. I couldn't believe what they did to that script. They totally re-wrote it and if you read their version, you wouldn't know it was the same story. They re-wrote it for the talented Tony Award-winning actor Jim Dale whom Disney had under contract.

The rest of the cast consisted of Don Knotts, Karen Valentine, Jack Elam and John Williams. It was directed by one of Disney's finest, Robert Butler, and produced by Ron Miller with co-producer Christopher Hibler. Jim Dale gave a good performance but unfortunately the camera didn't like him. He had one of those faces you'd never remember and I don't recall him doing anything else. It was just one of those strange things. The stage was Jim's forte. The film was made and released several years later like the successful comedy style western films Disney produced previously, *The Shakiest Gun in the West*, *The Apple Dumpling Gang*, and *The Return of The Apple Dumpling Gang*. These motion pictures did well at the box office, so I guess that was the only way to go with *The Perfect Target* which was given a new title, *Hot Lead and Cold Feet*. To this day, I believe Audie and I could have brought an entirely different and quite successful movie to the screen and one that opened up our careers to playing more comedy, as well. It was another case of "Hollywood experts" at work.

44
... Fireplaces?

Harlow, **in 1965, was a biopic** on the life of film star Jean Harlow played by talented actress Carol Lynley. The transformation was jarring when she donned a blonde wig and full makeup. It was done live, utilizing a TV kinescope process called Electronovision.

It was hurriedly assembled to capitalize on the distribution of this film through Magna Pictures before a Paramount Studios feature was released of the same name. It was photographed using more than one camera by one of the best multiple camera directors, Alex Segal. The screenplay was written by Karl Tunburg and produced by Bill Sargent Jr. and Lee Savin. We had an excellent cast in Ginger Rogers, Efrem Zimbalist Jr., Barry Sullivan, Hurd Hatfield, Lloyd Bochner, Hermione Baddeley, Audrey Totter, John Williams, Jack Kruschen and yours truly. I played Jean Harlow's gigolo lover, a young stud named Ed. Ginger Rogers replaced Judy Garland to play Jean's mother. Judy came to rehearsals the first day and read beautifully. I thought she did an excellent job, but she seemed very nervous and unsettled.

The next day her agent, Guy McElwaine, came to the set just before rehearsals and announced that Judy was bowing out because of health reasons. Ginger replaced her and in two days she had everything memorized and did a terrific job. I invited Ginger to have lunch with me one day and she apologized but said she couldn't, because all she ate for lunch was celery and carrots. She was on a vegetable diet and she still had that beautiful dancer's figure.

Barry Sullivan played Jean's stepfather, Marino Bello. I had a lot of fun teaching Barry how to roll his R's, so he would sound Italian. Efrem Zimbalist Jr. played a thinly disguised William Powell, who refused to allow his name or likeness to be used. Hurd Hatfield played producer Paul Bern, who Harlow marries only to have him commit suicide due to his impotence. When she finds that out, she comes running to Ed (me) to satisfy her needs. Quite a few talented people in the business told me that the seduction scene between Carol Lynley and me was one of the best they'd ever seen.

We were rehearsing that scene right up until we were finished for the day at the end of the first week of shooting. Toward the end of the seduction scene, I gently take Carol and place her on a beautiful white polar bear rug in front of a lit fireplace. It played out like a ballet. Alex Segal came to me just before we quit for the day and asked me to come up with an improvised line just before I set her down on the rug. He said to go home and think about it over the weekend and come up with something for Monday's shoot. I went home that weekend and as I lit my fireplace, I came up with something that was perfect.

It was my pleasure to play Carol Lynley's lover in Bill Sargent's Electrovision version of Harlow.

I couldn't wait to get to work on Monday to share what I had in mind. Alex asked me if I wanted to tell him and I said no, let's shoot the rehearsal. I told Carol it wasn't anything physical. It was just a psychological gesture and Alex called for action. Just toward the end of the scene, I set her down gently on that beautiful white polar bear rug, so she is now on her back, looking straight up at me.

The camera is on an extremely close up shot of my face and spoke the line I improvised, "Do you like… f… fireplaces? I held on the letter 'f' a little longer; a psychological gesture. I'm sure you get the idea.

Alex came running down from the control booth and kissed me on the cheek. He then thanked me and said that was one of the greatest improvised lines an actor had ever given him. I was thrilled to be appreciated for creativity and again, less was more. After we finished the picture, producer Bill Sargent threw a huge wrap party and invited few members of the press. Ginger walked down to the area where there was food and drinks with a friend of hers, and mingled in with the crowd. She wasn't getting much attention so she went to her dressing room and made a grand entrance wearing a beautiful blue-green dress.

She looked gorgeous! Everyone in the room turned to look at her and the press gathered around her for the rest of the evening. She was a professional and a star, and little did I know it, but this was her goodbye to Hollywood. She never made another movie again.

Years later when I heard Alex was quite ill and hospitalized, I called him and wished him well. He was a lot sicker than he let on. We reminisced about *Harlow* and I told him again how much I enjoyed working with him. Being the gentleman he was, he returned the compliment. I will always remember his energy and enthusiasm. Alex passed away shortly after that in 1977 at the age of 62. Hollywood, for whatever reasons, claimed a lot of lives at such an early age.

On the Ponderosa

The same year, 1965, I got the opportunity to guest star in my favorite western series, *Bonanza*. It was all about family and cast extremely well with Lorne Greene, Michael Landon, Dan Blocker and Pernell Roberts. The stories and production values were first class under the guidance of executive producer David Dortort. The entire country looked forward to seeing the show every Sunday night and did so for fourteen years.

The segment I appeared in was entitled 'The Brass Box' with the former star of the original motion picture *Ben Hur*, Ramon Navarro. The character I played was a well-educated Mexican by the name of Miguel Ortega.

He was schooled back east and returned to live with his uncle, played by Ramon Navarro, near the Ponderosa Ranch. Miguel's uncle was being mocked by the local people because he told them that the Ortega's owned all the land in the area, including the Ponderosa Ranch and he had the documents to prove it. I returned home to find my uncle being ridiculed, abused and threatened for telling such lies.

Mr. Cartwright hired me to work on his ranch, but I still didn't like their condescending attitude toward my uncle and I let them know it. I made it my business to find those important documents placed in a brass box in his ranch house. Everything my uncle said was true; the documents were authentic and the land belonged to him. The papers were authenticated by a local lawyer and agreed by the Cartwright family that the documents were legal. Some of the local characters decided to take the law into their own hands and attempted to kill my uncle. There's a shootout and Little Joe saves my life in the end. My uncle had every right to all of the land including the Ponderosa, but decided not to claim anything. He did not want to destroy what the settlers had developed, and what the Ponderosa and Cartwright family meant to that area.

In one of the sequences, I almost got decapitated. I had a long scene with Lorne Greene and Michael Landon, saddling my horse at the railing of the corral. At the end of the scene, I mounted on my horse and rode off in a full gallop. I had no idea, nor did anyone else, that riding underneath the entrance to the ranch archway was not high enough for me to go through without ducking. No one told me about it, but I was lucky. At the last second, I just made it through by quickly ducking my head underneath the archway. If I didn't, I wouldn't be alive today. That's what I almost got for being tall in the saddle at the Paramount Ranch.

One day while we were shooting interiors at Paramount and lounging in our chairs waiting for the next set up, I overheard Lorne, Michael and Dan talking about a business venture. It had to do with buying land and building condominiums along the shoreline in Marina del Rey,

I actually challenged the pugnacious Cartwright family, playing the highly educated but very arrogant Miguel Ortega. It was a fun role and the cast was great.

California, not far from Los Angeles International Airport. It sounded really good and they were all excited about closing the deal with their business manager, who I believe was Bill Loeb.

I leaned over to Lorne and asked him more about the minimum amount needed to invest. Unfortunately, I didn't have that kind of money to invest at the time, but they made an awful lot of money. It sounded like a winner the moment I heard the area in which they were talking about. I knew the exact location and could visualize the potential. Ah, the perks of stardom.

Immediately after I finished my last scene, I went to my dressing room to take off my wardrobe, when a knock came at the door. It was the assistant director.

"Mr. Dante, don't leave the lot until you see Mr. Dortort in his office. He wants to see you right away," I was told with a sense of urgency. I stopped to see Mr. Dortort and he congratulated me for doing such a good job playing Miguel Ortega.

"I would like you to do a series I'm producing called *High Chaparral* and so far, Cameron Mitchell is cast in the lead," he told me. I asked him what kind of character he had in mind for me to play. He said "The character is a Mexican called, Manolito Montoya."

I told him I wasn't interested because I didn't want to typecast myself in any specific culture. I wanted to be able to play a variety of characters and not pigeonhole my career. He told me to think about it for a day or two. I called the next day and told him I couldn't do it, but thanked him for thinking of me. He said he understood. I told him I knew that the show would be a success because he was producing it. Indeed it was, running for five consecutive years, 1967-1971 on NBC. The role David wanted me to play eventually went to a friend of mine, Henry Darrow, who did an excellent job.

To this day I never regretted not doing the series, although those five years of consecutive work would have helped my pocketbook. With that said, I was able to play so many different types of roles throughout my career without being typecast.

In September 2011, I was invited to The Annual Bonanza Roundup, an event that took place at the Marriott Hotel in Burbank, California. This extravaganza was so special because it was the celebration of the life of executive producer and the creator of *Bonanza*, Mr. David Dortort.

The loyal fans came from every part of the country and around the world to participate in all the events such as visiting the Autry National Center at Griffith Park, including the Hollywood Heritage Museum, visit locations where episodes of *Bonanza* were filmed; Bronson Canyon, Vasquez Rocks, and Paramount Ranch. There was a charity auction, episodic screenings of *Bonanza*, cast panels' visits to Michael Landon and Lorne Greene's gravesites and the unveiling of David Dortort's tombstone.

There certainly was an abundance of activities for the guests. Just a few actors and actresses were invited such as Gregory Walcott, Mariette Hartley, Morgan Woodward, Mitch Vogel, Peter Mark Richman, Richard Hatch, Dave Blocker (Dan's son), Barbara Luna, and me. All the original cast members with the exception of Mitch Vogel are all deceased. I'm just glad I'm still here to celebrate Bonanza's legacy and the people behind this magical show.

46
Get Smart

It wasn't long after my role on *Bonanza* that my agent called to tell me Leonard Stern, producer of the hit comedy show, *Get Smart* wanted to see me at his Paramount Studios office. I couldn't wait to get there because it was one of my favorite comedy shows, and I met and knew Don Adams from a party I attended at Jack Carter's house in Beverly Hills.

After meeting with Leonard he told me that I didn't have to audition and I already had the part. I went home to read the script and laughed aloud at every page. It was that hilarious! I couldn't wait to go to work. The show was so well produced and cast with Don playing bumbling secret agent Maxwell Smart, Barbara Feldon playing Agent 99 and Edward Platt as the Chief.

This comedy, crime, mystery segment was being directed by Gary Nelson and written by two fine comedy writers, Stan Burns and Mike Marmer. The title of the episode was called 'Kisses for KAOS,' starring yours truly playing the lead character, an art gallery owner, Rex Savage. My associate in the episode, Mondo, was played by the fine character actor John Abbott.

Allow me to be a little long-winded about this show because I had the most fun and the biggest laughs in my entire career as it was the first time I was cast in a comedy TV show. The story was that buildings were being blown up in Washington D.C. by paintings that include explosives from my art gallery artist, Mondo. The Chief assigns Agent 99 and Max to check it out, portraying a socialite and her chauffeur. They arrive at the gallery and try, in vain, to take a picture of me as well as get my fingerprints during their stay. Max's fumbling behavior lead me to believe there was something awfully strange about him, as he fails to take the picture or get a fingerprint. What didn't help him was that my character always wore gloves.

I invited Agent 99 on a date to take a drive with me up to Lover's Lane on Mulholland Drive. While getting intimate and caressing her face with gloved hands, Agent 99, wanting to get my fingerprints, asks, "Rex, the gloves are rough and scratchy, do you mind removing them?" I said, "Not at all." I take off the gloves and reach into my pocket for a softer, smoother pair. It was hysterical. In the meantime, Max, observing our date, is sitting in his car with a life-size inflated doll that looked like a woman so it appeared as if he were on a date. He was approached by a police officer who asked him what he was doing there. The funny scene ends with Max trying to explain, saying; "Well, you see officer…" drowned out by lots of canned laughter.

Then, pretending to be attracted to me, Agent 99 invites me to her apartment for dinner to attempt again to get my fingerprints and take a photo. Maxwell Smart poses as her butler and places a bowl of soup with a hidden camera in it, right in front of me.

"Try the soup Rex, I think you'll like it," Max says. I asked him, "What kind of soup is it?"

He answers, "Cream of Technicolor." I laughed so hard, I cried!

We all broke up and couldn't stop laughing. After a couple of takes, we got it right. And needless to say, my associate Mondo and I did not succeed in blowing up the Pentagon.

The show was purely satirical, fun to film and the producers and cast were more than happy with my performance. I really liked doing comedy and wished I could have done more throughout my career. Every time I saw Don socially, we always exchanged a smile and a laugh about the punch line, "Cream of Technicolor."

Maxwell Smart, played by Don Adams is attempting to photograph me from a camera inside his cap as Agent 99, Barbara Feldon tries to make me look in his direction. Didn't work.

47
Crazy Horse

The following year, I guest starred in more episodic television shows and in 1967 I got a call directly from one of my favorite producers, David Weisbart. He bypassed my agent and wanted to discuss what he had to offer to me personally. He produced *Kid Galahad* and we got along well. He was easy going, talented and always a gentleman. I remember him thanking me for the good job I did on that film and he said, "We'll work together again, for sure."

David was one of the finest men in the business, including producing the classic *Rebel Without a Cause* with James Dean. Anyone with a track record like that, you pay attention to.

"I'm going to be the executive producer of the series, *The Legend of Custer*, and I would like you to play the role of Crazy Horse. Up until that time, I didn't want to do a series, but I read a lot about Crazy Horse and I immediately became interested.

David said the two main characters would be Crazy Horse and Custer. It wasn't an easy decision for me to make because I didn't want to get myself into another type casting situation. I told David I would sleep on it overnight and call him back the next day.

I thought about it and rationalized I had done enough work playing many different characters in my young career so far, so I wouldn't be identified only with Crazy Horse. I called David the next day to tell him I would do it. I knew I was in good hands because he was at the helm. He said he would contact my agent and the rest is history.

We had a good cast with Wayne Maunder, an unknown actor playing Custer. He had the same physical build as Custer and looked just like him. He was perfect for the part. The rest of the cast, Slim Pickens, Peter Palmer, Robert F. Simon, Grant Woods, and I were all experienced actors, cast as regulars. After the first couple of weeks the show was moving right along and getting strong ratings.

We were working on location at the Malibu ranch and just before we finished one day, Slim Pickens said that his wife and two daughters were coming to visit the set the following day. He asked me if I didn't mind taking a picture with them. Did I mind? I was flattered that Slim Pickens was asking my permission to pose for a photo with his family.

Slim's family arrived just before lunch hour and I had the pleasure of meeting them. His wife was an attractive blonde and his two daughters were flat out gorgeous. For the next couple of days the whole cast kept ribbing Slim and telling him, "Thank God the girls didn't take after you." He laughed and took everything in stride.

Wayne and I were doing a scene together that called for us to escape from a tribe that had held both of us hostage. We got to the river and at this point, I had to dive into the water while Wayne went in another direction to escape the oncoming pursuit.

Starring as Crazy Horse in the TV series Custer. *Contemplating the survival of his people, the Ogala Souix.*

Crazy Horse's war strategies are used in training the troops at West Point to this day.

The starring cast of Custer. *Top left: Slim Pickens / Top right: Peter Palmer / Middle: Wayne Maunder as Custer / Bottom right: Robert F. Simon / Bottom left: Crazy Horse.*

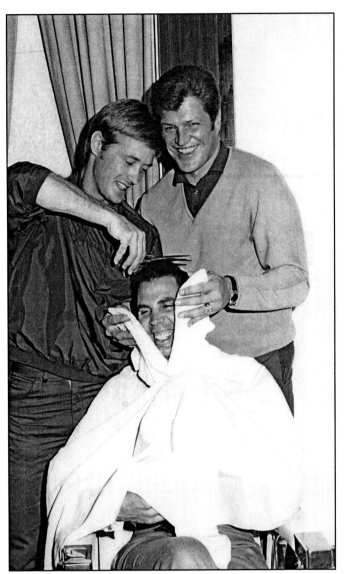

Getting a trim at Harry Drucker's famous barbershop in Beverly Hills, California, by co-stars Wayne Maunder and Peter Palmer.

When I dove into the water my buckskin shirt caught on a limb underwater and as I pulled away to come to the surface, I couldn't break free, so I pulled my shirt from the limb as hard as I could and freed myself. I was out of air at this point, and if I couldn't wriggle out, I would have been in serious trouble.

About the tenth week of shooting we received terrible news that our executive producer, David Weisbart, died of a heart attack on the golf course. The atmosphere on the set for the duration of the series was never the same. We all grew to know and love David, his wife and daughter. He left us at the early age of fifty two. It wasn't long after that the show became the victim of a new political correctness. The character of Lieutenant Colonel George E. Custer was ripped apart by the critics, and the show was off the air after 17 episodes. I was well aware of what was happening with the attitude and behavior of the young people in America at the time. In addition, with the use of drugs and their know-it-all attitude; the young people were rebelling against middle-class ideals. It was totally against the principles my mother and father taught me. Because of the love and respect I had for my mother, father and family, I never once indulged in taking drugs. I would never let them down as long as I live. This change in society limited my social activities because so many in Hollywood jumped on the bandwagon.

That said, the show and the character I played, Crazy Horse, served me well several years later when producer, director Charles B. Pierce saw my work and cast me in the title role, my favorite role of all my films, *Winterhawk*. Sometime after the Custer series went off the air, 20th Century-Fox and ABC decided to edit four of the episodes and make it into a full-length feature film for domestic and foreign distribution. It was called *Crazy Horse and Custer—The Untold Story*. It was also released for television, video and later on DVD. I was okay with that because they had to pay me a salary for a feature film. Through it all, there were some positive career changes that emanated from the series for me.

As always, the best was yet to come.

Live Long and Prosper

After I did my last segment of the *Custer Series* in 1967, producer Gene Roddenberry wanted to see me at his office at Paramount.

I walked into his large, colorful office with *Star Trek* memorabilia and photos displayed on the walls, the counter tops and on his desk. Being around the sci-fi genre of filmmaking was a first for me. Gene said he saw me on a television show a couple of nights before and would like me to guest star with Julie Newmar in a segment of the original series of *Star Trek* entitled 'Friday's Child.'

"You don't have to read for the part because I know and like your work. Read the script and if you like it, you got the part," Gene said. I read the script that night and I loved it, especially with Julie Newmar playing my pregnant wife. I called my agent the next morning to tell him to make the deal. It was a well-written script that had drama, action and comedy. We were the leaders of the Capellan tribe, a group that were tall, handsome and highly intelligent.

The first day of work took place on location at Vasquez Rocks, just north of the San Fernando Valley in Southern California. It was only a 45-minute drive from the studio, but it looked like another planet. It was a popular location for filming science fiction TV shows and films and western movies, as well. We were surrounded by extraordinarily large tan and grey colored boulders. They were so big and tightly packed together that it was difficult for even a small breeze to come and go between the cracks in these rocks. The temperature that day in that dry, sunken, confined area reached well over 100 degrees.

As a matter of fact, our body heat was somewhere around 120 degrees because our wardrobe costumes were heavy and fitted to our bodies with no open areas. I drank all the water I could and still lost seven pounds that day. The cast, crew and the director had a difficult time working throughout the whole day. Joe Pevney, an ex- actor, was our director and a good one at that.

He was having the most difficult time of all, and first aid had to put ice packs around his neck and shoulders to keep him from passing out. Joe was blocking us through a scene, whereby I forfeit my life by getting zapped by Tige Andrews of an opposing tribe called the Klingons. Tige was one of the regulars on the successful *Mod Squad* series. We were all ready to go when Julie suddenly said what every director hates to hear, especially in blistering heat.

"Why am I walking down to this mark? What's my motivation?" Julie said. I looked over at Joe and thought he was going to have a heart attack.

"Julie, it's too damn hot for methodology, just walk slowly to hit that mark and trust me everything will be covered," Joe said firmly.

In Star Trek, *different kinds of outer space weapons were used. Maab is examining, with much suspicion, the Klingon disrupter.*

Joe was right. It was too damn hot to explain everything. It was a piece of mechanical direction and that was all, but Julie, as an actress, was still looking for an answer. It was so hot my boots were squishing with sweat every time I took a step. The cameras had to be iced down by placing padded canvas underneath ice pads to keep the machinery cool. It was one of the hottest and most humid days I ever experienced working throughout my career.

The original *Star Trek* series lasted only three years, but because it ran in syndication for so long, many people thought it was on television much longer. Several years later, I was invited to appear at *Star Trek* Convention in Pasadena, California. Thousands of 'Trekkies' came from all over the world to seek autographs, photos and memorabilia. It was a site to behold. Some were even in costumes worn by their favorite characters in one of their favorite episodes.

The fans stood in line and waited for hours. I asked many of them if they were tired and disappointed to have to wait so long. Not one of them complained. They always made new friends while waiting and had so much to share with each other. I got the biggest kick out of a number of the fans that knew the dialogue I spoke as the character, Maab in 'Friday's Child.' I've appeared at many film festivals and conventions, and without a doubt, the Trekkies never fail to show up in full force and are always the most devoted and faithful fans.

In 1968 my brother, Anthony's daughter Kristen, just turned five years of age and I asked her what she would like to do on her birthday. She answered immediately, "I'd like to go to the San Diego Zoo," which was not far from where they lived in Newport Beach. When her younger brother, John heard where we were going he wanted to come along so the three of us journeyed to San Diego.

It was a beautiful day and we were looking at a variety of birds in a giant birdcage, when I turned and looked over my shoulder. There were four people pointing in our direction and whispering. When we saw enough of the birds in that cage, we moved to the next one directly to our right. I looked over my shoulder again and that same group was much closer now. They were all smiling, giggling and pointing at me. I had no idea who they were as they began to skitter toward us, shouting, "Maab." Then I knew; they were Trekkies.

What was most amazing was that they carried their picture portfolios and prized *Star Trek* possessions to the zoo. I was somewhat bemused and asked them why they were carrying their "stuff" with them to the zoo. Their answer was simple; they carry their portfolios with them all the time because they never know when they might run into one of their favorite *Star Trek* actors. I autographed the picture of Maab that they each had in their portfolios.

Trekkies tell me that this is their favorite original series episode and can actually quote much of my dialogue. I am frequently asked if I still have my wardrobe but it belonged to Paramount Studios where we filmed the show.

The autograph signing and the purchase of memorabilia at the conventions earned a lot of money for Mr. Roddenberry and the principle cast of *Star Trek,* much more than the salaries they received during the three year run of the series. The amount is in the millions and still going strong. I have met a lot of Trekkies during my appearances and they are not only loyal but quite special.

In 2004, I accepted an invitation to a *Star Trek* convention located on the beachfront area of Bellaria, Italy, a resort town about two hours from Bologna on the Adriatic coast. My wife, Mary Jane and I thought we would make it a business and pleasure trip. I accepted the invitation and we immediately began making out our plans.

We stayed in Milan the first night we arrived and the next morning, enjoyed an early train ride to Venice. We stayed four days in Venice, marveling at everything in sight. We spent time people watching in St. Mark's Square, watched the gondoliers rowing and transporting passengers through the waterways and canals, shopping from one end of the city to the other, and enjoying the gourmet food surrounded by so much history and Italian culture. We also enjoyed the water taxi to the outer islands of Murano and Burano. I got a kick from watching the glass blowers in Murano, the handed down art of glass blowing from one generation to another, as told by our group guide on the premises. It was so interesting because one had to work as an apprentice for many years before becoming a master glassblower. It was fascinating to see all of their fine work on display in the different rooms where one could purchase anything they saw.

We left Venice after four beautiful days and headed to the mountain top town of Assisi in a rented car, taking in all the beauty Tuscany had to offer along the way. It was one of the most beautiful drives we have ever encountered. As we approached Assisi, we could see it was located at a higher level from our point of view. We arrived at the point of entry to go to the hotel where we were staying. Cars were not allowed to stay in the area; only to unload luggage and park outside the center of town in the parking lot behind the hotel. I dropped Mary Jane and our luggage in front of the hotel and went to park the car. By the time I got back, Mary Jane had entered the hotel and tripped on the cobblestone entrance.

As she was falling, headfirst, a man exiting the hotel at the same time grabbed her arm, saving her from serious injury. When he lifted her up, Mary Jane thanked him for saving her life.

"I didn't save your life, St. Francis did. You'll see," he said. I arrived a couple of minutes after this happened. Mary Jane told me all about it and we never saw the man again. The clerk at the front desk of the hotel was an aspiring actor who recognized me and knew I was an American actor. He to went on the computer before our arrival and was well aware of my work and who I was.

The hotel staff treated us with open arms. The clerk directed us to a local family owned and operated restaurant for dinner that was superb. All the vegetables, fruit and wine were local and so fresh. The homemade pasta with fresh red tomato sauce and the potatoes and hand fed, local veal, should be a national treasure, it was that flavorful and good. The service and the atmosphere could not have been better. It was a most delicious and memorable experience. After dinner we decided to walk to the church where St. Francis of Assisi is entombed to get our bearings before going to mass the next morning. There is little, if any, change in the town of Assisi since the 15th century.

We heard beautiful music as we got closer to the church and on our left, there were people standing along a stone wall and down below the wall there was an amphitheater with a concert going on. Just as we got there, two people standing next to the wall in the front of a crowd of people watching the concert left and we fell right into their empty space, right up front. The performer was

Maab forfeits his life to save his tribe as he shouts, "Klingon!"

unique and outstanding. He sang and played violin and there were only two other performers on stage with him; a guitar player and a percussionist that played about ten drums rotating from one to the other. I've never heard any anything like it, it wasn't jazz, reggae or pop, it was a combination of all of the sounds and it was fabulous.

The artist had a beautiful crop of grey hair, wore a gorgeous Italian gray silk suit and performed barefoot. His name was Eduardo Branduarte. It was the 750th anniversary of St. Francis of Assisi, and we, without having any knowledge, were there to celebrate this one and only historical event and concert occasion. There were no posters or signs in town advertising the evening. It was just meant to be.

Our quaint hotel had a lovely room for us with a loft where the bedroom was located with the living room and a bath below. There were stairs that led from the living room up to the loft and they were rather steep. Early the next morning before the sun came up I woke up to go down to the bathroom and the room was dark.

Half asleep, I was not familiar with the angle of the steps and fell head first destined to hit my head on the marble top platform at the bottom of the stairs. I threw my arm out and luckily grabbed the post near the bottom of the steps and saved myself. Mary Jane woke up and asked if I was all right and I told her what happened.

"Oh my God, St. Francis saved us again," she said. The man that saved Mary Jane from injury in the lobby upon our arrival was right.

We walked to the magnificent, old world church that was made of stone, marble pillars and stained glass in a fine mist of rain to attend an early morning mass all in Italian; we viewed the aged tomb of St. Francis downstairs, located beneath the church and digested our incredible experience in Assisi over breakfast back at the hotel.

We checked out and just before we were leaving the lobby, the desk clerk came running after me with this huge, beautiful book in his hands.

"Mr. Dante, you must not leave without this book," he said. "It is my gift to you for the many times I've enjoyed your work in the movies and on television." It was the most beautiful hard cover pictorial book about the history of Assisi and St. Francis, which I cherish to this day. We left Assisi experiencing and believing in miracles.

Our next stop was Siena where there is the running of the horses in the square once a year. We got there just in time to enjoy lunch and to linger and people watch for a couple of hours before we left for Bologna. We watched people from all over the world coming and going, enjoying the Siena experience. We only had pizza and a cool drink, but you just can't get a bad meal anywhere in Italy and again, the atmosphere was like being transcended into another time. We continued on and stayed in Bologna for one night.

The next day we were picked up at our hotel and driven by two members of the *Star Trek* committee, who took us to Bellaria. It was a picturesque two-hour drive to the Adriatic side of Italy.

We encountered what looked like old, carefully maintained, large homes made of stone on many acres of beautiful land surrounded by the rolling hills that are so picturesque and typical of the Italian countryside called Tuscany. It was May, the weather was pleasantly warm and there were still fields of sunflowers and pretty wildflowers dressing parts of the landscape along the way. There was not a lot of traffic on the highway so we arrived in good time. We were given a lovely hotel room on the second floor of our hotel overlooking rows of bocce courts, white sand and the Adriatic Sea. The scenery looked like a postcard; picture perfect. There were many bright colored umbrellas pitched into the sand for protection from the sun. Lots of adults and children were at the beach enjoying the day. Men were playing Bocce, an Italian lawn bowling game. It was very amusing. We commented about the contrast at the beach in Italy because the beach scene in Southern California is quite different. Surfboards, bikinis, boardwalks with restaurants and amusement parks with merry-go-rounds, high cliffs and big waves are what we were always used to seeing at the beaches in California.

We were greeted warmly by fans from all over Italy, England and Germany. The convention started at ten in the morning and stopped at twelve noon for a two-hour lunch that consisted of two different kinds of pasta with either red sauce or white, salad, meat, fish or fowl and potatoes served with white and red wine. A variety of desserts were also served with coffee or cappuccino. At two o'clock in the afternoon we went back to our tables to meet Trekkies until five o'clock in the evening. We had time to freshen up and return for dinner at seven o'clock until the singing began two hours later.

This went on for the four days we were there. The convention directors and volunteers were charming and gracious. The Trekkies are pretty much the same no matter where we went, warm, polite, patient and vociferous. It was an awesome experience to remember.

We were driven back to Milan by two lovely ladies, Roberta and Danielle, big fans of mine and *Star Trek* who lived in Milan. We stayed there for two days and got to see the magnificent Duomo in the center of the city that is surrounded by one of the fashion capitals of the world.

One could spend a week scrutinizing and appreciating the engraved front of the five doors of the Duomo. The Duomo, the main Cathedral, is in Cathedral Square, which is the main piazza in Milan. The Duomo took six centuries to complete, but is still under construction to this day.

In 2013, I was cast in the film, *Unbelievable!!!* It's a homage and parody of B-rated Science Fiction films of the 1950s and 1960s. As one of eight in an ensemble of the original series *Star Trek* guest stars plus a special appearance by Captain Kirk, William Shatner, we all gathered and waited for a phone call from a producer for all of us to be cast in a movie called *Unbelievable!!!* The dialogue was hilarious and the play on words in the script was brilliant. We are all over the age of 70 yet we had fun like a bunch of kids. It was hysterical!

In character as producer Michael Dante in 2013's Unbelievable!!!!!

49
The Brotherhood

I received a call in 1968 from director Martin Ritt's office at Paramount Studios. On the line, was his secretary Golda, who I adored. She was a big booster of my work and always kept after Marty to hire me.

Marty got on the line and asked me to come to the studio immediately. I knew Marty for quite some time and had breakfast with him on several occasions at the famous Nate 'n Al's Delicatessen in Beverly Hills, California. He was a big baseball fan and knowledgeable about the game. We both enjoyed our long-winded baseball conversations.

I always respected Marty's opinion and straightforward attitude about any subject matter and of course, his body of work. Some of his films include *Norma Rae, The Black Orchid, The Great White Hope, The Long Hot Summer,* and *The Spy Who Came in From the Cold.* He respected my acting ability and finally found a good role for me to play.

I drove to Paramount as quick as I could and entered his office, met by Golda, who had a big smile on her face. Marty's door was open and he asked me to enter. As usual, we greeted each other warmly.

"I've got a good part for you in this picture. I want you to take the script home and read it over the weekend. Get here around 12:30 Monday afternoon to have lunch with me and Kirk Douglas." I read the script and the part. Marty wanted me to play Kirk's younger brother. We were going to portray Sicilians in a Mafia environment. I thought it was the best part in the script.

On Monday, I drove to Paramount Studios and entered Marty's office at the appointed time. The smile on Golda's face was not there this time around and she wasn't her usual bubbly self. Her chin was down and when she looked up she could barely say hello. I knew as God made apples, something was wrong.

"Is that you Michael? Come on in. What did you think of the script?" Marty asked. I told him it was a terrific part and that I could knock the part out of the ballpark.

"Come on Michael, we'll go to lunch."

"Okay, but where's Kirk?"

"I have some bad news, I'll tell you at lunch," Marty said, barely audible.

We sat down and he told me Kirk didn't want me in the picture. And the reason was that I was much taller, more forceful and my looks made him feel insecure. I couldn't believe what I was hearing because when he ran *Harlow* at his home, friends of mine were there that evening and Kirk told them how much he admired my performance. He wanted to film *One Flew Over the Cuckoo's*

Nest, a script he owned, just the way Bill Sargent filmed in Electronovision, the same way *Harlow* was photographed.

"I know Michael. If I owned the property I would tell him to go to hell, but I don't," Marty said. "He owns the property, and he's the producer so there's nothing I can do."

I thought, having all my great attributes, it would be a compliment to him, but Kirk's ego wouldn't allow it. That was another good role that could have elevated my career to a much higher level at that time. It made me even more determined and more knowledgeable about how cold-blooded some people in Hollywood could be. The movie was called, *The Brotherhood,* produced by Kirk Douglas and released through Paramount Pictures. My friend Alex Cord was eventually cast in the role and did a good job.

And this wouldn't be the last time I lost a movie due to actor's insecurities.

50

My Dancing Career

In 1968, I did an episode of the long running successful series *The Big Valley* starring Barbara Stanwyck, Richard Long, Peter Breck, Linda Evans and Lee Majors. The title of the segment was 'Deathtown.' I played a flamboyant happy-go-lucky character by the name of Francisco.

It was the second time I danced in a western. It was outdoors under the romantic starlit skies in cowboy boots and I spoke in a rather thick Mexican accent. I adapted the accent without any problem, but had to improvise the flamenco dancing on the set near a fire where the scene was to be shot the first day of filming.

Don Taylor, who worked for many years, directed the episode. It was not only the first day of filming, but the first shot of the day. We didn't have a technical advisor or someone to teach me, so I just kept kicking my boots into the dirt and clapping my hands until he said, "Cut." That was some workout; I was completely exhausted after we finished the scene.

The next day the producer Lou Morheim saw the rushes, and came down to the set to discuss with Don why he didn't take more footage of my dancing sequence. They got into a heated discussion and Lou let Don know exactly how he felt. To my surprise, he wanted to see more of my dancing because he thought it was really good. It was unfortunate because there wasn't extra money in the budget of the show to do re-takes for this kind of a scene. So much for my dancing career!

It wasn't all dancing and fun in the script because someone was murdered and I was the accused killer. Richard Long was the star of this episode. He was in hot pursuit of my girlfriend and me thinking I was the murderer and trying to run away.

In the end, Richard's character finds and kills the real murderer, played by actor Jason Evers. Richard and I enjoyed working together because we socialized over the years, and he lived within a half-mile from me in Encino, California. Doug McClure was my neighbor, too. They would love to come to my house for a good homemade Italian dinner, made by yours truly.

Richard called me after the show aired and he teased me about my flamenco dancing. He was a good actor and a nice guy. He was a rarity in Hollywood.

51

Freezing Waters

I appeared in a 1969 episode of *Daniel Boone* opposite Fess Parker, for producer Barney Rosensweig, entitled 'For a Few Rifles.' All of the exterior locations were done at the 20th Century-Fox Studios Malibu Ranch. It was a vast piece of property with a majority of the land donated by Bob Hope. Also, parts of the ranch were purchased from Ronald Reagan. The site consisted of native plants such as sage, chaparral and California oak woodland. The area's habitat included mountain lions, mule deer and golden eagles. The whole ranch was "Old West" in the sights and the feel of the property. It still stands today as a protected area called Malibu Creek State Park.

In this segment, I played a character, Akari, a Native American who captures Daniel Boone's son, played by regular on the show, Darby Hinton. Fess Parker is in hot pursuit of tracking me down. In the process, Darby escapes and heads toward the lake where a canoe rests ashore. He succeeds in getting into the canoe and begins paddling away. I am not that far behind and dive into the water to stop him from going any further. When the stunt coordinator checked the temperature of the water while sitting in a rowboat, he only stuck his arm into the water and found that the first 6 to 12 inches of water was always warm from the hot sun. He didn't actually get in to the water to test it. He just stuck his arm in the water, so when I dove in and came up, I couldn't catch my breath, it was so bitter cold. My objective was to turn the canoe over to prevent Darby from going any further.

Unfortunately, he was not aware of what I was experiencing. If I had a bad heart, I would've gone down and never came up. I became more concerned about Darby. I turned the canoe over and had him in my grasp, but he was now gasping for air. Knowing we would not be able to do another take, I turned Darby and my head away from camera and started to tread water toward shore, where the camera was set up.

Darby was reacting to the shock of the cold water as the 40 yards to shore felt like 40 miles, with my buckskin leather outfit weighing me down. I treaded water with all the strength I had with my right hand and held Darby around the neck with my left arm as we finally made it to the water's edge. I lifted him up and had to carry him while sliding on extremely slippery rocks past the camera lens; I was so elated to finally hear the director yell, "Cut! Print." Everyone came running, including Darby's mother, who was standing next to the camera the whole time. Darby spewed out, "Mommy, mommy, Michael saved my life…he saved my life!"

He was shivering and immediately blankets were wrapped around both of us and we were shuffled off to our dressing rooms to put on dry clothing. The prop man gave me a shot of brandy to warm me up. It was a strange feeling and a close call, but we got the shot. Darby's mom thanked me profusely and we both realized that still water runs deep and very cold.

52

Joltin' Joe and the Rock

In the summer of 1969, I arrived at home late in the afternoon after having enjoyed a couple of sets of tennis with my pals Lloyd Bridges, Ron Ely and Charlton Heston at Dr. Omar Fareed's Beverly Hills home. Dr. Fareed had a beautiful tennis court, where he hosted competitive games all week long. All we had to do was show up and there were always enough players for a good doubles game. Fareed was the doctor for the Davis Cup Team for many years and was well known, loved and respected by everyone in the professional tennis world.

Just as I walked in the phone rang and it was a good friend of mine, San Jose restaurant owner Jack Allen.

"Joe DiMaggio and Rocky Marciano want to talk to you, but first we would like you to jump on a plane and come to the restaurant to have dinner with us. It's only about a 40 minute flight," Jack said.

I told him I wasn't necessarily concerned about the flight but the traffic getting to the airport and parking the car would take much more time. Besides, I had made previous plans that I would have had to cancel for the evening.

"Hang on, Joe wants to talk to you," he said. Joe got on the phone and we chatted a bit. He said the same thing, "Come and join us for dinner." Then, Rocky got on the phone and I told him that it was impossible for me to get there in time for dinner.

"If I knew a day ahead of time I'd be there now," I said, letting him know there was no place I'd rather be, but it was almost impossible to fulfill their wish. Rocky said he was going to be in Los Angeles for two weeks after he celebrated his 46th birthday on September 1, at home with his family in Florida. I told him he was welcome to stay at my house in Beverly Hills and he gladly accepted. We were both looking forward to spending time together. Sadly, Rocky never made it to his home in time to celebrate his birthday.

He was killed in a small plane crash in Newton, Iowa, just outside of Des Moines on August 31, 1969. Rocky was the only undefeated heavyweight champion of all time and a warm, gentle human being. He was another extraordinary person that left us too soon.

I did have the opportunity to get together with Joe Di Maggio a few years before when Jack Allen called me to put a celebrity softball team together to play against Joe's All Star Team in San Jose, California. There were quite a few ex-big league ballplayers living in the San Jose area and Joe put his team together with Hall of Famer Joe Gordon, ex-New York Yankee and Cleveland Indians great second baseman, Dolph Camilli, Dodgers first baseman, Gus Triandos, Baltimore Orioles and Yankees catcher, Don Larsen, Yankees pitcher, Sal Taraomina, San Francisco Seals outfielder, Eddie

It was a joy to call baseball great Joe DiMaggio, my friend. How many kids grow up to know and become close with their idol, no less one of the greats of all time?

Bressoud, San Francisco Giants shortstop, along with some of his ballplayer friends from the San Francisco area. I brought singer, actor Frankie Avalon, Peter Brown, of the *Lawman* series, Norman Alden, a fine character actor, Paul Picerni, a regular on the *Untouchables* series, Doug McClure, a regular on *The Virginian* series and yours truly.

We played the game at the San Jose Bees ballpark the home field of the Class C professional team in the California League. It is now called the San Jose Giants Municipal Stadium, the home ballpark of the Class A affiliate of the San Francisco Giants organization. We had a good game going and were down by three runs in the ninth inning. I came up with the bases loaded when Joe Di Maggio called timeout and came in from the outfield to pitch to me.

It was a dramatic moment as Joe spun one up to the plate and I hit it over the left fielders head, clearing the bases for an inside the park home run, scoring all four runs. We beat the All Stars 8 to 7.

I am the only one in the history of baseball to hit a home run with the bases loaded off Joe Di Maggio. Of course, it was a lob softball game but I couldn't imagine a more memorable moment and I never let Joe forget it! We all celebrated at Jack Allen's restaurant in his private dining room after the game and thanks to invited guest jazz violinist, Joe Venuti, we were entertained royally by his prankster stories and jokes. It was some weekend!

53

Willard and the Rats

I appeared in the original movie _Willard_ directed by Daniel Mann in 1971. Danny had directed two dozen films during his successful career, some of which included _Butterfield 8, The Last Angry Man, Teahouse of The August Moon, Our Man Flint_ and _The Rose Tattoo_ to name a few. We had a good cast, which included Academy Award winner Ernest Borgnine, Bruce Davidson, Sondra Locke and yours truly.

Surprisingly, I grew to like the rats, who were the real stars of the film. I had an educational experience about the critters during the filming of _Willard_. The trainer brought me to the area on

The whole cast of Willard, _literally screaming as the rats were coming into the office. Rats love peanut butter and that's how they're trained to act on command._

the set where he caged them. I was so surprised to see how warm and affectionate they were to each other. They cuddled the whole time waiting for their turn to work. The trainer said that he could tell in five minutes which rats were trainable. He employed the Pavlov method, which used a buzzer to discipline them in the area of work. If they didn't stay in that area, he would hit the buzzer, which meant they would not be given food to eat unless they got back into the working area. They caught on very quickly.

When the rats climbed on Willard's shoulder and then nibbled on his ear to appear affectionate toward him, it was accomplished by 'movie magic.' The trainer did it by placing a small amount of peanut butter on the outside of Willard's ear. On film it looked as though the rat, 'Ben' was giving him little kisses on his ear. It was so interesting to watch the communication between the trainer and the rats. He was so professional and it was obvious he liked his work. He was really responsible for making everything work and making those sequences look so real. I had a much better opinion of rats after we finished the film. I'm always in awe of the many talented people that train and work with animals in our business to make the final product so believable.

The movie was a box office hit and a cultural sensation. One critic gave an interesting review of the film and wrote, "Michael Dante's talent was totally wasted because there wasn't enough of him in the film." I couldn't agree more!

54

Killer Clown

The following year I starred in another film playing a role disguised as a clown who was the thief and murderer in *Thirty Dangerous Seconds* with Robert Lansing and Marj Dusay. I played him with the fantasy of my favorite clown Emmett Kelly, Sr. I saw him perform more than once and he was absolutely brilliant. It was interesting for me to hide behind the comedic-looking innocence of a clown when beneath that makeup lurked an evil character. The role was challenging and like nothing I had done before.

The film was shot entirely on location in Oklahoma City, Oklahoma. It was written and directed by a new filmmaker, Joseph Taft, who was a local. It was the first time I'd ever been to Oklahoma City and found it to be a pleasant place to work in terms of production. We never had any problems with traffic control or any of our 'night for night' chase sequences. The film commission and the city welcomed us with open arms since Joe was a long-time resident and they certainly wanted the business. All of his friends and people in the area were rooting for him to succeed.

One afternoon just before lunch, a friend of our director, Joseph came to visit him on the set and asked us if we liked barbeque ribs. He said he had a special place to take us and these ribs were the best.

We broke for lunch and our host, Joseph and I were off and running to this special place. We drove for a good 20 minutes, weaving in and around oil pumps in an oilfield. We finally came to a stop at this huge gray shack with smoke coming out of its chimney and reeking with the most magnificent aroma. I knew I was in for a treat. There were several other people there enjoying their slabs of ribs and two men standing over this huge fence barbecue pit, cooking away. I ordered a slab of short pork ribs. They were indeed the best barbecue ribs I ever had and the best meal I had in Oklahoma City. Needless to say, Joe and I went back a couple more times before I left for Los Angeles.

Another day, an interesting thing happened to me while shooting in front of the state capitol building. Our assistant director called me aside and said someone wanted to talk to me about a potential project. I met the man and he wanted me to do a commercial for local use only and said it would only run for two weeks.

He asked if I didn't mind coming to his combination antique and jewelry store, located about fifteen minutes away. If I decided to do the commercial, it would take no more than an hour. I had a couple of hours break before the director needed me, so I went with him to his store to see

As an evil clown, a murderer and thief in Thirty Dangerous Seconds.

what we had to offer. He had a beautiful antique shop with gorgeous jewelry placed on black velvet cloths throughout the room. He said he would pay me in cash or we could trade for one of the antiques in the store that I might like. I saw a beautifully hand carved oak bishop's chair that looked like it came from a monastery a century ago. I flipped over it. The price of the chair was the same amount he was going pay me to do the commercial. I told him if he would ship this regal chair to my residence we'd have a deal. He agreed and I still have the bishop's chair in my home. It's worth much more now than when I bartered for it in 1972.

Joseph Taft was a well-liked man and a competent director and I thoroughly enjoyed working with him, but unfortunately the script was the problem. Commercially, it didn't reach the studio's

Going to work in Thirty Dangerous Seconds.

or the public's expectations. On occasion, when I sit in my bishop's chair, I can easily remember the taste of those ribs barbecued in that gray shack stretched out on that oilfield in Oklahoma City. That almost made the experience with it alone.

Directing Triplets

After I finished the movie *Thirty Dangerous Seconds*, I guest starred in an episode of *My Three Sons* starring Fred Mac Murray, William Demarest, Stanley Livingstone and Beverly Garland. The title of the segment was 'TV Triplets.' I was especially excited about doing the show because it was another comedy, and I would be playing a director by the name of Perry Prigrine.

In the story, Perry's job was to direct a commercial in a grocery store with adorable, identical triplets. These boys were little rascals and they sure lived up to their reputation. In the script they had to knock over cans of food that were nicely stacked and, as director, he had to deal with all of the turmoil, several times. The actual director of the segment, Earl Bellamy, had to direct me directing the triplets, so you can imagine this was a bit surreal. It was a hoot and we had a lot of laughs working with these talented children and their stage mother, who was guiding them along the way.

I was looking forward to working with wonderful actor, Fred MacMurray, but unfortunately, he was not in these sequences with me. We played in quite a few celebrity golf tournaments together and I enjoyed him and his actress wife, June Haver. Fred really loved the game of golf. June was always warm and gracious. Fred was a gentleman and was laid back, quiet and reserved off the set. He was noted for his comedy, but showed an awful lot of versatility playing the antagonist as in *Double Indemnity* with Barbara Stanwyck. I enjoyed doing comedy, but unfortunately I was not cast in that genre as much as I would have liked. When I did get the opportunity, my excellent timing and acting ability allowed me to succeed and as Milton Berle, someone that I knew and liked would say, "I got a lot of laugh."

56

The Six Million Dollar Man

In the winter of 1974, I starred in an episode of *The Six Million Dollar Man* entitled 'Dr. Wells Is Missing.' The location sequences were filmed in the mountains of Lake Arrowhead, California, and it was really cold with snow on the ground during the filming. The only accommodations at that time were old cabins, which were heated by gas.

The first night I went to sleep in a warm-up suit, covered myself with heavy blankets and lit the gas heater because it was so cold. Luckily, I woke up about an hour after I went to bed. I heard a hissing sound coming from the heater and noticed the pilot light was out. The smell of gas began to fill the room. I called the office and woke up the manager to come to my cabin right away. I had him change my cabin immediately. I was so fortunate that I wasn't asphyxiated or blown up. He was so apologetic and shaking when he told me I woke up at the right time to shut that gas heater off or God knows what could have happened.

Lee Majors was a real professional and an excellent athlete. He could do many things that his character, Colonel Steve Austin, demanded of him physically. Several months later Lee and I were among the several celebrities invited to Anaheim Stadium to participate in a touch football charity game. I played quarterback, and threw several passes to Lee and I was amazed at the speed he possessed. His cousin was the legendary All-American running back, Johnny Majors, so it was in the genes. I can recall one terrific catch he made on a post pattern I called and he made one of those over the shoulder catches for a touchdown. We easily beat the other celebrities, because of his blazing speed. I did two more shows with Lee when he starred in the successful *Fall Guy* series a few years later. Lee, like most of the young actors who were good athletes, chose to do their own stunts until they began to age a little and injuries began to occur.

I was one of those young actors, but I learned fast that it certainly wasn't worth the risk and also deprived the stunt man of making more money. If the actor had a good double you couldn't tell the difference anyway.

As Julio Tucelli guest starring on the TV series, The Six Million Dollar Man *in the episode,* 'Dr. Wells is Missing'.

57

That's the Way of the World

I got a direct call at my home from producer/director Sig Shore in the summer of 1975. He wanted me to do a movie in New York City about the music business entitled, *That's the Way of the World*. Sig produced and directed the big box office hit *Super Fly*. What made this job so special were the locations; one sequence was shot in my hometown of Stamford, Connecticut. We filmed it at the Rockrimmon Country Club, one of the places where I caddied when I was growing up. Sig was able to put a good cast together for this low budget film, which included Harvey Keitel, Ed Nelson, Bert Parks, Jimmy Boyd and yours truly.

The rest of it was shot in New York City with the exception one sequence at a huge roller skating rink in New Jersey. We began that sequence at midnight and finished at six o'clock in the morning. It was packed with die hard roller skaters, rolling to all the hot musical numbers of the time. The place was a mixture of young and old, who were all having the time of their lives. This was a scene about my character catching up with record producer, Harvey Keitel, about some unfinished business with my uncle's music company. I tracked him down to this roller skating rink. The music was so loud and deafening; I couldn't wait to get out of there. Those skaters danced the whole evening and loved every minute of it. We had a beautiful sunny day to shoot several scenes at Rockrimmon. It was a meeting that took place where no one could hear what the subject matter was about. It was a fun day for me and brought back a lot of memories.

I was able to get several of my friends jobs as extras riding in golf carts and caddying. Now, they could tell all their friends that they were in the movie. Sig made sure two of my best friends Mario DeCarlo and Canio Carlucci were placed closest to the camera. It was so special; friends and family came from all over to watch a day of filming. The rest of the film was shot in skyscraper offices in the Big Apple.

Our locations were so convenient since we were staying at the Warwick Hotel, located on West 54th Street. Since we worked six days a week, my friends came to pick me up Saturday night at the hotel to spend the next day with them or members of my family. We went straight to Stamford, which was only 45 minutes away, to enjoy each other's company and eat some of my mom's good home cooking.

Monday I was back to work and the weather was perfect. Ed Nelson and I decided to pick up some food at the delicatessen near Central Park and eat outside in the park. We were standing waiting for the light to change opposite the park when a thief ripped the pocketbook by the strap off a lady's shoulder standing right next to me and ran as fast as he could in the opposite direction.

At the cast party for That's the Way of the World *with Bert Parks and producer, director Sig Shore with his wife Barbara.*

The poor lady yelled and screamed to no avail. There was nothing Ed or I could do, it happened so fast and he was long gone.

Life in the big city, I guess.

58
Winterhawk: My Title Role

A surprise call came from my agent in September 1975, and it changed the direction of my career and life. He said the agency was sending me a script overnight entitled *Winterhawk*. It was going to be filmed in Kalispell, Montana. He asked me to read it and to call him immediately afterward.

As soon as I read it I called him to convey my enthusiasm. They were interested in me playing the title role of *Winterhawk*. Not very often does an actor have the chance to play the title role in a film. Less than 1 percent of all actors that ever lived have that opportunity. He told me they wanted to see me as soon as I got back to California.

I finished *That's The Way of the World* on a high note and flew to the West Coast with great expectations. I unpacked my bags, rested for a day and caught a plane to Montana to meet Charles B. Pierce, the producer, writer and director of *Winterhawk*. As I walked into the production room where he and his staff were sitting at a long table, Charles stood up and pointed at me as I got closer to him and proclaimed, "You're Winterhawk!" That was the fastest acceptance for a role that I ever had.

After meeting everyone, he said, "We're still doing some re-writing and you will get those changes ASAP. You'll be traveling on September 2 and our first day of shooting will be the following day." I told them that this was a good luck picture for all of us, because September 2 was my birthday.

The weather and location for the film could not have been better. The Big Sky country was in the midst of a beautiful Indian summer. There was no rain or snow and no cold weather to speak of. The sun would shine on the Kalispell trees and turn them a profoundly sparkling golden hue. Nature was the true background for our film, giving us beautifully warm weather to shoot in for September. For quite some time we enjoyed fall temperatures from 70 to 80 degrees. That was really rare for that time of year in Montana.

Our director possessed a wonderful visual talent and took advantage of all that area had to offer. The beauty of the Glacier Park, Flathead Lake, wildlife consisting of elk, deer and buffalos and the golden Kalispell trees made for a perfect background.

We had one of the finest casting of character actors ever assembled in this genre of film. The cast included: Leif Erickson, Denver Pyle, L.Q. Jones, Dawn Wells, Woody Strode, Elisha Cook, Arthur Hunnicutt, Dennis Fimple, Sacheen Littlefeather, and Chuck Pierce Jr.

Winterhawk was not written as a spiritual man. I incorporated that into my characterization with every decision I made for my people, I relied on a greater essence than ego. As a result, I gave the character more color and nuances. This was the first written material I had the opportunity

As young Blackfoot Indian chief and the leader of 'The People' in the title role in Winterhawk.

to make that marriage with this noble leader. Speaking of marriage, the beautiful black and white leopard Appaloosa I rode along with our terrific stuntman, Bud Davis, throughout the film, was half thoroughbred and half Arabian, which gave him the perfect combination of speed and endurance. He was so powerful and spirited, the wranglers had to exercise him two hours every morning to wear him down before shooting. From the first day I rode him, it was like a marriage made in heaven.

He was the most powerful horse I've ever ridden. This was not an animal anyone could ride. I was sitting on him relaxed one afternoon with only my left foot in the stirrup waiting for the camera man to set up his rig to film a close-up of me on the horse by the river's edge. Suddenly, the horse lodged his left hoof between two logs and reared straight up. Luckily I slid off his back side, but not without straining ligaments in my left knee. If I didn't get my foot out of that stirrup in time, I would have been torn to pieces. He bolted out of there like a streak of lightning. The director had to work around me for the next ten days. I had to wear a full length leg cast and go for whirlpool treatments every day. The ligaments were stretched to the limit, but not torn, so I was as good as new after the treatments. The day they removed the cast, I brought it to Elisha Cook's room. I thought we'd have some fun putting it on his leg, and have Woody Strode wheel him into the dining room for everyone to see. I stayed in the background and watched everything unfold. Charlie Pierce almost had a heart attack when he saw Elisha with that full-length cast on his leg.

We all had a good laugh and it was back to work the next day. There was a lot of tracking scenes to be done with the mountain men, so there was no time lost. For several weeks, a fine artist, Bob Wood, followed me to get the right background he was looking for to paint a life-size portrait of me as *Winterhawk*. I remember the day he was behind me, clicking his camera as fast as he could and kept saying, "I got it, I got it." I was standing on a bit of a rise looking at the blue and red Montana sky above beautiful Kalispell trees full of golden leaves. He was so happy with all smiles and said, "Now I have the background I was looking for and I can start painting the portrait." All he wanted in return was the publicity. I told him I would have the Associated Press and United Press there when we had an unveiling. A couple weeks later, Governor Thomas E. Judge was having a dinner party for the whole company at the Governor's mansion. I asked him if we could have the unveiling of the portrait that evening.

He thought it was a great idea and had his staff make all the arrangements to have the necessary press there to cover the event. The artist, Bob Wood was grateful for the exposure. He expressed his thanks for getting more coverage and recognition than he had ever dreamed of. Bob did a fantastic job and to this day the portrait sits above my fireplace to remind me of the many memorable days I enjoyed making *Winterhawk*.

We finished eight weeks of filming, which brought us into November and we didn't have any white stuff to shoot our snow sequences. Charlie Pierce was patient and thought we would have snow any day but two weeks past and still nothing. There wasn't snow in the whole country at

Winterhawk sitting on his magnificent leopard appaloosa, half Arabian and half thoroughbred.

Winterhawk leaving for battle dressed in full warrior regalia.

With portrait artist Bob Woods and his wife at the unveiling of his portrait of me as Winterhawk at Governor Thomas E. Judge's mansion in Kalispell, Montana.

the time and he was thinking of taking the company to Alaska. He had to do something, because everyone was on the payroll and not working. During that period we spent a lot of time at our headquarters, The Outlaw Inn.

They had a terrific country and western band playing there during our stay and the place was packed night after night. Everything about it was western. They played the song "Delta Dawn" three times a night and everyone danced and sang to it every time. One night Woody Strode had

Ahhhh… finally, above the title billing after twenty years in the biz!

a few too many drinks and shot two arrows into the dining room ceiling. The last time I looked before we left, they were still embedded.

At the end of the second week we got word that there was snow in Purgatory, about 20 miles south of Durango, Idaho. The whole company packed up and drove in tandem to the location. It was a cold, rough ride and when we arrived there Saturday night, it was snowing so hard we could hardly find the lodges. We rested Sunday and started shooting Monday morning. The United States ski team was training there, because that was the only place that had snow in the whole country at the time.

Leif Erickson, Woody Strode, and I were sitting side by side having breakfast in the commissary in western costumes and me in full Blackfoot regalia facing the entrance door when several members of the ski team entered shaking the snow off their boots and making their grand entrance. They were speechless and couldn't believe what they were seeing. We all broke up laughing and explained what we were doing in there.

Before I left for home I asked Charlie Pierce if I could buy the Appaloosa, and he said no because he was taking him back to Texarkana. That was the last thing I said to him before I said goodbye, was, "Make sure you let only an exceptionally good horseman ride that animal or he will hurt someone or himself." Just before Christmas of 1978, the phone rang at my home in Rancho Mirage late at night while I was asleep. It was Charlie Pierce on the other end to tell me the sad news about the Appaloosa. He said he let a friend ride the horse on his ranch and he threw the rider to the ground. The rider held on to the end of the reins while the horse was throwing his head from side to side and hit a pole, breaking his neck.

"They had to put him down," Charlie said. My heart just sank and the image of that magnificent animal galloped before me in the dark. That was the last time I ever spoke with Charlie. Sadly, he passed away in 2011.

An actor friend of mine by the name of Len Di John asked me to meet him for lunch at the famous Hollywood restaurant, Musso & Frank's Grill on Hollywood Boulevard. After lunch, he asked me to walk down the block because he wanted to show me something. I had no idea what he was talking about until I was surprised and thrilled to see my name above the title of *Winterhawk* on the marquee outside a Hollywood movie theater. It was the first time my name was above the title of any of the films I had done. It was an awesome sight to behold and one of the most rewarding highlights of my career.

Superstars Competition

59

In the spring of 1976, I received a surprise phone call from producer Shelly Saltman at ABC-TV. He asked me if I'd be interested in competing in the celebrity *Superstars* competition in Rotonda, Florida. At the time it was a popular Saturday afternoon show and allowed audiences to see the more human side of celebrities and sports stars by placing them in fish-out-of-water experiences. I said I would like very much to go and in a couple of days I was on my way.

I was in good shape because I was jogging six days a week and playing tennis in between. The flight to Florida was smooth until we got into the Atlanta, Georgia, area where it was raining so hard and thundering and lightning that we couldn't land. The plane was actually hit by lightning and we had to circle the airport for two hours before touching down. We finally landed but I missed my connecting flight. There was a later flight to Fort Lauderdale and I was grateful that American Airlines provided a driver to take me to the other side of the airport to catch that last plane. I had called ahead to producer Don Ohlmeyers' office to tell them I would be on the last flight to Fort Lauderdale. I landed in Fort Lauderdale after a bumpy ride and was greeted by a driver from the network.

I was exhausted, stressed out and for the next 90 minutes I was driven to Rotonda West where the competition was being held. We got there around 4 a.m. and had to wake up the night clerk to show me to my room. We were all staying in condominiums. He escorted me and gave me an itinerary and schedule for the following morning. I barely got to sleep and had to get up at seven o'clock, ready for competition at eight sharp.

I dressed as quickly as I could in the uniforms they provided and headed for the commissary for a quick continental breakfast. I was starving and only had time to gulp down a glass of juice, piece of toast, cup of coffee and I was on my way to play my first tennis match, but not before we were all introduced to one another. The introductions began with ABC-TV producer of the tournament Don Ohlmeyer, hosts O.J. Simpson and Keith Jackson followed by the competing celebrities, Peter Benchley, Oleg Cassini, Chris Connelly, Robert Duval, Peter Duchin, Kent McCord, Kenny Rogers, and Bill Withers. We had to choose to compete in five of ten events.

I selected tennis, bicycle racing, bowling, weightlifting and a homerun-hitting contest. I broke National Football League Hall of Famer Franco Harris's homerun hitting record, one I still hold to this day. All of the highest scoring celebrities competed in the final obstacle course event on the last day.

I was the only celebrity who scored in every event in which I competed. O.J Simpson asked me why I didn't run the hundred yard dash. I told him I was afraid I might pull a muscle because I had been on the plane all night, had no time to prepare or stretch, unlike the others had, who were preparing for several days before.

Publicity headshot during the Superstars Competition.

Hitting the record-breaking homerun previously held by NFL Hall-of-Famer Franco Harris. It's a record I still hold to this day.

I was awfully tired the final day competing in the obstacle course event and was only one point behind Robert Duval, who won first place in all of the swimming events. I got over the wall quickly, but lost my concentration and timing, straddling the rubber tires. I had to go back and do it a second time. That cost me quite a few bucks. Robert Duval placed first winning $14,600, Kent McCord, who played football at UCLA, finished second, banking $9,500 and I finished third, taking home $6,500. Despite the frenetic schedule and harrowing experience on the plane, I had a competitive good time and made some money too.

But the biggest windfall I received was on ABC who televised the event. They played a scene from *Winterhawk*, which featured a huge close up of me. That's publicity you simply cannot buy. Needless to say, the producer/director, Charles B. Pierce was thrilled with the results. It was a big plus for us at the box office.

Hoisting 150 lbs. over my head in the weight lifting category of the competition.

After a very close and exciting bicycle race, celebrating here with Robert Duvall, Keith Jackson and Kent McCord. We were all completely exhausted.

My Celebrity Tennis Tournament

Tennis swept the country in the 1970s and it was certainly one of my favorite pastimes as well. One of my best friends who later became the best man at my wedding, Mario De Carlo, asked me if I would host a celebrity tennis tournament at the Italian Center in Stamford, Connecticut. I gladly accepted. The money raised would go toward transporting underprivileged children to and from the Center. They would have access to all the recreational facilities there; the gym, swimming pool, tennis courts, baseball field and equipment.

I was asked to bring several celebrity tennis players and their wives to the tournament. I rounded up a wonderful group of players; Lorne Greene and his actress wife Patricia Evans, Eric Braeden, Ben Murphy, John Marley, Huntz Hall, Cornell Wilde and his actress, wife Jean Wallace, Gary Crosby, Robert Loggia, Ed Ames, Ron Ely, Doug McClure, Bert Parks, heavy weight boxing contender Jerry Quarry and Joe DiMaggio.

We all left from the Los Angeles International Airport except Joe DiMaggio, who came in from San Francisco. We arrived Friday night in Stamford and the tennis matches started Saturday morning and finished Sunday evening with a wonderful dinner and the presentation of the winners. Bert Parks did an outstanding job as the Master of Ceremonies and he and his wife Annette generously donated $5,000 to the charity.

That was the first time there were that many big name Hollywood celebrities attending a single event in Stamford. It wasn't a huge financial success because of the costs of accommodations and transportation from one coast to the other, but on every other level, it could not have been better. The tennis, food, the camaraderie between the stars, the players and the attendees went extremely well. The participants had several opportunities to communicate and play tennis with the celebrities, which was the icing on the cake. We had a large autograph table roped off so the fans could take pictures and get autographs from the stars in a comfortable orderly fashion.

The most popular of all the stars was Joe DiMaggio. Even the celebrities were in awe of him. He had that special charisma and dignity that set him apart from all other athletes. I can't describe how happy I was that he was able to attend, even though he never lifted a racket. He was also a close friend of our mutual friend, Canio Carlucci, who knew more jokes than Milton Berle. That weekend Canio had Joe laughing the whole time.

Joe really enjoyed himself and always reminisced about what a nice time he had in Stamford at my tennis tournament. Years later, after I married my wife Mary Jane in 1992, he always insisted we sit with him at many of the celebrity golf tournaments we attended together.

Making a crisp volley while hosting the Celebrity Charity Tennis Tournament at the Italian Center in Stamford, Connecticut.

Congratulating the winners of the men's doubles matches, Lorne Greene and Chris Connelly.

With heavyweight contender, boxer Jerry Quarry and, chairman of the Michael Dante Charity Celebrity Tennis Tournament, Mario De Carlo, who years later was the best man at my wedding.

Mary Jane and me with Joe DiMaggio at the Warner-Lambert Celebrity Golf Tournament in Florida.

Thank you, Joe. Since seeing you play for the first time when I was a youngster at Yankee Stadium, it was a dream come true getting to know you. In my opinion you were the greatest all-around baseball players of all time.

61

John Wayne Charity

While *Winterhawk* was playing in the theaters I received a phone call from Pilar Wayne, wife of actor John Wayne. She asked if I could help raise money for her husband's favorite charity for child abuse. It would be held at a restaurant in Newport Beach, California. I had the pleasure of knowing Pilar, Patrick, Michael, Aissa and Marisa Wayne from celebrity tennis tournaments we all participated in, but had never met "Duke." How could I say no to such a great American icon, whose movie *Stagecoach* just happened to be my favorite all-time western? I gladly accepted and was looking forward to meeting Mr. Wayne. She told me Patrick and I would be auctioning all sorts of ladies items donated by the local merchants in the area.

When the time came, Pilar introduced me to a warm and receptive audience and praised my performance as the star of *Winterhawk*. Most of the ladies in the audience saw the movie because it had been recently released in the area. There were no men invited to this luncheon-benefit except the owner of the restaurant, Duke, Patrick and myself.

Pilar introduced me to Duke and he grabbed my hand firmly with his big paw and said, "Michael, all I want to be is your friend."

"Yes, Mr. Wayne, I want to be your friend, too," I smiled, shaking his hand.

"Call me Duke."

"Yes, Mr. Wayne." I was in awe and had so much respect for him I just couldn't call him Duke until I got to know him better and earned it. I had met some legends in my day, but none were bigger than Duke Wayne.

Patrick and I had a lot of fun auctioning all the items and doing a good job, as a matter of fact. During the course of that afternoon we netted $51,000 with 100 percent of the money going to the Duke's favorite charity. Mr. Wayne sat there at the front table with a big smile on his face the whole time, enjoying our auctioning of the items and our clowning around on stage.

Duke was happy with the results and thanked us both for doing an excellent job. It was a special afternoon and we were all proud and happy for the children. The following year Pilar called me again to assist Mr. Wayne and this time my co-host was actor Jack Kelly, who played James Garner's brother in the *Maverick* series at Warner Bros.

Jack and I knew each other well. Everyone seemed to enjoy the fun auctioning off all the goodies. When everything was all said and done, we raised $52,000 the second year.

A few months later, I was visiting my brother Tony, his wife, Jan and their two children, Kristen and John, in Newport Beach. We went out to dinner at Matteo's restaurant located on the Pacific Coast Highway. We walked into the restaurant and sitting alone in a booth at the far corner of the

My friendship with John Wayne was one of the great honors of my life. 'The Duke' was truly a living legend and a gentleman.

room, waving his hand, beckoning us in his direction, was John Wayne. We went to his table and I introduced him to everyone.

"I finally got a print of *Winterhawk* from Charlie Pierce and we saw it at my house a couple of nights ago. You did a terrific job," he said. "Let me tell you if I didn't know you, I would've thought you were an Indian. I've got a great script you and I are going to do. It'll take a while to put it together. I'll be able to tell you more about it when I see you at the next luncheon." I was so happy and excited I was speechless. Another one of my dreams was about to come true; there was no other actor in the world I'd rather work with than John Wayne. I walked on air the rest of the evening.

The third and last charity we did was at the same place with only the ladies invited again. Patrick Wayne and I again teamed up to do the last one. We raised another $51,000. There was never any publicity or fanfare for these charity luncheons and other events he supported. Duke thanked me again and said he was going to Hartford and would contact me about doing a movie together when he got back. That was the last time I ever spoke with him. I received a note from Duke a few weeks later saying that he had some things to take care of and he would be in touch with me. He never mentioned his illness and in 1979 at the age of seventy-two he passed away from cancer.

Duke Wayne was a very special man and a giant in the movie industry. What you saw is what you got. I wish I could have gotten to know him even better, but I'll cherish our short-lived but meaningful friendship.

62

Grand Marshal

The winter of 1976, I was invited to be the Grand Marshal of the Winter Carnival in Whitefish, Montana, less than hour drive from Kalispell. They played *Winterhawk* in the theater while I was there and the film was a big hit in the community. It was a riot because everywhere I was invited to in the town, we went by sled. The snow was hard-packed and perfect for sleigh rides. The rides reminded me of something out of a storybook and a movie I saw when I was growing up called, *Christmas in Connecticut*. It was magical.

I was asked to go to breakfast, lunch and dinner with various dignitaries and committee members that were involved in making the annual Winter Carnival a success. I was even given skiing lessons, ski clothing and skis at the Big Mountain ski resort, located near Whitefish. It was all part of the business agreement I made with them for my appearance in the parade and the honor of being their Grand Marshal.

In three days, I learned to ski and had the time of my life. Since then, I have skied in Colorado, Utah, California and Idaho many times, thanks to my short, fun-filled stint as Grand Marshal of the Winter Carnival in Whitefish, Montana.

Washington, D.C.

On January 27, 1977, I was invited by Connecticut House of Representatives Christopher J. Dodd to attend the National Prayer Breakfast in Washington, D.C., held at the International Ballroom in the Washington Hilton Hotel honoring the incumbent President Jimmy Carter. It was sponsored by the United States Senate and House of Representatives prayer breakfast committee. I was told that representative Christopher J. Dodd was a movie buff and he had seen *Winterhawk* and enjoyed it very much. I had never been to Washington D.C and the prospects to visit the Smithsonian Institute as well, so I accepted immediately. At that time Washington D.C. was being inundated with people coming from all over the world and I had a difficult time finding a place to stay.

I finally found a hotel room the size of a matchbox. I think it might have been a supply room at one time. I literally walked into the room sideways to get to the closet and bathroom, it was the only room left in all of the nation's capitol and I was lucky to get that. I arrived the night of January 26 and the next morning I took a taxicab to the Washington Hilton Hotel. I entered the International Ballroom and was ushered to my assigned table. I was greeted by and gifted with one of the most pleasant surprises of my life, when I was seated next to Bishop Fulton J. Sheen, one of the most prominent, brilliant, charismatic Catholic leaders in American history. He was undoubtedly one of thee most important Catholics of the 20th Century. We talked briefly before the official commencement of the breakfast. People surrounded the table to talk, take pictures and gathered to get an autograph from Bishop Sheen.

He was the hit of the floor; people remembering the many years he radiated his humor, charm, intelligent and acting skills throughout the years of his successful television series, *Life is Worth Living*. I was a big fan of the Bishop's for many years.

The bell rang at 9:09 a.m. and we all stood up to greet Texas House of Representatives James C. Wright, Jr. to deliver the introduction of President Jimmy Carter. He began with several quotes from the Bible without any assistance from notes or a teleprompter. He finished but not before he introduced and brought President Carter to the podium. Again we all stood up and were seated to hear the president quote the Bible just as Representative Wright did. When President Carter finished we all stood up as he made his exit, Bishop Sheen turned to me and said, "Michael, I think we inherited a couple of preachers."

That same year, 1977, Bishop Sheen had open heart surgery and went to heaven in 1979 at the age of 84, but not before he wrote 66 books and countless articles. The good Lord enriched my life again by allowing me to meet this totally brilliant and holy man, Bishop Fulton J. Sheen.

I wasn't the only one from Hollywood that was invited to the President's Breakfast. Actor Dean Jones and his actress wife, Lory Patrick, were also invited. Dean Jones was known for his lighthearted roles in several successful Walt Disney movies, most notably *The Love Bug*. Coincidently, we were both under contract to MGM Studios at the same time and had small parts in our first movie, *Somebody Up There Likes Me* starring Paul Newman. We were escorted by one of Representative Dodd's aides to several historic and most interesting Washington landmarks such as the Supreme Court and the Senate and House of Representatives floor. Time was running short and I rushed to visit the Smithsonian Institute, albeit brief, before I caught my plane to New York City to spend a couple of weeks with my family. It was another special experience I will always cherish. Maybe even a small miracle.

The Farmer In Atlanta

Next role after *Winterhawk*, I co-starred with Gary Conway and Angel Tompkins in the movie, *The Farmer* (1977). It was filmed outside of Atlanta, Georgia. *The Farmer* was the most violent film I ever worked on, but was happy it was a part of my filmography. As the story goes, Kyle Martin, played by Gary Conway, returns from Vietnam as a "Silver Star" hero. He realizes that running a one man farm is not profitable and the bank wants to foreclose on his property. My character, Johnny O, a degenerate gambler, has a car accident near Kyle's farm and Kyle saves his life. Johnny O offers him $15,000 to keep his farm but it's not enough. To help Kyle, Johnny O bets on a horse race for $50,000 but in doing so he angers a local mobster bookie involved. The mobster, played by George Memmoli and three of his henchmen blind Johnny O (me) with acid for past-posting, which is betting off-track on the winning horse just before he crosses the finish line. He tells his girlfriend, Angel Tomkins, to convince Kyle, who was quite capable of the assignment from his war training, to kill the mobsters one by one for revenge and to get the $50,000 back.

During the filming, it was the baseball season and the Atlanta Braves ballpark was about a 45 minute drive from our hotel. The Braves were hosting a home stand playing against the Pittsburgh Pirates. I had an off day and called Donald Davidson the road manager for the Braves, who I knew from my playing days. Donald was delighted to hear from me and invited me to the ballpark. I told him I needed a good workout and asked if he would mind if I worked out with the team.

"By all means," Donald said. "I'm looking forward to seeing you."

Donald was aware of my transition from baseball to the acting profession. We stayed in touch over the years and got to see each other on several occasions. It was a beautiful and sunny day and I suited up, ready to go to work. I was in good shape because in those days I was jogging at least five days a week. I got out to my shortstop position and none other than Hall of Famer Luke Appling began to hit me ground balls. I still had a lot of range and he moved me around pretty good. He didn't know who I was, but I learned later from second baseman Marty Perez and third baseman Darrell Evans, how much he was impressed with my hands and range. Coming from Luke Appling, it was some compliment. Looking to my right in between ground balls, I could see Pirates Manager Danny Murtaugh talking to General Manager Joe L. Brown at the top of the Pittsburgh Pirates dugout steps.

They began to look in my direction and I could almost feel the wheels turning in their heads with Danny asking, "Is that the former ballplayer Ralph Vitti who became an actor and came to spring training in Huntsville, Texas, with us when I was managing New Orleans in the Southern Association?" They both came walking toward me, smiling and I jogged in their direction with a big grin on my face.

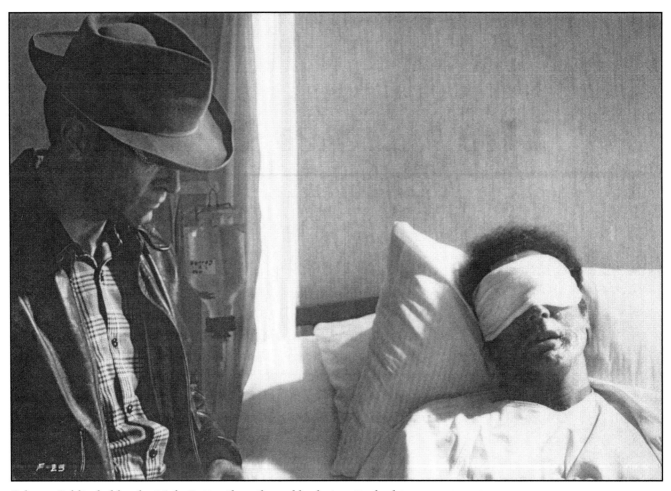

Johnny O blinded by the Mob. Better than the ankle chain attached to cement contract.

"Yes, it's me, but now the name is Michael Dante," I said. They said they knew because they had been following my career. They were impressed that I stayed in shape and hadn't changed a bit since they last saw me. I told them what I was doing in Atlanta and invited them to come to the location where we were filming. Unfortunately, they were leaving after the game that night and couldn't make it. I later had a chat with Luke Appling and he thought I was a new infielder just brought up from the minor leagues.

I gave him a brief rundown of my background and told him I used his S2 model bat when I was playing. "I was hoping one day I would meet you, to tell you about using your model bat and becoming a better hitter. Looks like I got my wish," I told him. He smiled and said, "You still have great hands!"

65

Cruise Missile

My next gig came along in 1978, an urgent call from producer Ika Panajotovic's wife, Elena, who was instructed by her husband to hand deliver a script to me entitled *Cruise Missile*. Ika wanted me to read it right away. He said if I liked it and agreed to do it, I would be on a plane to Teheran, Iran, in less than forty eight hours.

Mike Connors of *Mannix* was originally cast in the part but he bowed out and returned home. I read it and found the character to be a new and different one for me. I would play a Russian KGB agent, co-starring with Peter Graves, Curt Jurgens and Iranian actress Pouri Banai. The film was going to be directed by Les Martinson, who I had worked with several times at Warner Brothers. It was a co-production project with the Iran, Austria, Spain and American participation. We were scheduled to film five weeks in Teheran, Abadan and Esfahan in Iran, five weeks in Vienna, Austria, and two weeks in Barcelona, Spain. I had never worked in a film outside of the U.S. before. It sounded like an adventure, as well as working with two actors whose work I respected.

Ika called me from Iran and we made a deal over the phone without speaking with my agent. He told me to buy a couple of suits that I would wear for the character's wardrobe in the film and charge it to his account, which I did. Forty eight hours later I left on a plane from Los Angeles to New York City. There I had a two hour layover and then flew nonstop to Teheran in fourteen hours. There was plenty of room on the plane, so I laid out several pillows and blankets across four seats, lifted the armrests and got several hours of good sleep before I arrived in Teheran the next morning. When I arrived, there was no Ika to meet me. I waited about 20 minutes and all of the passengers from plane had left. Luckily, I had the phone number of the hotel where the company was staying in my wallet. I got Ika on the phone and read him the riot act. "I got confused with the time schedule," he said apologizing and arrived about a half hour later.

I knew we were in for some interesting times because there were Russians staying at the same hotel and we were involved in a cold war with Russia at the time. I had dinner with Ika that night and several of the Russian soldiers were singing folk songs at the top of their lungs in the dining room and could not have cared less who didn't like it. Several nights later, a member of our crew played piano and we sang American songs as loud as we could in their presence. On one occasion, I thought we were going to get into a donnybrook with the Russians and thanks to management that was squelched. After a few drinks it was obvious both sides did not particularly care for each other. About a week into shooting, a member of the Iranian crew who did not speak English approached me, barking out Farsi words, which sounded like he was angry with me. Our first assistant director, Amir, spoke perfect English and Farsi. I looked at this character and asked him what the problem was. All of the Iranians around who heard what he said began laughing and I said, "All right, let me in on the joke." Amir, through fits of laughter, said, "Michael, he would like to invite you to his home to meet his family and join them for dinner on Sunday."

I learned then and there that Farsi was not the easiest language in the world to understand, by any means. Yes, the joke was on me. I met his wife and two children. The food was good and they couldn't have been nicer.

Tehran was not a good city to film exteriors. The daily traffic was bumper to bumper with cars, trucks and scooters mixed in with horns blowing constantly. There were accidents every day in the city; mostly people riding scooters trying to weave in and out of traffic.

When I had a day off, I went window shopping for a pair of old dueling pistols to take back to the States. I found an antique shop close to the American Embassy, where I enjoyed observing two of our U. S. Marine's standing at attention outside of the entrance. This is where 52 Americans were taken from and held captive for 444 days by radical Iranian students.

For as long as I live, I will always remember the front of the American Embassy, where it all occurred. We finished shooting in Tehran and flew to the oil business city of Abadan to film some scenes there for several days. The hotel accommodations there were not the best but they did have a clay tennis court on the premises. The oil executives flew from Tehran to and from Abadan in their private jets on a daily basis after doing business, rather than stay at the local hotels. Our producer, Ika, was one of the greatest tennis players Yugoslavia ever produced. He was a member of their Davis Cup Team and destined to make his mark in the tennis world. He was 6 feet 5 inches tall with great range, speed and possessing all the shots.

While in the service in Yugoslavia, he went home on furlough to be with his family and unfortunately got into a terrible automobile accident and suffered a broken leg. He was never the same player again, but he still could play excellent social tennis. The local tennis pro and his assistant challenged Ika and me to a match. We had a pretty good audience watching and we beat them handily.

They couldn't comprehend that a producer and actor beat two Iranian professional tennis players in two sets after we had already finished our day's work. We were not professionals, but we knew how to play tennis well, in addition to our other talents.

The following morning was a Sunday and we had a day off, and I certainly wanted to sleep in. About eight o'clock that morning there was a hard, loud knock on my door. I opened the door only to be greeted by two sullen men. It was the two professional tennis players we had beaten the day before, demanding a rematch. I told them that we would accommodate them later in the day.

I got in touch with Ika and a couple of hours later we were on the courts again and beat them in two straight sets. They took the losses extremely hard and personal. It really was an indication of the machismo mentality of the Iranian male—something President Carter didn't quite understand at the time. We were lucky *we* weren't held hostage.

We finished our work there and left to film the rest of our Iranian locations in the city of Esfahan. We stayed in a Taj Mahal domed hotel called the Shah Abbas. There was a lot of history associated with the hotel and we had the privilege of staying there only one year after it was renovated. All of the interior murals and paintings were done by fine Italian artists imported from Italy. It took them quite some time to finish their work. The Shah built it for his wife and it was their getaway to the tranquility of the desert. It was magnificent and of course, extremely expensive. Many, many years before the hotel was built, different tribes came to Esfahan with their merchandise to trade with one another and enjoyed their extended stay in the city, as well.

We filmed several of our interior sequences in the hotel, surrounded by all the beautiful Italian artwork on the walls and the ceilings. We filmed a couple of sequences on the streets in the city of Esfahan and a location about 45 miles east to the Varzaneh desert. On our return to the Shah Abbas after work one day, while riding through the desert in the front seat of the company limousine, I noticed a person jogging on the road. I asked the driver to slow down. The jogger had a sweat suit on and a white towel around his neck.

His car was about a half a mile down the road ahead of him and I imagined that was his destination. It was about 115 degrees outside our air conditioned car and I turned to see who the maniac running in triple digit temperatures was. It was none other than actor Anthony Quinn, who had just arrived a couple days ago and was staying at the Shah Abbas Hotel, too.

He was starring in a film entitled *Caravans*, a screenplay adapted from the James Michener novel of the same title. The rest of the cast consisted of Michael Sarrazin, Christopher Lee, Jennifer O'Neill and Joseph Cotton.

I played tennis with Anthony a couple of times in the past, once at director Daniel Mann's house in Malibu, California and another time in a mixed doubles match at Robert Stack's house in Bel Air with Rosemary Stack and Edgar Bergen's, wife Francis. Quinn was paired with Rosemary and Francis was my partner. Quinn was so competitive and we always beat them. He was a blamer and pretty tough on Rosemary, but we always wound up laughing and had a good time.

I saw Quinn briefly at the hotel before we left for Athens, Greece, for a couple of days of R&R. We stayed at the Hilton Hotel in Athens and my room was on the fifteenth floor. I remember the howling wind out on the terrace that almost blew me off my feet. I could see the Acropolis from my window. It was all lit up at night and it was a sight to behold.

The next day we visited the Parthenon and spent some time at the Scipio where they kept the lions and where the gladiators trained. It was a unique and wonderful experience to fantasize, walking among 2,000 years of history.

We left there for a walk in the market place and enjoyed a typical Greek salad for lunch with black olives, feta cheese and pure Greek olive oil. I topped it off with a thick cup of espresso that was so strong it made my teeth rattle, but the taste was coffee, coffee. We really enjoyed ourselves taking in as much as we could of Athens and the Greek people, food and the surroundings in such a short period of time. Two days later we landed in Vienna to an entirely different culture and atmosphere. Curt Jurgens, his mistress, Peter Graves with his wife and I stayed at the famous Sacher Hotel in the heart of Vienna, opposite the Vienna Opera house. The hotel was the home of the famous and delicious Austrian pastry, the Sacher Torte.

I liked everything about Vienna including the hotel and the people, the opera house, the Lipizzan Arena, where they trained the beautiful Lipizzaner stallions and of course, the food. St. Peters Church was spectacular and the unique experience of tasting the wines from giant vats beneath the surface of a rock formation at one of our locations was all new to me.

We filmed 'night for night' sequences at the gambling casino in the spa town of Baden, a short distance from Vienna.

I also enjoyed the small Lugwig van Beethoven Museum. Beethoven enjoyed spending summers in Baden, and partook in scenic walks near the Museum. The outside and inside of St. Peter's Church was just magnificent. It is a Roman Catholic parish and the interior with several altars was all Baroque. If you don't get the feeling of reverence while you're there, you never will. The same applies to the St. Augustine Church, full of ornately carved wood. It was the first tasting of the wine in Vienna and Curt Jurgens with his mistress, decided to give himself a birthday party

As Konstantin, a KGB agent in the film, Cruise Missile *with actor Peter Graves on location outside of a mosque in Tehran, Iran.*

in the caverns where those huge vats were located.

There were several plateaus with tables and chairs with different kinds of food as you descended deeper into the ground. They invited all of the cast, the press and several of Curt's friends in the area. They were charming, entertaining, and possessing exquisite taste with every choice they made.

I've never attended another birthday party that ever came close to that experience. Curt played a Baron in the film, and he was certainly treated like one in Vienna.

One of my favorite character actors, John Carradine, joined us to work in the warehouse sequence where the cruise missile was being held. I never met him before and was looking forward to getting to know him. We were filming several scenes at night inside a theatrical warehouse across the street from the Vienna Theatre. The warehouse was used to store theatrical sets, wardrobe and props that belonged to the theatre. It was the coldest indoor set I ever worked in. They did everything they could to heat the place and it still remained ice cold. In a conversation with a couple of Austrian crew members, they told us Hitler held meetings there at the beginning of his political career.

When we were not needed in the scene, I invited Carradine for some fresh Sacher Tortes and cappuccino at a coffeehouse across the street. He told me a few stories about John Barrymore and several of his drinking cronies.

One story that stood out in my memory occurred when Barrymore died and his body was lying in the coffin. On a lark, they decided to remove him and prop him up in a chair, making it appear as if he was alive and well. They were all pretty fractured at the time and sitting around telling stories that included him as if he were alive. Carradine was getting on in age, but was still a fine actor and fun to be around. I can still see his cold breath and hear that great voice of his, speaking his dialogue in that ice cold warehouse.

Just before we finished our shoot in Vienna, Curt Jurgens invited me to have lunch with him in the private dining room at the Sacher Hotel. The moment I entered the front door, I was greeted by the maître d' and escorted in to the dining room. Curt was already there, seated at a large, round table and in the center of the table was a bottle of Dom Perignon champagne.

We talked about Hollywood and a lot of the people that we both knew. The different wines that were served with every course were unbelievable. Our first serving was pheasant marinated in a Viennese sauce and then a light sorbet was served in between every course to change the pallet. The next course was venison steak with potatoes, onions and mushrooms. Again, the wine was changed to compliment the venison. A delicious salad changed our taste buds again. The captain gave an explanation why he served each wine with each course. The dessert was a combination of specially made Viennese pastries served with cappuccino and a choice of cordials.

During the luncheon, Curt told me about the business deal he had with the producer of the Clarence Darrow one-man play he was performing in on the weekends. When he finished working with us during the week, his producer would fly him in a private plane to the city where he was performing next. The deal he and his agent made was that for six months he would work for no salary, just expenses and the next six months all the box office receipts were his.

The play was a huge success and he performed to a full house every night. Curt said that it was the greatest deal his agent ever made for him. He commented on how he needed the money to keep up his lifestyle. He owned a home in Staad, and Baden Baden, both in Germany, and an apartment in Berlin and another one in London.

He was a class act, living a full life and seemingly enjoying every moment of it. We finished the two hour luncheon and Curt asked for the check. The captain was as gracious and charming as he could be and said, "Mr. Jurgens and Mr. Dante, we are honored to have you as our guests today." Nothing Curt said could have convinced him otherwise.

We were escorted to the front door and they thanked us again for dining there for lunch. There was no doubt Curt Jurgens was the number one favorite male movie star in all of Austria and Germany. That was the most lavish luncheon I ever had.

We left for Barcelona, Spain two days later to finish the last two weeks of the film. Barcelona had expanded with a new section to the city and our company was located in the new part of town, but I liked the architecture and the atmosphere in the old section better. On our off day, Peter Graves and his wife, Joan, Ika and I took a long walk to the fish market on the wharf. Along the way, we stopped at a calamari stand and enjoyed a taste of the fresh calamari catch of the day. Their calamari stands were similar to our hot dog stands back home.

We enjoyed a tasty lunch on the wharf where all of the fresh fish sits on a long bed of ice for you to choose from. You pick out your own fish and they cook it the way you like it. After lunch, we meandered over to the black market section with all kinds of vender booths for shopping, which was close by and we all bought gifts to bring back home to our respective families. The quality and the prices were right, without having to pay any taxes on the items.

The first couple days of filming our director, Les Martinson, thought he would try to exercise his poor Spanish with the local crew and he wasn't getting anywhere. He was holding up production and thought he was speaking well enough to communicate what he wanted them to do in Spanish. After an hour's delay, the assistant director, very politely looked at him and informed him that his ego needed to be checked at the door.

"Mr. Martinson, you are wasting your time. We all speak English fluently," he said. It was a little embarrassing for Les, but we'd still be there if the assistant director didn't speak up. It all ended with polite group laughter and from then on only English was spoken whenever direction was needed.

About a week into our shooting schedule, two of the stars of a flamenco dance team came to visit the set and were introduced to the director, producer and the cast. They invited us to be their guests at the nightclub where they were performing. We all attended and had a wonderful evening. They really put on a special show for us and delighted in introducing us to the audience. It was the first and last time I had the opportunity to see that type of dancing, up close. They were sensational.

On our last day in Barcelona, we worked long after our regular time to quit for the day. We were already behind schedule. It was nearing midnight and Ika decided to rewrite a scene that included Curt Jurgens. It was late and Curt was dead tired. He told Ika, that he would do the scene if he were paid over time. Ika apologized and said he didn't have any more money. Curt also apologized and began taking his wardrobe off and threw the beautiful cane he used as a prop throughout the picture on the sofa nearby. He thanked and said goodbye to everyone, before he left. I picked up the cane and Ika said, "Be my guest, it's yours." To this day I have that gold engraved cane hanging on the wall in my den as a reminder of my work with Curt Jurgens and *Cruise Missile*.

The producer, Ika, the director, Les Martinson, Peter and Joan Graves and I left Barcelona by plane for Madrid and had a two-hour layover before we left for New York en route to California, and we prayed there would be no delays so we could all be home for Christmas. We were fortunate to leave Madrid on schedule because fog was moving into the area so rapidly we were literally on the last plane to leave the airport.

The pilot made that announcement once we were airborne. I remember it was a pretty rough ride. We hit a lot of turbulence and headwinds before we landed safely in New York. The plane was late and by the time we arrived at customs, our plane for Los Angeles was long gone. We went to the airlines auxiliary counter near customs and found out there was only one last plane leaving for Los Angeles and it was completely full. They were ready to board passengers and it was Christmas Eve. I told everyone not to despair, as I sized up the employees at the customs turnstile.

I chose the guy with a Brooklyn accent because I knew a lot of people from that area. I told everyone to get behind me and I'd take my bags to him first. I told Peter to get out some 8 x 10 pictures and be prepared to sign some autographs. In my street vernacular I greeted him with all the gusto I could muster.

"Hey, how you doin' pal?" He looked at me and he couldn't believe it.

"Ain't you Mikey, the actor?" he asked.

"Yeah," I said energetically.

"Larry Ciaffone invited you to come to the Avenue U Club in Brooklyn to sign autograph pictures for the kids and you got stuck in a snow storm in the Bronx a while back," he said. I complimented him on his memory and reminded him I was going to visit the club the next time I came to the East coast.

I immediately called Peter Graves over and introduced him. Turned out this guy was also a big *Mission Impossible* fan. I told him about our plane being late, and there was only one more plane going to Los Angeles and they said it was full. He was the shop steward on the floor at the time and he called one of his assistants to take over his turnstile. He told me to get everybody together and be ready to move quickly. He went over to the auxiliary counter to talk with whoever was in charge and returned shortly. He told me when my name and party was called, to go to the counter immediately.

"They will call your name over the loudspeaker to come there to pick up your tickets for the next flight to Los Angeles."

I got his name and address and told him I would send him some autograph pictures as soon as I got home. Peter autographed a couple of his 8 x 10's and he was the happiest guy on the planet. We didn't even have to check through customs. We were rushed to board the plane the moment they announced my name to pick up the tickets at the auxiliary counter.

He managed to get us five seats across the back of the plane near the galley. I don't know how he did it, but we managed to arrive in Los Angeles in time to be at home on Christmas Eve. As a matter of fact, I dropped my bags off at my home in Beverly Hills and took all the gifts I brought from abroad to my brother's house in Newport Beach, about a two-hour drive from my home. I arrived at 11:30 p.m. to a late Christmas Eve party and couldn't believe how I got there before midnight.

By the time I contacted Larry Ciaffone, my old teammate when we were with Washington Senators at his home in Brooklyn, he had already heard what took place. I sent him a whole bunch of 8 x 10 autographed pictures and heard that all the kids were happy. It was without a doubt one of the nicest Christmas gifts I ever received.

66

Beyond Evil

Along the way, I was proud of myself for not allowing anyone to typecast me because I enjoyed the wide variety of roles I played. In 1980, I co-starred in *Beyond Evil*, a horror flick with John Saxon and Lynda Day George. My character Del, the owner of a real estate developing company, gives his newlywed friends a haunted colonial mansion as a wedding gift. Linda, as the wife, is possessed and inhabited by the female evil spirit who is seeking revenge for being murdered by her carousing husband there. The reign of terror and series of horrifying deaths, including mine, take place during their stay in the house.

Some of the interiors were shot in a real old and spooky looking house in the Hollywood Hills. It wasn't far from the famous white Hollywood sign above the freeway. The producer really picked the right house, for we all got spooky vibes while we were filming there.

The consensus was that something very strange, perhaps similar to the story we were filming, happened in that house a long time ago. The stuntman that did the fall for me from the second floor balcony down to the street when I was killed miscalculated his landing on the air filled mat below him. He landed too close to the edge and bounced off and was unconscious when

In 1980's Beyond Evil, *I portray Del Georgio, a flashy engineer.*

224

we all reached him. Luckily, he was only out momentarily; a couple more feet and it could have been fatal. That was the first and only time I've ever witnessed a close mishap by a stuntman. It was so hot working in that old stuffy house. Lynda had a huge fan on her all the time when she was not working and caught a serious respiratory infection and the director had to shoot around her for a few days. John and I stayed away from Lynda as well as the fan, so we wouldn't get sick, too. Maybe there were still evil spirits at work there?

Beyond Evil was the first horror picture I ever appeared in and it was also the last. It was interesting and fun to do, but not for the faint of heart.

67

License To Be

The year 1980 proved to be a fruitful one, and my next project was a TV movie entitled *The Kids Who Knew Too Much* for Walt Disney Studios. It featured actress Sharon Gless, Jackie Coogan and three young model-building aficionados played by Dana Hill, Rad Daly and Christopher Holloway. It was directed by the talented Robert Clouse, who helmed many projects for Disney Studios. Sharon did her usual good job playing a reporter in this two hour movie. She later went on to star with Tyne Daly in the successful series *Cagney and Lacey*.

The kids made the acquaintance of ace reporter Sharon Gless who was investigating a murder. Gless and the kids discovered that the murder was committed to hush up a major political conspiracy.

I played a bad guy by the name of Ross. This character was mean and ultimately paid the price in the end. I always liked playing these parts because I had the license to be a real bad guy and didn't have to go to jail for the crimes I committed. It's the only place in the world I wouldn't have to suffer the consequences for my wrongful actions.

I remember one scene when I ran and chased after the three youngsters and didn't succeed. My partner in crime and I had to hightail it to our car before the police arrived. My sidekick who was driving the getaway car arrived a little before me, quickly put the car in gear and took off just as I was getting inside. The door was only half shut when he sped away and I almost got thrown to the street. I held on to that door with all my strength and managed to muscle my way back into the car and shut the door. It looked great on film but it was a close call. I was darn fortunate to escape serious injury, *again*.

68

Building My Library

In 1982, Joe Wallenstein, one of the line producers of the long-running television series *Knots Landing,* called me to meet the executive producer of the show at MGM Studios. I knew Joe and he liked my work but the executive producer wanted to meet me, so he asked if I would mind coming in to read for the part of Captain Alving, the head of the Swat Team in an episode entitled 'Night' AKA 'Nervous Breakdown.'

We discussed the character for a while and I gave a good reading to land the part. It was an extremely dramatic script written by John Pleshette, cousin of actress Suzanne Pleshette, a semi regular on the show. He was to star in the episode as well. The drama began with an argument between Richard played by John and Laura played by Constance Mc Cashin, which led to Richard having a nervous breakdown and threatening to commit suicide at the cul-de-sac location used in many episodes. Richard was irrational and held a gun to his head. At this point they called in the SWAT team to deal with the situation.

My job was to make sure he didn't harm anyone else. The scene took place on the front porch of the house. A child was on the second floor so I had to get to her first and bring her to a safe area before dealing with Richard. It took Laura and everyone else a lot of time to convince him to put the gun down. It was an extremely emotional and dramatic story. John did an exceptional job writing and acting in this episode. I enjoyed playing my character because I had never portrayed someone like Captain Alving before. He was a disciplined, cautious and highly trained officer. I always looked forward to building my library with a variety of characters to display my versatility as an actor. The Captain was another good addition to my repertoire.

69
Chicago

I did two films with actor, producer, director Fred "The Hammer" Williamson. The first one was called *The Big Score* in 1983, which was filmed on location in Chicago, Illinois.

Fred had a gift for casting highly talented actors in his films. He had a way of convincing actors how much he respected their work, even though he didn't have the budget to pay them their regular salaries. Fred was able to circumvent paying the actors their regular salaries by arranging their scenes to shoot back-to-back for a week or two, instead of staggering their appearances throughout the whole filming schedule. Fred worked with three cameras and saved a lot of extra camera setups and close-up shooting.

The starring roles in *The Big Score* belonged to Nancy Wilson, John Saxon, Richard Roundtree, Ed Lauter, and Bruce Glover. This was a talented cast for a low budget crime, drugs and murder story that took place in Chicago. All of us were recognizable names and highly-respected professional performers.

I was jogging six days a week at the Beverly Hills High School track in those days, so I brought my gear with me just in case I had a day or two to jog up and down Michigan Avenue. Coincidentally, there was a chase scene when I escaped from a shootout with Fred Williamson. I played a drug lord named Goldy and Fred played detective Frank Hooks. I took off as fast as I could and when I turned around to see where Fred was, he was way behind me. I didn't realize Fred, who was a former NFL player, couldn't keep up with my pace, as I was in such good shape. I later teased him about it and we had a good laugh. We had to do the scene again at a slower pace and sped up the camera. We had a pretty good jog through the city, until he caught up to me, crossing an empty lot and then shot me dead. I had the next day off, so I got to jog up and down Michigan Avenue; weaving through pedestrians along the way. It was a beautiful sunny day and I loved every minute of it.

Chicago was and is a special city to film motion pictures, because its film commission is so cooperative. And the food wasn't too shabby, either. During my stay I enjoyed dining at Stefano's and Sabatino's, two of my favorite restaurants in the windy city.

70

Four With Lee

I guest starred in four episodic television shows with Lee Majors, *The Big Valley, The Six Million Dollar Man,* and two *Fall Guy* segments entitled 'Hollywood Shorties' in 1983 and 'Baja 1000' in 1984. Other cast members of the *Fall Guy* included Douglas Barr, Heather Thomas and Markie Post.

The "Hollywood Shorties" episode was about a drug dealer (me) who needs a 'little person' to retrieve his drug stash. I played a character by the name of Tommy and actor Robert Fuller played Lieutenant Ryan. He was in hot pursuit of tracking me down. I remember chasing two of the 'little people' and finally catching up with them with my drug stash. When I caught up with them, the director told me to pick the last one by his belt buckle and throw him on top of several boxes in the room before shutting and locking the door. I was reluctant to do that for fear of hurting the actor, but the little person actor said it was okay because I was going to throw him on top of boxes that would cushion his fall. It added a little comedy to the scene, and I was more than pleased he wasn't injured.

The episode co-starred my good friend, actor Billy Barty. He served as a strong advocate for Little People in the movie industry and nationally brought much needed public attention to their needs. Billy was talented and a beautiful human being. I played in his celebrity golf tournament for many years to raise awareness on their behalf. I have fond memories of Billy and I miss seeing his smiling face. He was a little person, but a giant of a man.

'Baja 1000' was directed by Daniel Haller, who helmed quite a few episodes of the series. Lee played a Hollywood stuntman Colt Seavers, who doubles as a bounty hunter in this adventure series. This was an interesting story because the director, Dell Loomis, who gave Colt, the character Lee Majors plays in the series, his first job as a stuntman. Dell has been taking advantage of that situation for years to get Colt to work in his new low budget movies.

Now he wants Colt to take part in a desert auto race, supposedly to get more footage. But what he didn't tell Colt was that he made a large bet with someone in Las Vegas in favor of this bad character to win the race that Colt sent to prison several years ago. I portrayed a bad dude named Oscar Fields. This was a fun sequence, because I got the opportunity to throw hand grenades from a biplane at Seaver's (Lee Majors) racing car during the Baja 1000 race to prevent him from winning.

Of course, I didn't succeed but I had a good time trying. It was rewarding working with Lee, because he enjoyed his work, was always very professional and we worked well together.

My friend Billy Barty was small in height but was a giant of a man. He possessed a lot of heart and did great work on behalf of Little People in the movie industry.

71
Soaps

Way back in 1963, I was offered the starring role of Dr. Steve Hardy in the soap opera television series *General Hospital,* created by Frank and Doris Hursley for the ABC network. It began as a 30 minute live show, which centered on the life of Dr. Hardy, the staff doctor at General Hospital in Port Charles, New York.

Frankly, I didn't want to do a soap opera series for several reasons. One, it was filmed "live" five days a week, which meant I had to memorize dialogue, night and day to be prepared to work each day.

I was working quite a bit in television and motion pictures at that time, so I was in demand elsewhere. I was single, making enough money freelancing to pay my bills and could afford to choose. I wanted to do motion pictures because I liked the time to develop a character and rehearse as much as possible. Doing television didn't give the actors enough rehearsal time because of budget constraints. That meant that the filming always had to hurry along. Also, I didn't want to be locked into playing one character for many years, which could adversely affect my future by pigeonholing me, which I avoided for so long.

It was clear that *General Hospital* had the potential to be on the air for decades and still on the air today. I was happy when my good friend, John Beradino was cast to play Dr. Steve Hardy, where he remained for the next four decades. With humor, he always reminded me that I made him a star by turning down the role.

Almost 20 years later, I received a call from my agent that producer Gloria Monty wanted to see me about doing a number of shows playing a character by the name of Dr. Moreno. He was trying to cure Luke Spencer, played by Anthony Geary, who was partially paralyzed from the waist down as a result of a skiing accident. I was excited about playing a doctor, which I had never done before.

I went in to read for the part, my attitude for the character was just right and I got the part. My scenes with Geary were very dramatic and after all the trials and tribulations, I got him to walk again. We had time to rehearse and conditions were a lot better than in 1963 when the show first started.

The Soap Gods were smiling upon me because that same year, 1984, when I received a call from the producers of *Days of Our Lives.* I was cast to play Barney Jannings, the alcoholic father of Pete and Tess, two regulars on the show. Barney was a bitter and abusive man when he drank.

I jumped at the opportunity to play Barney Jannings, because it was a creative challenge for me to play an alcoholic and it was also the first time I was a father on screen. The character was

As Dr. Moreno in the daytime TV series General Hospital.

Barney Jannings, the alcoholic father of Pete and Tess in the daytime TV series, Days of Our Lives.

a huge departure for me and quite rewarding. He had a lot of psychological problems and used alcohol to bury his feelings. He was not a good father to his children because of his drinking problem. I had a difficult time with one of the scenes with my daughter, Tess. In this particular scene, we got into an argument and I slapped her in the face. I was sensitive about the abusive action even though my hand would cross in front of her face and the camera lens to make it look like I hit her. I had never struck a woman in my life; just the thought of it was awful. I had another confrontational scene with my son, Pete.

During an argument I had a drink in my hand and at one point threw what was left in the shot glass in his face. This character was a huge challenge for me because I never got drunk in my life. I got sick once when I was a teenager and I swore I would never drink like that again. To this day, I'm happy to say, I've kept my word to myself. It was a great experience working with the talented actors on the show and it was another new character I could proudly show on my demo reel. My versatility kept me alive for a lot of years in the business. I was proud of myself for staying on course.

72
Where Did the Time Go?

Academy Award winning actor and friend, Sidney Poitier, directed a film in 1985 called *Fast Forward*. It was cast with unknown talented young actors, singers and dancers. The movie was produced by John Veitch and Melville Tucker. It was written by Richard Wesley and Timothy March for Columbia Pictures. The story was about eight young dancers from Ohio who formed a dance troupe that traveled to New York to compete in a national dance competition. The dance sequences were creatively choreographed by Allegra Glinsky. The leading cast members were John Scott Clough, Don Franklin, Tamara Mark, Tracy Silver, and Cindy Mc Gee. The theme song, "Long as We Believe" was awesome.

In Fast Forward, *I play a snooty maitre'd. The 1985 film was directed by Sidney Poitier.*

Sidney asked me to do a cameo that would take place in a nightclub sequence. I played the maître'd dressed up in a tuxedo, making sure everything went well in the room. During the course of the evening, eight young dancers somehow bypassed me through the back entrance and managed to perform their act on the dance floor of the nightclub without permission from the manager. I had no way of stopping them and had to call the manager to get down to the main room, fast.

By the time he got there, the people in the nightclub were enjoying every minute of it, including me, plus the troupe got their dress rehearsal before a packed house. I thought Sidney did a terrific job working with these young and talented performers. When he spoke with them you could hear a pin drop, they had so much respect for him. After all, he was one of the best in show business. I don't know why the movie didn't do well at the box office as it was well done and entertaining. And I often wonder what happened to those young performers and where they are now because their careers were so promising.

Sidney and I enjoyed a good deal of quality time playing tennis in Beverly Hills and we also played golf over the years. He didn't grow up playing golf and tennis, learning later on in life, which was more difficult. However, Sidney applied himself and played well competitively. He was always the consummate gentleman and a good sport. He was a much better athlete than he gave himself credit for. During the time I was living in Beverly Hills, if we weren't playing tennis or golf we would "do lunch," as Sid would say. Those were fun days, Sid had a nice sense of humor and we would talk, laugh and enjoy our lunches together, managing to stay healthy along the way. Sidney attended our wedding twenty years ago at the Good Shepherd Catholic Church in Beverly Hills, California. With all these wonderful memories, I can't help asking myself, "Where did the time go?"

73
Tonsillitis

In 1986, executive producer John G. Stephens, whom I'd known for several years, asked me if I would be interested in portraying a tennis player in an episode of *Simon and Simon* entitled 'Tonsillitis.' He knew I was a good tennis player and thought of me for the part right away. I wasn't the guest star of the show, but he would pay me top dollar to play the role. He said he needed an actor who could act and play tennis well. I didn't have to read for the part, I just had to pick up the script and start working on Monday. It sounded sweet to me.

The regular stars on the show were Gerald McRaney, Jameson Parker and Mary Carver. This popular drama/action series was about two brothers Rick Simon; a scruffy eccentric character played by McRaney and A. J. Simon; a clean-cut and ambitious guy, played by Jameson Parker. Together they partnered in a struggling private detective agency in San Diego, California, that was in constant competition with other agencies.

In this particular segment, Rick Simon violently protests when the doctor wants to remove his tonsils. While he is under anesthetic he sees what he thinks is a murder and no one believes him.

I played a character by the name of Tobias; a tennis professional, who Rick and A.J. came to question in connection with the murder Rick witnessed. I just had one scene to do and I was done for the day, and got razzed about what a tough job I had. It was the most money I ever made in my career at that time for a day's work and had a good workout at the same time. There was another nice surprise about my character Tobias; he was not guilty of any wrong doing after all. Oh, the sweet life of a versatile actor.

74

Brown Paper Bag

In 1986 I co-starred in my second film with Fred Williamson entitled *The Messenger*. This film was also cast extremely well with Cameron Mitchell, Christopher Connelly, Val Avery, Joe Spinell, Peter Brown, Sandy Cummings and yours truly.

Fred produced, directed and starred in this picture about a former Green Beret by the name of Jake Turner, who becomes a self-styled avenger and takes on the mob. Jake's wife is murdered by the Casa Nostra mob for her failure to complete a big time drug deal. Jake swears revenge, vowing to nail every lowlife whoever got near her. He launches a one-man crusade for justice that takes him from Italy to Chicago, Las Vegas and Los Angeles, where he proves he hasn't lost his deadly touch. That is, until a powerful Don attempts to do away with Jake permanently.

I played a character by the name of Emerson, who is a part of a big drug operation and winds up on the short end of his ambition. Fred didn't have a large staff and on this particular day, we did a rewrite before filming a scene. We didn't have the luxury of a script person on the set, so I picked up the nearest thing I could write on, which happened to be a brown paper bag. That drew a hearty laugh from the cast and the crew. Every time I think of that scene, a broad smile comes to my face. It was all about money.

Fred was extremely easy to work with, which stemmed from his respect for the actors he cast. He listened and allowed the cast to change some of the dialogue if it was better than what was written in the script. If you had an idea about the scene you were working in, he was all ears and welcomed anything that might make it better.

Unfortunately, his pictures weren't mainstream because I think Fred was ahead of his time. If he were producing his films in today's market, he might've been more commercially successful. The African-American leading men acting in today's films have developed a far greater audience than in the 1980s and '90s.

75

Single Parent

I guest starred in a 1987 episode of the successful television series, *Cagney and Lacey* entitled 'Right to Remain Silent.' The crime drama series starred two talented actresses, Sharon Gless as Detective Sgt. Christine Cagney and Tyne Daly playing detective Mary Beth Lacey. The show was produced by Barney Rosensweig, whom I previously worked for when he produced *Daniel Boone.*

This story was about a deaf teenage girl suspected of murder. I played the character Paul Bennett, a sheet metal worker and single father of the teen. This was only the second time I played a parent in a television show or motion picture. Cagney and Lacey are both emotionally affected while investigating the deaf teenage fugitive. The segment was directed by Sharon Miller, who worked for the producer/director Joseph Taft on the film, *Thirty Dangerous Seconds.*

I remember talking with her on the set in Oklahoma City and how she expressed her desire to become a director. Well, she certainly succeeded and directed quite a few of the *Cagney and Lacey* episodes. She worked long and hard and eventually reached her goal. I was pleasantly surprised and happy to learn she was directing 'Right to Remain Silent.'

In the episode, Cagney and Lacey came to question me about my daughter at the sheet metal factory where I was employed. I wasn't pleased about the police questioning me about my daughter's whereabouts and certainly didn't appreciate them trying to implicate a deaf teenager of murder. In addition, they accused me of being a neglectful parent. This scene involved me cutting sheet metal on this old and clumsy machine while being questioned, which took a lot of coordination. One mistake and you could cut your hand off. There was a problem with the machine just before lunch and the producer was going to strike the set and move to another location, which would have been costly.

The machinist said he could fix it and I volunteered to forgo my lunch hour to perfect my timing, learning how to operate the machine and spewing out a lot of dialogue at the same time without cutting myself to ribbons.

Barney Rosensweig accepted my offer and when they got back from lunch I did the scene in one take. Barney thanked me more than once and said I saved the company a lot of money.

There was a pathetic and dramatic twist to the end of the story. With all the sympathy and concern Cagney and Lacey expressed for my deaf daughter, we learned that she actually was guilty of murder. Sharon Miller did a fine job directing this dramatic segment and I had another different role in the can.

Beverly Hills To Malibu

76

I was just minutes away from leaving my house in Beverly Hills to play tennis when the doorbell rang. It was a building contractor who was renovating and building houses in the neighborhood. He introduced himself and handed me his card and flat out asked me if I would like to sell my house.

"I'm not a real estate agent, but a builder and if you're interested in selling, there won't be any fees or commissions involved," he said. "I'm going door to door because I'm interested in building two story single family houses in the neighborhood. You can keep everything inside the house because I'm going to tear it down and build my houses from scratch."

I couldn't believe how easy he was making everything sound. He didn't pressure me at all. He told me to think about it and he'd call me in a couple of days. I thought about it and two days later he called and came by the house. I threw a large figure at him. He hesitated for a moment and said, "It's a little high, but we've got a deal."

This was my third house I had bought and sold. It was by far the easiest, most profitable real estate deal I ever made. I had no intention of selling the house, but I went along with the flow as if the good Lord sent him to tell me it was time to move on. I called my lawyer and made all the arrangements, and I had ninety days to look for a place to live.

About a month before escrow closed, I went to visit with Tino Barzie, Pia Zadora, her husband Meshulam Riklis and their two children Kady and Kristofer, at their home in the Trousdale Estates in Beverly Hills. During our conversation Pia asked me where I was going to live. I told her I didn't know yet, but I had to make up my mind in the next thirty days.

"We have a beach house with a guest house in the Malibu Colony. You're welcome to stay in the guest house, just take care of your phone bill and utilities," she offered. It was like an invitation from an angel and I immediately accepted. I was living in the Malibu Colony two weeks later.

It was a whole new experience living in the colony. Through the years, I liked visiting the ocean but not living on the water permanently. There was something about the dampness in the wintertime that didn't agree with me, it sort of went through my bones. Now, the summertime was a different story. The sun was warm and the colony was filled with a lot of interesting and talented people during the time I lived there. Some I knew before I moved in and others I got to know shortly thereafter. I knew Rod Steiger, Michael Landon, Jack Warden, Bruce Dern and got to know producer Lou Shaw, Bob Mac Leod who now owned and operated a successful public relations business, and actor Larry Hagman, who lived in the next house. Lots of competitive doubles tennis matches took place on the weekend and during the week with whoever was not working at the time. I jogged down the old

Malibu Road six days a week and continued to stay in shape while I lived there. Larry Hagman and his wife had a beautiful beach house next door to Rik and Pia's house.

One day Larry and I were both out on the patio of each other's houses at the same time and I introduced myself. Occasionally, we would chat and the strangest thing I learned about Larry was that he didn't talk on Sunday. He told me he saved his voice for work and did not speak a word all day.

He and his wife designed the interior of their home. Each room and the cove sitting area was decorated completely different and done in exquisite taste. I didn't get to know them well, but they were always warm and friendly. For a while I drove into Beverly Hills to have lunch at the Café Roma on Canon Drive with my buddies, with whom I enjoyed being with when I lived there for many years. The regulars were Norm Crosby, Jerry Vale, Shecky Greene, Al Martino, Leonard Gaines, Morris Diamond, Blackie Segal and on occasion, Rodney Dangerfield. The conversation was always interesting with a lot of teasing and laughter. It was the perfect luncheon and meeting place for a lot of actors on a daily basis. I saw Milton Berle, Sean Penn, Mickey Rourke, Jackie Cooper, Jed Allen, Robert Clary and Arnold Schwarzenegger having lunch there many times.

When I went into town I always brought my tennis gear with me, and after lunch, I joined the guys at Dr. Omar Fareed's house for tennis. I did that for quite a while until I got tired of fighting the traffic going to and from Malibu to Beverly Hills. Senator Ted Kennedy and John Tunney came by the tennis court when they were in town. Ted and Omar were close friends and Ted enjoyed the competition and caliber of play we had to offer. He was pleasantly surprised that actors Charlton Heston, Lloyd Bridges, Ron Ely and I were good players. Ted was competitive and demanded perfection from his doubles partner, John Tunney, who happened to be an A player. I had the opportunity to play with both of them on two occasions and enjoyed our matches. They were both personable and fun. Several months later, I was sitting in a popular and extremely crowded southwestern restaurant, the Malibu Adobe, with two casting agents Joe D'Agosta and Lou DiGiamo, whom I knew for several years. This attractive, eclectic restaurant was designed and decorated by actress Ali McGraw.

Lou had offices in New York and came to Hollywood on business and called to have lunch with Joe and me. It was a beautiful day and the place was packed with people. We were sitting where the band was set up in the evening, the closest seats to the railing, having lunch when Ted Kennedy walked in. I could not miss seeing him, because our table was set up high and facing in his direction. He was obviously looking for someone as he surveyed the noisy room slowly then turned and looked in my direction. He recognized me and worked his way through the crowd to where I was located. The noise diminished as he got closer to us. He skipped up three little steps of stairs to where we were sitting.

"Hello Michael. How are you and how is your tennis?" he asked.

I was so surprised he remembered my name because I only played tennis with him twice. I introduced Joe and Lou to Ted and asked him how his back was. He said he was having a lot of problems with it and he wasn't able to play any tennis at all.

We chatted a while and he said, "I stopped by to meet with someone but he isn't here." We shook hands with him and I said, "I hope to see you at Omar Fareed's for tennis as soon your back gets better." When he walked away I could see he was really favoring his back by leaning forward. Joe and Lou were so impressed that he recognized me from across the room and came directly to the table to say hello. I think most of the people in the room were impressed as well. That was the last time I ever saw him. To this day I often think of Ted Kennedy, the charismatic person that he was, and his friendliness toward me.

I went to play in a celebrity golf tournament in Indian Wells, not far from Palm Springs and was hitting some golf balls on the practice tee when a familiar voice behind me called out my name. It was Nancy Chaffee Kiner, the former ladies indoor national tennis champion. She was with two other ladies, LPGA Golf Hall of Famer Amy Alcott and CNN anchor Kathleen Sullivan, who was married to Nancy's son Michael at the time. They have since gotten divorced.

I met Nancy years ago at Clint Eastwood and Merv Griffin's Celebrity Tennis Tournament in Pebble Beach, California, and we remained good friends ever since. After a brief chat I told her what I was doing there and she invited me to a barbecue party she was hosting at her home in Rancho Mirage that same afternoon. I told her I would finish playing golf in plenty of time and I'd call her from my hotel to get the directions.

On the way to Nancy's house and on the same block where she lived, I turned to look out of the car window and I noticed a small "For Sale" sign on the garage door of an attractive shake roof house, about four houses from where Nancy lived. I stopped the car and wrote the phone number down. When I got to her house, I asked her if she knew the people with the for sale sign on their house. I told her I was interested in getting a place in the desert and asked her if she'd mind calling them to ask what price they wanted. She knew the people and called immediately, but they weren't home at the time.

I had such a good time at the barbecue and left excited about the prospects of buying that house. Nancy was just as excited I was, because I would be her neighbor if I bought it. My drive back to Malibu took about two-and-a-half hours. About 10 minutes after I arrived home, the phone rang and Nancy was on the other line. She said she spoke with the owner of the house and told them I might be interested in buying it if the price was right. Two weeks later I drove to Rancho Mirage walked in the house, and 15 minutes later I gave them my offer. There were no real estate agents involved and it was another clean-cut real estate deal I was fortunate to make with the owner. I contacted my good friend for many years, actor Harry Guardino, who was living in Palm Springs. I told him I just bought a house in Rancho Mirage, and needed someone to paint my house.

He gave me the name of the guy who painted his place, and I hired him to paint the house inside and out. I also hired a contractor that Nancy knew to do some construction work to build a wall and a gate on the side of the house. Two months later, on December 24, 1988, the house was ready for me to move in. My mom made a special trip to visit and help with getting everything furnished properly like no one could. Lucky me!

I took all of my furniture I had in storage from my Beverly Hills house and brought it to Rancho Mirage. I rented a truck and with the help of a buddy of mine and moved everything in one fell swoop. I was still living in Malibu, but on the weekends I went to my home in the desert to check the house and make sure everything was okay.

The next film I did, *Cage,* in 1989, was being released and the producer Lang Elliott asked me if I would plug the picture while I was in the Palm Springs area. I did an interview at the KNEWS radio station and the manager was a fan of mine. After I finished the interview, he asked me if I was interested in hosting a weekly celebrity talk show. I told him I didn't know anything about radio, except I knew I could always give a good and interesting interview.

He said I had a good speaking voice and personality, knew a lot of celebrities and I was the right guy he was looking for. He said he would teach me all the technical things before we got started. I tried to discourage him and told him I was only coming to the desert on the weekends.

"That's when I want you to do the show; every Saturday for thirteen weeks," he said. We agreed on the salary and started doing the first show two weeks later. A week before I started my first show I received a phone call about two o'clock in the morning in Rancho Mirage from my ex-roommate Mickey McDermott when I was with the Washington Senators and introduced me to Tommy Dorsey. Mickey was known to drink in his day and he sounded the same, whether he was drinking or not. I thought I had to go and rescue him from some ungodly place. I was half asleep and the first thing I asked him was if he was sober.

"I'm as sober as a judge," he said. He told me to "hold on to the bed" because I just hit the Arizona lottery for $7.5 million dollars.

I could hardly believe the good news, and to think two weeks ago he called me to tell me how happy he was getting $100 raise on his next major league baseball pension check. Being the thoughtful guy that he was, the first thing he asked me was if I needed any money. I politely declined but thanked him for his generosity. I told him how happy I was for him and to come when he could to visit and see the new house in Rancho Mirage. What an unbelievable gift for Mickey, a big-hearted and exceptional human being.

My first two guests on my radio show were my pals Phil Harris and Alice Faye. After 13 weeks of doing live radio, the manager wanted to renew the contract for another 13 weeks. I got smart and decided to get my own sponsors, pay for the airtime and conduct my own radio show calling it *The Michael Dante Classic Celebrity Talk Show*. All the friends I made throughout the years through Hollywood in entertainment and the sports world were invited to be my guests on my radio show, and the list was long and prestigious.

After 12 years, I had completed over 300 top name interviews. I only had one turn down by a celebrity guest all those years, which was due to a working conflict. The one-hour interviews are one of a kind, just like fireside chats, warm, friendly and truly classic, as well as a three-minute show with the same guests called *Michael Dante on Deck*. It was my third successful career to date.

77

Return From the River Kwai

Also in 1989, I had the privilege of doing a war movie called *Return from the River Kwai*. It was produced by Kurt Unger and directed by Andrew V. McLaglen. We had an outstanding cast with Timothy Bottoms, Nick Tate, George Takei, Edward Fox, Chris Penn, Denholm Elliott and me, playing Commander Davidson. This was the second time I played an officer on board a submarine. The way I was cast in this film was interesting.

I met the producer Kurt Unger in Mesholem Riklis's office in Beverly Hills when I stopped by to visit Tino Barzie, actress/singer Pia Zadora's manager and former manager of Tommy Dorsey. Mesholem and Pia were married and were two of the nicest people I ever knew. Mesholem was in the office that day and introduced me to Kurt. He told him to find a part for me in his soon to be produced film, *Return from the River Kwai*.

Mesholem was an investor in Kurt Unger's motion picture company. Rik, Pia and her two children saw *Winterhawk* and were big fans of mine. He responded immediately saying that he had a good part for me as a submarine commander. He said he would be in touch and that the film will be photographed entirely on location in the Philippines. A few months later I heard from the producer, Kurt Unger, with all the details.

The screenplay *Return from the River Kwai* was based on a true story and adapted from a best-selling novel written by Joan and Clay Blair Jr. My orders as the submarine commander were to torpedo any ship flying a Japanese flag. While searching for the enemy, we picked up a Navy pilot by the name of Lieutenant Crawford played by Chris Penn, brother of Sean Penn, on a raft at sea.

He reported he had escaped in a Japanese plane, ran out of gas and had to ditch it in the ocean. As Commander, I had to make a most difficult decision to find those transports and torpedo those ships, knowing there were American and our allies on board. Even though I was acting, I got the strangest feeling in my stomach about what I had to do. Since it was a true story, my heart went out to the Commander, who had to make that tough decision and all the lives that were lost. On the positive side many were rescued, sadly those were his orders and he had no choice.

After several days of work I had a day off and visited a tailor shop that was not far from the hotel. Being a clotheshorse, I hustled over after breakfast and picked out half a dozen pieces of material for my dress shirts and eight pieces of material for my trousers. During my conversation with the salesman, I mentioned I was only going to be in Makati for another two weeks and asked when I needed to come back for a fitting. He looked at me with a puzzled look and said, "You don't need to come in for a fitting we have all your measurements. Everything will be ready in forty eight hours." I couldn't believe it. Two days later I went to pick up everything and tried on one shirt and

Got a role on a submarine again. This time it was on location in the Philippines. I just love submarine films.

one pair of trousers and they fit perfectly. I saved more than half of the money that I would have had to pay to have those shirts and trousers made back home.

Makati was an awfully smoggy city. The Jeepneys, a small version of our golf carts that they drove around the city in, gave off a cloud of black exhaust. They were used to transport people very economically in and around Makati, but breathing in the exhaust was extremely unhealthy.

We had an international cast and everybody did a fine job, but unfortunately a problem arose with the distribution of the picture. Columbia Pictures and producer Sam Spiegel filed a lawsuit against producer Kurt Unger and his film company claiming they were trading on the title *The Bridge on the River Kwai*. I could never understand why there was a lawsuit because *Return from the River Kwai* was a bestselling novel based on a true story. The lawsuit went on for a few years before the film could be distributed in the USA.

Unfortunately, the film was not a box office hit. There was no doubt in my mind, the lawyers wound up with most of the profits. It was another interesting experience for me about the trials and tribulations of the film industry.

78

Cage Fighting

I starred in a 1989 film directed and produced by Lang Elliott entitled *Cage,* with Lou Ferrigno and Reb Brown. The story was about two American soldiers who fought together in Vietnam. Billy Thomas, played by Lou Ferrigno saved his buddy's life, Scott Munroe played by Reb Brown. In the process Billy is shot in the head and the injury resulted in brain damage. The injury left him as a simpleton and Scott becomes his caretaker upon their discharge from the service. Billy's mental disability got him mixed up with illegal cage fighting.

In Cage I had fun playing Tony Baccala, a degenerate gambler in debt to the Italian and Chinese Mafia.

I played a degenerate gambler by the name of Tony Baccola who, along with my partner, lured Billy away from his house when Scott left to run some errands. I convinced Billy, who is a physical specimen, to cage fight for me against the Chinese Mafia's cage fighter, to make enough money so he and Scott could purchase a neighborhood bar.

The matches were filmed in various warehouses in downtown Los Angeles and only the lawless were invited. The majority of the loot they bet gambling on their man was drug money. My character was heavily in debt to the Chinese and the Italian Mafia, and desperately squirming to pay off both debts to save my life.

Scott finds a way to rescue Billy and fights in his place. Billy is getting beat up in the cage fight and because of his mental disability, doesn't want to hurt anybody. Together they managed to come out on the winning end after the Chinese and Italian Mafia kill one another in a shootout. Unfortunately, I get killed in the crossfire.

I had never met Lou Ferrigno before we started filming. He approached me and said his uncle and I played professional baseball together in spring training camp at Myrtle Beach, South Carolina and spoke highly of me.

His uncle was Sonny Giordano, a right-handed pitcher from Brooklyn, New York. Sonny was not only a teammate, but a good friend. He was an outstanding prospect before he developed a sore arm that ended his career.

Sonny and I kept in touch for many years. He got married and raised two lovely daughters. He, his wife and daughters came to visit me while I was living in Encino. Sadly Sonny suffered a fatal heart attack at his daughter's wedding while on the dance floor. We both shed tears when that subject matter came up. Lou did an outstanding job in the film and showed he had a lot more talent than just *The Incredible Hulk*.

79

Mary Jane and Me

The Southern California Sportscasters Broadcasters Association met the last Wednesday of each month at the Lakeside Country Club in Burbank, California. There was a different theme every month with invited guests from the sports world. The sportswriters would learn about the backgrounds of the guests and enjoyed meeting them as well.

On July 26, 1990, the topic for the luncheon was about former professional athletes that made the successful transition to show business. Those of us that were invited were Chuck Connors, Esther Williams, John Beradino, Chuck Essegian and yours truly. We were all actors with the exception of former Los Angeles Dodger outfielder Chuck Essegian, who became a show business lawyer and was employed at 20th Century-Fox. He was a classmate of Richard Zanuck at Stanford University, a successful producer and the head of studio operations at the time. The phone call and invitation to be a guest at the monthly sports luncheon came from the man that was in charge of gathering the troops, Goldy Norton.

He called me about a month ahead of time and I said I wasn't sure I would be available to make it because there was something on my calendar I tentatively committed myself to. I told him to call me back in another week or so and I'd see if I could get out of my commitment. A week later he called and I thank the good Lord I was able to get out of my commitment.

That Wednesday I was greeted by Goldy Norton, whom I met for the first time. He was as nice in person as when I spoke with him over the phone. He told me the President of the Association, Stu Nahan, who I knew for many years, was unavailable to chair the meeting because he was on vacation and Chuck Bennett and Chuck Benedict would be pinch hitting for him. A loud voice rang out across the room and it was Chuck Connors, summoning me to his table. I had not seen him since I moved from Beverly Hills to Malibu. He had a condominium just a block away from my house on Canon Drive when I lived in Beverly Hills.

We talked about baseball and our love for the game until it was time to call the meeting to order. I got up to leave to go to the table I was assigned to and Chuck wouldn't let me leave.

"You're sitting here with me," he said. I told him I had an assigned seat and he got up and went to my table, picked up my name card and put it on his table and said, "See, you're supposed to sit here." Goldy was standing by and he looked at me, smiled and said, "It's alright, I'll take care of it."

Throughout the luncheon we were introduced individually and went to the podium to tell the story of how we made the transition from professional sports to acting. Then we answered questions from the attendees. Everyone was gracious and gave us a standing ovation. There certainly was enough for the sportswriters to talk and write about. At the end of the luncheon Chuck and I were

For Michael Dante many thanks From a big Fan

Our mutual professional baseball backgrounds and the love of the game bonded Chuck Conners and me the first time we met.

That smile on my face was for real, because on September 26, 1992, I made Mary Jane Scott my bride for life.

standing near our table talking with some people, when an attractive lady and her lovely daughter in a beautiful blue dress, approached Chuck. They introduced themselves as the wife, Dorothy and daughter Mary Jane of the late sports announcer Mark Scott.

Mark was the announcer for the Hollywood Stars baseball team in the Pacific Coast League and the host of the original television home run hitting contest show, *Home Run Derby*. Chuck and Mark were very good friends. As a matter of fact, Chuck visited their home on many occasions in Burbank. For a moment, Chuck went into shock.

"Oh my God, of course I remember you Dorothy and Mary Jane. You were just a little girl at the time," he said. He then introduced me to Dorothy and Mary Jane and began to tell a couple of stories about Mark. Time was running short for Mary Jane because she had to get back to work at Disney Studios, where she was working as an assistant editor. Mary Jane said to Chuck, "I'd like to hear more stories about my father. May I have your phone number?" Just at that moment, someone grabbed Chuck's arms and turned him away to ask him a question. Mary Jane had a paper and pencil in her hand, and so did I. I asked her if she was married and she answered the question with a question.

"No, are you?" she asked. I liked her approach.

"No," I smiled. I then asked her for her phone number and if she would like to have lunch. Before we knew it, Chuck was gone and so was everyone else. The meeting had adjourned. The next day I called Mary Jane to have lunch with me, but she said she was going to Europe the next week for the first time and had too much to do. She was leaving the following Tuesday. I was always pretty fast on my feet, especially when it came to beautiful women, so I came up with a simple solution.

"You have to eat before you go, so how about dinner on Monday night?" I asked. Mary Jane accepted my invitation and we hit it off. At the end of the night, we both knew.

Twenty two years later, we still know.

Northridge Earthquake

I was engaged to Mary Jane in 1991 and moved from Malibu to a condo we shared in Toluca Lake, going back and forth to the desert on weekends to do the radio show. The shows were getting better and better because I was learning more about the technical aspects of conducting a radio show and feeling more comfortable with each interview.

I did encounter a problem hiring a sound engineer to work on Saturdays and I couldn't find a good technician in the desert at that time. In a short period of time, Mary Jane learned all the machinations necessary to keep a balance of the sound throughout the show and she was much better than the so called professionals I hired. We became a good team and everything became so much more fun to do, working together.

Around the same time, I met Scott Warren in a golf tournament and he and his sponsor, the Holiday Inn asked me to be their celebrity host for their first annual celebrity golf tournament benefiting their charity, Give Kids the World. The tournament would eventually be called The Annual Michael Dante Celebrity Golf Classic.

The terminally ill children and their immediate family members were invited to spend six days at the Holiday Inn Kids Village in Kissimmee, Florida. Their transportation expenses were also taken care of. There were cottages at Kids Village that were filled with thoughtful amenities for the child and their families were served three meals a day. The Disney characters Pluto, Mickey and Minnie Mouse from Disneyland came by to entertain the children twice a week.

I accepted the offer and the responsibility for the next three years. I am so proud to say we raised approximately $70,000 each year. I personally went to Florida with Scott Warren, the Holiday Inn chairman of the tournament the first year, to see Holiday Inn Kids Village. We met all the people involved and personally presented Give Kids the World with a check.

It was sad, but yet so rewarding to be able to grant all of those children's dying wishes. The Village also had a biplane and a pirate ship on the premises. All of the hedges were shaped like the Disney characters that all the children knew and loved.

The first time I met the children and spent some time with them, I had to excuse myself to go to the men's room to shed my tears in private, before I was able to compose myself and return to them, smiling again. They had no idea that their days, weeks or months were numbered. They played and were all having a joyous time, but were gathered at a certain time to take a nap.
Their energy level was much lower than a normal child because of their treatments and medication. Before I left they all came around and hugged me to say goodbye. I always shed tears when I think of those kids… God's little children.

For the next five years thereafter, I continued to host The Annual Michael Celebrity Golf Classic raising money for various charitable organizations such as Leukemia, Emmanuel House, Guide Dogs of The Desert and the last two years with Swing for Life. Between the radio show and hosting celebrity golf tournaments, Mary Jane and I were two of the busiest people in the desert.

After eight years of hosting my golf tournament, Mary Jane and I were burned out. I had a volunteer committee that helped a great deal, but most of the work always reverted back to the two of us and the pressure was exhausting. All the people on the committees had good intentions, but their lives took them in other directions and so many times the jobs they were assigned to were left unfinished. We had to pick up the pieces and do what had to be done. In the end, we were proud of the success and the funds we raised that went to the various charities.

During those eight years, we never handled the money or took a salary for our services. We did it for the love of the people that benefited from each tournament. As a matter of fact, it cost us money each year out of our own pocket, but that was okay and most rewarding. Every charity was financially rewarded from our dedication and hard work during those years. The participants and the celebrities complemented us as to how much they enjoyed the golf, food, gifts and the entertainment compared with many other tournaments.

I know it's because we did everything from our hearts. I continued to participate in countless charity golf and tennis tournaments over the years. It was time to give back and I wanted to help as many people I could.

For the next two years we were living five days a week at our Toluca Lake condominium, because Mary Jane was still working as an assistant editor in the trailer department at Disney Studios and spending the weekends at our home in Rancho Mirage.

In the desert, we had a new guest to interview every Saturday for my radio show. We had to deliver it to the radio station so it could be aired every Saturday at 2 p.m. on KGAM 1450. We always had two or three shows recorded in advance in case we were unable to get away for the weekend. On Sunday, January 17, 1994, Mary Jane and I returned from Rancho Mirage to our condominium in Toluca Lake and arrived just before midnight. About 4:30 in the morning, the Northridge earthquake struck with such a vertical force that the small television set that was sitting on top of the bureau in our bedroom went flying across the room like a piece of paper and went smashing into the sliding closet door. If it came in our direction it would've killed us for sure. We could hear everything breaking that was in the china cabinet and all the dishes from the cupboards in the kitchen.

I stopped Mary Jane from getting out of bed in time to put on our tennis shoes that were nearby because we were about to encounter thousands of small pieces of glass spread all over the kitchen and living room floors. If we walked without putting those thick rubber-soled shoes on, our feet would have been shredded. The center beam in the living room buckled and looked like a ski jump. Thank God we were not hurt, but the condominium was a total loss. We cleaned up the mess the best we could and went on with our lives. The condominiums were in a horseshoe shaped design, eight, on each side of the entrance way. All the condos on our side were totally demolished and the condos on the other side only had broken windows. The force of the earthquake determined the extent of the damage. I felt the good Lord was trying to tell us something. Shortly thereafter, we moved permanently to our home in Rancho Mirage and we never looked back.

81

Palm Springs Walk of Stars

Twelve dear friends of mine came from my hometown of Stamford, Connecticut, to play in my 1994 celebrity golf tournament. Mario and Fran De Carlo, Mike and Gloria Tiscia, Lou and Lorraine Greco, John and Edith Darling, Pat and Marion De Nicola, Joe Riccicci, and Judge Bill Strada arrived ready to have a good time. It was the first of two trips they made to the Palm Springs area to visit with Mary Jane and me. They were always so supportive of us, my career, the charity events, and we always had so much fun. They all gathered at my house to swim, have lunch, dinner and play bocce. I had a regulation sized Bocce court in my backyard and even some of the ladies played for the first time. They were having more fun than the guys and played better, I might add. For lunch, I served antipasto with fresh, warm Italian bread and plenty to drink. We had gorgeous days and the evenings were so balmy and beautiful that we could eat outside under the awesome desert sky, at poolside. I made one of my favorite dishes that everyone loved; Pasta Fagiole and a mixed green salad with olive oil, red wine vinegar with crumbled blue cheese.

Mario De Carlo, who was the best man at my wedding, made his favorite whipped cream and strawberry short cake for dessert that was scrumptious. The golf tournament Pairings Party, with dinner and entertainment could not have been better. The entertainment consisted of singer Peter Marshall, comedians Jack Carter and Norm Crosby, and singer/mime Scott Record. The evening ended with a standing ovation for these talented performers. That year I was able to deliver a check for $40,000 to the charity recipient, Emmanuel House. They were a multi-denominational religious organization in dire need of money to purchase the real estate that they were currently renting. Father Bill Faiella, a Catholic priest at Emmanuel House, gave free counseling services to anyone that had marital problems, drug abuse, anger management problems, alcoholism, family issues, etc. They wanted to have a 'home' to call their own.

I raised funds through my golf tournaments so they could purchase that house in Palm Desert, California, to provide their counseling services to the public.

Before my friends left for the East Coast, I was given a huge surprise by the Palm Springs Walk of Stars committee, my wife, sponsors of my radio show and good friends. They presented me with a sidewalk star on the "Walk of Stars" on Palm Canyon Drive in downtown Palm Springs.

I couldn't have been happier to receive that honor with my friends from my hometown there to share it with me. To this day, I can't figure out how Mary Jane kept it a surprise until I read it in the newspaper the morning of the dedication while having breakfast. The article was a press release that said that I was going to receive a star on the Walk of Stars that same afternoon. Then my wife told me the whole story and what to expect. I didn't have a clue that Mary Jane was coordinating

253

At my Palm Springs Walk of Stars sidewalk star dedication on June 19, 1994. This magical day was officially designated by the Palm Springs Mayor and City Council as Michael Dante Day. I was surrounded by actor Kem Dibbs, Gerhard Frenzel, the Walk of Stars originator, actor Gene Barry, actor Alvy Moore, Mary Jane Dante, singer Jerry Vale, executive producer William T. Orr, musical director Johnny Mann and TV host Geoff Edwards.

A close up of my Walk of Stars block on Palm Canyon Drive in Palm Springs, California.

the event with Chairman Gerhard Frenzel. It was an impressive ceremony with a proclamation read and then given to me in a frame by the Mayor of Palm Springs proclaiming June 19, 1994 as "Michael Dante Day" in Palm Springs. We all had a terrific luncheon reception afterward. It was the start of many awards I was going to receive in the coming years.

82

My Four Careers

I am blessed to have had four professional careers, so far; professional baseball, television/ movies, radio talk show host and writer. In 1994, Mary Jane and I were busy rounding up a celebrity guest every week from show business or the sports world to interview on my radio show, *The Michael Dante Classic Celebrity Talk Show.*

We succeeded in recording an hour interview with a different celebrity every week. From my era, I was fortunate to know many people in the entertainment world and sports. I was able to call them at their home instead of going through their manager, publicist or agent.

Every show was recorded either in their home, a country club, restaurant or hotel and after the interview we always enjoyed more interesting discussions over lunch. Mary Jane did an excellent job of recording the shows on a Marantz recorder and mixing board. She also prepared the accompanying paperwork that was needed at the radio station to go along with each show. It was stimulating and an important learning experience for me to focus on listening, not talking. Most people think talk radio is more about talking if you are the host. For me, it was about listening. I learned early on that everything became much easier when I focused on listening and doing my homework the night before in preparation for the questions I was going to ask my guest the next day.

I wish I had learned the art of listening earlier in my acting career because I'm sure many more interesting, creative nuances would have manifested in the dialogue with another actor. When I learned that about myself, I looked forward to each interview with much

A radio show host gig in Palm Springs kick-started my fourth career into high gear.

more enthusiasm. People always ask me which interview was my favorite, and my answer has always been the same: they all were. But, one that stands out is my interview with my dear friend Jonathan Winters. It wasn't just an interview, it was a special performance. He was brilliant!

Guests of 'The Michael Dante Classic Celebrity Talk Show'/ Michael Dante "On Deck"

Maud Adams
Danny Aiello
Anna Marie Alberghetti
Norm Alden
Kermit Alexander
Jed Allan
Ed Ames
Bobby Anderson
Richard Anderson
Ray Anthony
Michael Ansara
Vijay Amritraj
Desi Arnaz Jr.
Ed Asner
Christopher Atkins

Jim Bailey
Kaye Ballard
Gene Barry
Billy Barty
Dick Bass
Don Baylor
Johnny Bench
John Beradino
Milton Berle
Yogi Berra
George Blanda
Pat Boone
Ernest Borgnine
Tom Bosley
Eric Braeden
Lloyd Bridges
John Brodie
Les Brown
Les Brown Jr.
Tony Butala (Letterman)
Dick Butkus
John Byner
Edd "Kookie" Byrnes

Rory Calhoun
Michael Callan

Bert Campaneris
Al Campanis
Glen Campbell
Jack Carter
Rosie Casals
John Castellanos
Page Cavanaugh
Sydney Chaplin
Don Cherry
Linda Christian
Gary Collins
Carol Connors
Mike Connors
Dick Contino
Gary Crosby
Norm Crosby
Tony Curtis

Vic Damone
Bill Dana
Alvin Dark
James Darren
Beryl Davis
Tommy Davis
Phyllis Diller
Tom Dreesen
Alex Drier
Ann Meyers Drysdale
Marj Dusay

Ron Ely
Roy Emerson

Ron Fairly
James Farentino
Bill Farrell
Ed Faulkner
Tom Fears
Norman Fell
Bob Feller
Vince Ferragamo
Rollie Fingers

Bob Flanigan/Greg Stegman
(of the 4 Freshman)
Rhonda Fleming
Tom Flores
Robert Forster
Anne Francis
Connie Francis

Kathy Garver
Steve Garvey
Dick Gautier
Al Geiberger
Larry Gelbart
Jack Ging
Kelsey Grammer
Gogi Grant
Buddy Greco
Shecky Greene
Lalo Guerrero
Bryant Gumbel

Buddy Hackett
Monty Hall
Tom Haller
Carole Hampton
Jim Hardy
Ron Harper
Pat Harrington
John Havilcek
Norb Hecker
Charlton Heston
Hope Holiday/Frank Marth
Anna Maria Horsford
Robert Horton
David Huddleston
Dick Hyman

Dennis James
Anne Jeffreys
Herb Jeffries
Ferguson Jenkins
Arte Johnson

Jack Jones
Sam Jones

Buddy Kaye
Lainie Kazan
Howard Keel
Harmon Killebrew
Ralph Kiner
Morgana King
Chuck Knox
Bernie Kopell
Martin Kove
Jack Kramer
Toni Holt Kramer

Frankie Laine
Dick 'Night Train' Lane
Ted Lange
Julius La Rosa
Tommy Lasorda
Rod Laver
Carol Lawrence
Mark Lawrence
Johnny Lee
Michele Lee
Ruta Lee
Hal Linden
Roberta Linn
Robert Loggia
Trini Lopez
Maurice Lucas
Johnny Lujack
Carol Lynley

Stephen Macht
Patrick Macnee
Johnny Mann
Mickey Manners
Eddy Lawrence Manson
Joe Mantegna
Ed Marinaro
Peter Marshall
Donna Martell
Tony Martin
Al Martino
Bill Marx
Ron Masak
Gene Mauch
Virginia Mayo
James Mac Arthur
Mickey McDermott
Gavin McLeod/Patti McLeod
Barbara McNair

Gerald McRaney
Don Meredith
Kenny Miller
Barry Minniefield
George Montgomery
Alvy Moore
Terry Moore
Jim Mora
Jaye P. Morgan
Robert Morse
Gary Morton/Susie McAllister
Don Most
Ben Murphy
Don Murray
Jan Murray

David Naughton
Dylan Neal
Don Newcombe
Julie Newmar
Andrew Neiderman

Carlos Palomino
Fess Parker
J.C. Parrish
Charlie Pasarell
Stack Pierce
Ross Porter
Mala Powers
Stefanie Powers

Dennis Ralston
Sue Raney
Frankie Randall
Scott Record
Debbie Reynolds
Pat Rizzo
Harold Robbins
Dale Robertson
Brooks Robinson
Andy Robustelli
Jimmy Rodgers
Mickey Rooney/Jan Chamberlin
Rooney
Bob Rosburg
Al Rosen
Steve Rossi
Richard Roundtree

Doug Sanders
Joe Santos
Jack Scalia
Sammy Shore

Enos Slaughter
Keely Smith
Robert Stack
Rod Steiger
Jan Stenerud
Connie Stevens
Stella Stevens
Elke Sommers
Joanie Sommers
Kathleen Sullivan
Don Sutton
Harland "Swede" Svare

George Takei
Ruth Terry
Donna Theodore
Alan Thicke
Constance Towers
Bill Tracy w/Paula Kelly Jr.
Fred Travalena

Kiki Vandeweghe
Ernie M. Vandeweghe
Mamie Van Doren
Dick Van Patten
Jerry Vale
Ken Venturi
Marlene Hagge-Vossler

Clint Walker
Shani Wallis
Joseph Wambaugh
William Wellman Jr.
Dawn Wells
Jerry West
Jack Whittaker
Nancy Whittaker
Julie White
Andy Williams
Barry Williams
Paul Williams
Fred Williamson
Billy Wilson
William Windom
Bobby Winkles
Jonathan Winters
Mark Woodforde (with
Tommy Tucker)

Ralph Young
Johnny Yune

Efrem Zimbalist, Jr.

"Remembering Friends" from my radio show

> Life is but a stopping place, a pause in what's to be,
> a resting place along the road to sweet eternity.
> We all have different journeys, different paths along the way,
> we all were meant to learn some things but never meant to stay.
> Our destination is a place far greater than we know.

Remembering my friends, who shared a small part of their journey with me on my radio interview show, *The Michael Dante Classic Celebrity Talk Show*. They are gone but not forgotten:

Norm Alden • Michael Ansara • Gene Barry • Billy Barty • John Beradino • Milton Berle • George Blanda • Ernest Borgnine • Tom Bosley • Lloyd Bridges • Les Brown, Sr. • Rory Calhoun • Al Campanis • Sydney Chaplin • Linda Christian • Gary Collins • Gary Crosby • Tony Curtis • Berle Davis • Phyllis Diller • Alex Drier • James Farentino • Bill Farrell • Tom Fears • Norman Fell • Bob Feller • Larry Gelbart • Lalo Guerrero • Buddy Hackett • Tom Haller • Jim Hardy • Norm Hecker • Charlton Heston • Dennis James • Herb Jeffries • Buddy Kaye • Howard Keel • Harmon Killebrew • Ralph Kiner • Jack Kramer • Frankie Lane • Dick 'Night Train' Lane • Mark Lawrence • Maurice Lucas • Johnny Mann • Eddy Lawrence Manson • Tony Martin • Al Martino • Gene Mauch • Virginia Mayo • James MacArthur • Mickey McDermott • Barbara McNair • Don Meredith • George Montgomery • Alvy Moore • Gary Morton • Jan Murray • Fess Parker • J.C. Parrish • Harold Robbins • Dale Robertson• Andy Robustelli • Bob Rosburg • Steve Rossi • Enos Slaughter • Robert Stack • Rod Steiger • Fred Travelena • Ken Venturi • Jerry Vale • Ken Venturi • Nancy Kiner Whittaker • Andy Williams • Billy Wilson • William Windom • Jonathan Winters • Ralph Young • Efrem Zimbalist, Jr.

83

Honors and Awards

In 2002, one of *the* most provocative films I starred in was given a re-examination. The film was *The Naked Kiss* from 1964 and was directed by the multi-talented Samuel Fuller. It was the director's choice at the Film Noir Film Festival in Palm Springs, California. The film was shown to a packed house. It was highlighted and closed the festival with co-star Constance Towers and me participating in a symposium with the audience.

Sammy Fuller's direction was excellent, handling the sensitive scenes perfectly, which allowed the audience to use their imagination. Unlike today's films that are quite graphic, Fuller used subtle nuances to make his point without showing any of the details. He did it through his classic direction and our acting abilities. It was an honor for me to work with one of the best directors in Hollywood, Sammy Fuller.

At the Stamford High School Wall of Fame in Stamford, Connecticut, with longtime pal, boxer Chico Vejar in 2002.

260

With NFL Hall of Famer Andy Robustelli, a dear friend who also hails from Stamford, Connecticut. Posing at my wall plaque and photo at Stamford High School, our alma mater.

That same year I was asked to return to my other hometown of Stamford, Connecticut, to be honored for my career accomplishments by my alma mater. My achievements were written on a huge plaque along with my picture and placed on the Wall of Fame in the main hallway of Stamford High School. I was indeed proud to be placed on the same wall as Andy Robustelli; National Football League Hall of Famer, Chico Vejar; who fought Chuck Davey for the lightweight championship of the world, my cousin Jimmy Ienner, a very successful record producer and Senator Joseph Lieberman. We all were proud graduates of Stamford High School. My immediate family was there for the dedication. We all enjoyed lunch after the ceremony and reminisced about all of our school days at Stamford High School. It was the only high school in Stamford during that period of time; today there are four high schools in the area.

That experience brought back a lot of fond and sad memories too. Several of my buddies I played ball with on the high school baseball and basketball team had passed away at a very young age. I was always aware of the time going by too fast. I had wished there was some way I could slow down that clicking clock to enjoy more of the those precious moments in my life. Getting up early in the morning was the most difficult time going school. Once I had breakfast and was on my way, I loved every moment of it.

Receiving the 2003 Golden Boot Award with my wife Mary Jane at my side.

The Golden Boot Award is considered the 'Oscar' of westerns.

In between recording my radio show, I kept up with my golf game playing twice a week and maintaining my ten handicap. I was the all-around winner of the prestigious Frank Sinatra Celebrity Invitational golf tournament in 2003. It is and has been the best celebrity golf tournament in the country for the past twenty five years. The needs of abused children were Frank and Barbara Sinatra's favorite charity. He and Barbara dedicated so much of their time, energy, money and love to building a child abuse center in Rancho Mirage, California called The Barbara Sinatra Children's Center. As a result of their efforts, thousands of children are treated at the center. No child is ever turned away. Mary Jane and I visited the center and were moved to tears of joy to see the beautiful facilities.

Since Frank passed away, Barbara and her staff have continued to do angelic work at the center. I have had the pleasure to be a celebrity participant in 24 of the Frank Sinatra Celebrity Invitational golf tournaments to raise funds for their center and have met and played golf with many luminaries, including President Gerald Ford.

I continued to enjoy a rewarding 2003. I received The Golden Boot Award, which is considered "the Oscar" of western films. One cannot solicit to receive that award. A member of the Awards Committee, made up of one's peers, contacts the artists who are selected for the award each year.

That picture-perfect swing came as the result of many hours of dedication on the links.

Mary Jane and me celebrating my victory at the Frank Sinatra Celebrity Invitational in 2004. There's nothing like the thrill of winning.

Golfing with President Gerald Ford at the Frank Sinatra Celebrity Invitational. Photo courtesy of Steve Kiefer.

The award is based on how well the actor, actress, director, writer, producer and stunt person has performed throughout their career in the western genre. I regard this award with my ultimate respect and high esteem because it is *not* based on one performance, but an entire career. Almost three decades ago this special event was founded by Pat Buttram and others to honor the individuals associated with western films and to contribute to the Motion Picture and Television Fund.

Mary Jane and I drove two hours from our home to attend the event and stayed in a hotel in downtown Los Angeles to relax and dress for the occasion. While we were getting ready, I decided to go downstairs and pick up a newspaper.

When I opened the folded *Los Angeles Times* newspaper, the first thing I saw was the obituary page and noticed a figure in a baseball uniform. It was a picture of Mickey McDermott, my ex-roommate with the Washington Senators. The paper said he had just passed away of a heart attack the day before in Phoenix, Arizona. We were saddened and shocked by the news and were disappointed his wife did not call to tell us what happened. As we drove to The Golden Boot Awards ceremony at the Beverly Hilton Hotel, owned by Merv Griffin at the time, we were heavy hearted. We arrived at the hotel and were greeted by the host who assisted us to our table. The ballroom was filled to capacity. The honorees that night where Tommy Lee Jones, Graham Greene, Kris Kristofferson, Sue Ane Langdon, William Smith, Chris Alcaide, Tommy Farrell, Kelo Henderson, Charles Champlain, stuntman Terry Leonard, The Sons of the Pioneers and yours truly. Each Honoree had a Presenter. Actor Andrew Prine introduced me and presented me with the prestigious award. We each spoke and thanked the people who helped us along the way to success.

Holding my 2006 Silver Spur Award for acting career achievement in the western film genre.

I fought back my tears and shared my story about the passing of one of my best friends and teammate Mickey McDermott. Without Mickey, I would not have been there to receive that award. Mickey introduced me to Tommy Dorsey and Tommy arranged a screen test for me at MGM Studios after I left the Washington Senators baseball club with an injury. The rest is history. I thanked and dedicated the award to both Tommy and Mickey. It was an extremely exciting and emotional evening, one in which I will cherish and fondly remember the rest of my life. The Golden Boot Award sits on a special table in my living room where I can see it and always be reminded of that most special evening. It's much heavier than it looks, sitting on a block of stained wood with the engraved inscription of the event on a small plaque in front.

That same year, 2003, I proudly received the Southern California Motion Picture Council Award for the "Best of the Best" in the entertainment industry and the performing arts. This award has been given to deserving artists since 1945. The awards ceremony that year took place at the Sportsman's Lodge in Studio City, California.

It was quite another exciting evening with honorees director Dan Petrie, actress Kathy Garver, comedian Marty Ingles and yours truly receiving this most prestigious award. Again, Mary Jane and I enjoyed seeing and conversing with people we hadn't seen in a while. It was an evening spent with people we had so much in common with. We all congratulated each other for being recognized and respected with such a complimentary and ongoing show business award.

In 2004, I was chosen to be the Presenter of the Golden Boot Award, posthumously, to one of my boyhood western heroes, Johnny Mack Brown. Johnny was not only a film star but an All-

My western boot prints embedded in cement at the Superstition Mountain Museum in Apache Junction, Arizona, in 2011.

In 2012, I donated the moccasins I wore in Winterhawk *and a life-size portrait in the title role to the Superstition Mountain Museum.*

American halfback at the University of Alabama. He was inducted into the College Football Hall of Fame in 1957. In addition, he was one of the world's gun spinning champions. The event took place again at Merv Griffin's Beverly Hilton Hotel.

Johnny Mack Brown's son, John, and widowed wife, Connie, were there when I made the presentation. I shared my story of sneaking into Stamford's Strand Theater every time Johnny Mack Brown appeared on the screen. He had a distinct speaking voice and was a natural for the western genre. It was such a pleasure to meet and spend the evening with Connie and John. It was another memorable gift of friendship and camaraderie in my lifetime.

Three years later, I received the Silver Spur Award in 2006. It is given by The Reel Cowboys, a volunteer organization dedicated to the preservation of the western film. The organization honors those who have contributed a lifetime of excellence on film in the western genre. That year, the Tri-Valley Special Olympics benefited from the charitable donations from the evening. The honorees were Morgan Freeman, Gerald Mc Rainey, Barbara Eden, stuntman Erik Cord, Don Murray and me. Dawn Wells, who played Mary Ann on *Gilligan's Island* and costarred with me in *Winterhawk* was my presenter.

It was another exceptional evening. This is another award I hold in high esteem because one cannot solicit it. A committee of our peers chooses the honorees. Again, it's a career award not based on *one* performance. My "Silver Spur Award" is mounted on a beautiful stained oak plaque with all the etched details pertaining to the award. I have it hanging on a western gun rack with my gun belt and six-shooter in my living room.

In 2007, I had the honor and pleasure to be the Presenter of the Reel Cowboys Silver Spur Award to Audie Murphy, posthumously, for all of his achievements to the western film genre. Audie Murphy appeared in 44 films in his career, most of them westerns.

Audie was not only a hero on the big screen, but in real life he was the most decorated soldier in World War II, receiving 33 medals including the Congressional Medal of Honor. It brought back a lot of fond memories of working with Audie and I had to hold back the tears again when I handed the Silver Spur Award to his widow, Pamela, and his sons, Terry and James.

Pamela has since passed away, but Terry and James are doing fine and we exchange holiday cards every year. I had the pleasure of being the guest of honor in 2012 at the Audie Murphy Cotton Museum in Greenville, Texas, for Audie Murphy Days, for my work and friendship with Audie.

I've been so fortunate to receive many awards and in 2009, I received the Spirit of the West Award honored by the *Wild West Gazette* and Bison Western Museum in Scottsdale, Arizona, in recognition of my work in western films. Lee Ann Sharpe and Bob Roloff presented me with a beautifully designed plaque that made me aware that I was one of two or three actors that ever lived, who portrayed the Native American, the good guy cowboy and the bad guy cowboy. No one looked better playing all three parts and was more convincing in those roles. I was extremely proud of this unique accomplishment when it was brought to my attention. I sincerely appreciated the recognition of my contributions and the honor of receiving this award.

In 2011, I was honored at the Superstition Mountain Museum in Apache Junction, Arizona, for my years of work in the western film industry. My cowboy boot prints were embedded into cement

Mary Jane and I are pictured in the Elvis Presley Chapel at the Superstition Mountain Museum standing next to the display of my portrait and moccasins.

Outside of the Audie Murphy American Cotton Museum in Greenville, Texas, in 2012, next to the huge Audie Murphy statue sculpted by Gordon Thomas and his son.

Standing alongside the statue of American war hero and movie star Audie Leon Murphy as the Guest of Honor at Audie Murphy Days in 2012.

With Audie Murphy's sister Nadine Lokey and the Color Guard inside the Audie Murphy American Cotton Museum.

and placed on the Wall of Stars in the Museum with all the other western stars I admired since I was a boy. What an honor to be among the greatest that entertained the world portraying cowboys and Indians in the movies and on television. It was a special day for me and my wife and for the large crowd of people who were there to witness the ceremony. In 1964 and 1965, Audie Murphy and I filmed *Apache Rifles* and *Arizona Raiders* in the area. It brought back a flood of memories of working in such a beautiful location. I am now part of the Superstition Mountain Museum forever.

One year later I donated the hand beaded moccasins I wore in the film *Winterhawk* to the same Superstition Mountain Museum in Apache Junction, Arizona. The moccasins are placed in a shadow box beside a life-sized portrait of me in the lead role on permanent display in the museum. *Winterhawk* was highly successful at the box office and contributed heavily to the advancement of my career. My memorabilia of *Winterhawk* at the Superstition Mountain Museum will live on display for future generations to appreciate.

In January 2013, I received the first Apacheland Spirit Award at the Gold Canyon Film Festival, in Apache Junction, AZ. It was given to me for my contributions to the area. I continue to support the people that preserve the history of filmmaking at Gold Canyon in Apache Junction and was graciously honored with this very special, first award.

A few months later, I was asked by the Mayor of Stamford, Connecticut, Michael Pavia, to be the Grand Marshal of the annual Columbus Day Parade. The parade took place the same weekend as the naming of a street in my honor, MICHAEL DANTE WAY. The Council of Italian-American organizations presented the Columbus Day Parade, co-sponsored by the Italian Center of Stamford.

It started with an Italian Mass at Sacred Heart Catholic Church. The parade kickoff began at Mill River Street at noon and finished at Main Street where Columbus Park is located. Mary Jane and I were driven in a beautifully restored brown and tan antique 1938 Buick convertible, owned by Mario De Carlo, from the start of the parade to Columbus Park, where all the entertainment and festivities took place.

Hundreds of Italian Americans marched behind us to celebrate their heritage and the arrival of Christopher Columbus in America in 1492. A ceremony honoring me was held in the park, followed by lots of music, dancing and delicious food. Again, I was blessed to celebrate all of this

Awarded the very first Apacheland Spirit Award for costarring in two outstanding films with Audie Murphy in Apache Junction and Gold Canyon, Arizona, and for my support of making future film projects in the area.

A main street in downtown Stamford, Connecticut, was named after me on October 7, 2011.

with my wife, Mary Jane, my immediate family, relatives and friends. This was another exciting and rewarding day in my life that I shall never forget.

On Friday, October 7, 2011, a street was named in my honor in my hometown of Stamford, Connecticut for my outstanding career accomplishments. Mayor Pavia declared "Michael Dante Day" in the City of Stamford. Mary Jane, Mario De Carlo and City Representative Robert "Gabe" De Luca introduced and developed the idea and coordinated the event with the Mayor and the City. Gabe and I grew up together on the west side of Stamford and played football on the same neighborhood team called the West Side Hawks. We were pretty good.

The mayor authorized The City of Stamford Board of Representatives to unveil a vanity sign inscribed, MICHAEL DANTE WAY, along with the current street sign of Prospect Street, in recognition of an exemplar Stamford native. Also in attendance were my three sisters, Carolyn, Rose, Yolanda, my niece Mary, my brother, Anthony and brother-in-law Harold, along with several close relatives and some of my best friends who shared in the wonderful celebration.

The street is a quarter-mile long and after the first sign was unveiled at one end, everyone walked up hill to the other end where they unveiled the other street sign, MICHAEL DANTE WAY. It was an emotional walk for me because I had to walk that street to get to and from Stamford High School every day that I went to high school. After the dedication, we all gathered at Pellicci's Restaurant, located on the west side of town where I grew up. I'll never be able to really describe the feeling, because I never thought or dreamed that something like this could happen to me and remain for all to see as a reminder of what I have accomplished in my lifetime. Of the many prestigious honors and awards I have received, the naming of MICHAEL DANTE WAY is perhaps the most rewarding of all.

My only regret was my mother and father were not alive to see and share it with me, but I know they were looking down and smiling. I could hear Mom say one of her famous lines, "You did good, son!"

The road to success was not an easy one. There were a lot of roadblocks, hard knocks and obstructions along the way. But, because I made some good choices and with the help of divine guidance, I am truly grateful and blessed for the continuous journey that has led me *FROM HOLLYWOOD TO MICHAEL DANTE WAY.*

Thank you for joining me down the trail and until we meet again, *live long and prosper!*

Bonus Chapter

My Recipes To Die For

Acting is my great love, but one of my favorite hobbies is cooking Italian food. These days, I do a lot of it.

My mom was a great cook and a baker too. The aroma that permeated throughout our house when she made her Italian sauce was so special. It had a flavor and a taste I knew I had to learn how to make and carry on her family recipes. Sunday was a very special day in our household. After church, we couldn't wait to gather around mom in the kitchen to observe which ingredients she was going to put in her sauce that made it so delicious and different than anyone else's. I learned how to cook by watching her and asking questions. Once I learned those ingredients, the tastes were always the same. Of all the Italian restaurants I had the pleasure of dining at, no one's tomato meat sauce compared to hers. My love of mom's cooking and the enjoyment of eating good homemade Italian food were the reasons Italian cooking became my hobby. If I was asked what I would like to have for my last meal on earth, here are some of my favorite Recipes to Die For.

PENNE PUTTANESCA

3 cloves garlic, chopped fine
1/2 cup of fresh parsley
1/2 cup of fresh basil
2 oz. can of anchovies in olive oil, chopped
8 Italian Roma tomatoes, peeled and diced
2 oz. can of chopped ripe olives—drained
2 oz. jar of chopped green olives—drained
1 tablespoon of capers
Add crushed red pepper to taste
One 16 oz. box of Penne pasta

Sauté garlic in small amount of virgin olive oil in deep skillet until tender; do not brown, garlic should be gold in color.

Add a little more oil to skillet, then add ingredients in the order listed: basil, parsley, anchovies, tomatoes, ripe olives, green olives, capers with small amount of its' own liquid and crushed red pepper.

Simmer for about 30 minutes, stirring frequently.

While sauce is cooking; prepare pasta according to package directions. Drain well. Mix desired amount of sauce with pasta to your liking. Sprinkle with grated Romano cheese.

One 16 oz. box of Penne pasta.

Serves 6 to 8.

PASTA FAGIOLI

2 cloves garlic chopped fine

2 16 oz. cans of peeled Italian plum tomatoes with basil

2 tablespoons of Italian parsley, freshly chopped

Pinch of black or crushed red pepper

One ½ tsp. of salt

15oz. can of Cannellini beans

One pound of Mezzi Rigatoni pasta

Chop 2 cloves of garlic very fine and sauté in a pan with enough virgin olive oil to cover garlic.

Do not burn garlic—keep it gold in color.

Add two large 16 oz. cans of peeled Italian plum tomatoes with basil, after you have blended the tomatoes in a blender on the 'chop' mode.

Add 2 tablespoons of fresh Italian parsley, chopped very fine. Add a pinch of black pepper and salt.

Add 1-15 oz. can of Cannellini beans with its own juice and mix it all in the blender.

Put it in a pot and bring to a boil and simmer for 30 minutes.

Serve with Mezzi Rigatoni pasta sprinkled with grated Romano cheese and crushed red pepper if you choose.

Serves 4 to 6.

PASTA SALSICCIA

Extra virgin olive oil

Six cloves garlic, finely chopped

Two 16 oz. cans whole peeled plum tomatoes with basil

Fresh Italian parsley, chopped

Tablespoon of each of salt and pepper

Two links hot Italian sausage, removed from casings

Two links sweet Italian sausage, removed from casings

In a medium-size pot, heat enough olive oil to sauté the garlic until it is almost gold in color, be careful not to let it burn. Put tomatoes in a blender to a 'chop' mode, add the crushed tomatoes to the pot with the garlic and olive oil. Add parsley, salt and pepper to your taste. In a frying pan quickly brown the sausage that has been removed from casings.

Quickly stir to brown, *do not cook*. Bring the sauce to a boil for 20 minutes.

Add the loose sausage to the tomato sauce and lower the heat to a simmer for one hour and 30 minutes. The best pasta with these ingredients is Perciatelli or Buccatini sprinkled with grated Romano cheese.

Serves 4 to 6.

Note: This sauce will taste better if you allow it to cool and refrigerate it overnight. It begets a better flavor the next day. Applies to most Italian sauces made with meat.

TRE CARNE SAUCE

Three cloves of garlic, chopped fine.

Use enough virgin olive oil to sauté garlic in a large pot. Do not brown the garlic. It should be gold in color.

Three 16 oz. cans of peeled plum Italian tomatoes with basil in a blender on the 'chop' mode.

Take the chopped tomatoes and put them in the pot with the sautéed garlic in olive oil.

Three tablespoons of Italian parsley, freshly chopped.

One tablespoon of salt.

A pinch of black pepper or crushed red pepper.

Quickly stir to brown, *do not cook,* ½ lb. of ground pork, ½ lb. of veal and ½ lb. of lamb together in a frying pan.

Boil the blended tomato sauce for 20 minutes.

Take the browned pork, veal and lamb mixture and put it in the tomato sauce and simmer for 90 minutes.

The best pasta served with this sauce is Mostacioli sprinkled with Romano cheese.

Serves 6 to 8.

Note: This sauce will taste better if you allow it to cool and refrigerate it overnight. It begets a better flavor the next day. This applies to most sauces made with meat.

LINGUINE AL'OLIO

Two cloves of garlic—chopped fine
One 2 oz. can of anchovy fillets
Two tablespoons of Italian parsley
Virgin olive oil
One small jar of Capers
One pound of Linguine
Crushed red pepper.

Boil water in a large pot.

Sauté chopped garlic in virgin olive oil in a large pan. Do not burn the garlic. It should be gold in color.

Add1/2 cup of hot water (Use the boiling water that you will use to cook your pasta) to prevent over cooking the garlic.

Add 2oz. can of anchovy fillets and stir until they have blended into the sautéed garlic.

Add 2 tablespoons of Italian parsley and stir with other ingredients.

Add 1/2 teaspoon of capers with a teaspoon of its own juice and let it blend with the other ingredients.

Sauté for about 20 minutes.

Apply four ladle spoons of boiling water from the boiling water that the pasta will be cooking in to thin out the oil. The success of this recipe is mixing the right amount of hot water to thin out the thickness of the oil and garlic so either one doesn't dominate the taste.

Serve with one-pound linguine pasta – always cooked *al dente.*

Serves 3 to 4 people.

MY HELPFUL COOKING SUGGESTIONS:

- Don't burn the garlic and don't let it dominate the taste.
- With Al'oilo, save the hot water when your pasta is done cooking to thin out the sauce, if you need to, before serving.
- Only use fresh ingredients. The flavor is noticeably different if you don't.
- When making a large amount of red sauce, let it cool down on the counter for two hours and then put the containers in the refrigerator for two days before using and freezing. The taste will be much better.
- Don't use parsley in the sauce if you are using basil and vice-versa. They have a bit of a conflicting taste.
- Always use extra virgin olive oil.
- A nice glass of red or white wine is always delicious. Red white with meat sauce and white wine with a fish sauce.

Motion Picture Chronology

Somebody Up There Likes Me – (MGM, 1956). Part of Shorty the Greek, director Robert Wise

Raintree County – (MGM, 1957). Part of Jesse Gardner, director Edward Dmytryk

Jean Eagles – (Columbia Pictures, 1957). Part of Sgt. O'Hara, director George Sydney

Forts Dobbs – (Warner Bros., 1958). Part of Billings, director Gordon Douglas

Born Reckless – (Warner Bros., 1958) Part of Cowboy, director Howard W. Koch

Westbound – (Warner Bros., 1959). Part of Rod, director Bud Boetticher

Seven Thieves – (20ᵗʰ Century-Fox, 1960). Part of Louis Antonizzi, director Henry Hathaway

Kid Galahad – (Allied Artists, 1962) Part of Joie Shakes, director Phil Karlson

Operation Bikini – (American International Pictures, 1963). Part of Lieut. William 'Bill' Fortney, director Anthony Caras

The Naked Kiss – (Allied Artists, 1964) Part of Grant, director Sammy Fuller

Apache Rifles – (20ᵗʰ Century-Fox, 1964) Part of Red Hawk, director William Witney

Harlow – (Bill Sargent's Electronovision Magna Distribution Corp, 1965). Part of Ed, director Alex Segal

Arizona Raiders – (Columbia Pictures, 1965). Part of Brady, director William Witney

Crazy Horse and Custer, The Untold Story – (20th Century-Fox, 1968). Part of Crazy Horse, director Norman Foster

Willard – (Cinerama Releasing Corporation, 1971). Part of Brandt, director Daniel Mann

Thirty Dangerous Seconds – (James H. Milligan Productions, 1972). Part of The Clown, director Joseph Taft

That's The Way Of The World – (Minerva, 1975). Part of Mike Lemongello, director Sig Shore

Winterhawk – (Howco International Pictures, 1975). Title role Winterhawk, director, Charles B Pierce

The Farmer – (Columbia Pictures, 1977). Part of Johnny O, director David Berlatsky

Cruise Missile – (Eichberg Film, 1978). Part of Konstantin, director Les Martinson

Beyond Evil – (IFI/Scope III, 1980). Part of Del Giorgio, director Herb Freed

The Big Score – (Vestron Pictures, 1983). Part of Goldy, director Fred Williamson

Fast Forward – (Columbia Pictures, 1985). Part of the Maître d', director Sidney Poitier

The Messenger – (Soul Cinema, 1986). Part of Emerson, director Fred Williamson

Return from the River Kwai – (Universal Pictures, 1989). Part of Commander Davidson, director Andrew Mc Laglen

Cage – (New Century Vista Film Co., 1989). Part of Tony Baccola, director Lang Elliott

Unbelievable!!!!! – (Industrial Entertainment/Archangel Films LLC, 2013). Michael Dante as himself playing a producer. Written and directed by Steven L. Fawcette.

To be continued…

Television Appearances

Cheyenne (three episodes)
Sugarfoot (three episodes)
Colt 45 (two episodes)
Tales of the Texas Rangers
Rescue 8
Lawman
The Adventures of Rin Tin Tin
Maverick (three episodes)
Westinghouse Desilu Playhouse
Death Valley Days (two episodes)
The Texan (four episodes)
Bourbon Street Beat
General Electric Theater
The Wrangler
Checkmate
The Detective Story
Cain's Hundred
87th Precinct

Hawaiian Eye
Perry Mason (two episodes)
Bonanza
Get Smart
Custer Series (17 episodes)
Star Trek
The Big Valley
Daniel Boone
The Kids Who Knew Too Much
Knots Landing
The Fall Guy (two episodes)
Six Million Dollar Man (two episodes)
Days Of Our Lives (12 episodes)
General Hospital (12 episodes)
Simon and Simon
Cagney and Lacey (two episodes)
Pilot—"G-Men"

*Appeared on approximately 45 television game shows and personal interviews

Index

*Numbers in **bold** indicate photographs*

CPSIA information can be obtained
at www.ICGtesting.com
Printed in the USA
FFOW04n1157020418
46141386-47241FF

9 781593 937560